THE BOXER
AND THE
GOALKEEPER

THE BOXER AND THE GOALKEEPER

Sartre Vs Camus

ANDY MARTIN

**SIMON &
SCHUSTER**

London · New York · Sydney · Toronto · New Delhi

A CBS COMPANY

First published in Great Britain by Simon & Schuster UK Ltd, 2012
This paperback edition published by Simon & Schuster UK Ltd, 2013
A CBS COMPANY

ISBN: 978-1-84739-425-5
ISBN: 978-1-84983-588-6 (ebook)

Printed and bound by CPI Group (UK) Ltd, Croydon CR0 4YY

For a binary praxis of non-antagonistic reciprocity

'A binary praxis of antagonistic reciprocity'

JEAN-PAUL SARTRE

'The tragedy is not being alone, but rather *not* being alone'

ALBERT CAMUS

Contents

I

What it Feels Like
to be Alive

FOR A LONG WHILE I fully expected that this massive illusion would come to an end and everyone else in the world would just disappear, give up the ghost, and leave me all alone to play with the cars and planes and trains. (Quite how all the cars and trains and planes came to be there in the first place, without the existence of other people, did not give me serious pause.)

On the whole I thought this great vanishing trick would be a good thing. (At other times I would wake up in a cold sweat. Has everybody gone? Come back! Which they duly did.) A few practical details remained unclear. Sometimes I wondered what would become of their shoes and socks – when all these plausible simulacra faded away – if they would just be left there, vast piles of shoes on every street corner, or if they too would disappear back into the void along with the 'people' wearing them.

And yet, inexplicably, other people remained stubbornly *there*. But what were they all doing? What was the point of other people exactly? Perhaps a giant wave would sweep up the Thames and carry them all off, leaving me alone on top of a mountain somewhere. It took a few egocentric years before I started to wonder if, on the contrary, *I* was the illusion. What if, after all, *they* are real and I do not exist? I started to feel that I was not altogether palpably, tangibly, incontrovertibly, *there*. They were there. They were real, I was the ghost: an invisible man among the masses. Perhaps everything was a dream and I (or they) would eventually wake up and all would be revealed.

It was in the midst of this state of confusion that I entered the bookshop.

It was a small family bookshop, on a peaceful back street in a small town on the fringes of London, close to my school, run by real human beings, the kind that doesn't exist so much now. Like something out of Dickens. I treated it as my own personal library, and I would sit there for hours on end, often on the floor, usually not buying anything, then walk out. I loved that bookshop, but I still rue the day I first went in there.

I had a particular soft spot for the foreign-languages section down in the basement. It was like going somewhere far away, but without having to go to the trouble of getting on a boat or a plane – like a foreign land in itself, reassuringly other, strange, barely comprehensible. On this particular day, around the sixteenth year of the life I thought of as a dream or a prolonged hallucination, I went down to the basement. There was no one else around; I had it all to myself. For some reason I pulled the fattest book I could find off the shelf and sat down on the floor with it. It was a big book but the print was small. There were so many words and names in there I had never come across before. But there was a special kind of music to it that instantly played in my head. It sounded to me like a remix of '21st Century Schizoid Man' and 'Je t'aime . . . moi non plus'. I had an irresistible feeling of *déjà vu*.

This book changed my life (whether it ruined it or redeemed

it, I am still not sure). I couldn't understand too much of it, and not just because it was in French, but I felt as if it could understand me. At some visceral level we spoke the same language. Up until that point I had been a generally law-abiding citizen. Suddenly, stealing a book began to seem like not only a subversive, quasi-revolutionary act of some sort but also a way of rectifying matters, correcting some original, unspecified injustice. Like standing on the barricades in '68 and throwing a Molotov cocktail.

Not long before – like everyone at one time or another – I had been stood up. Waited for a girl to turn up at a local coffee shop, only she didn't. Her name was Sylvie. Then, riffling through the pages of *Being and Nothingness*, I read this, with an electrifying feeling of identification.

I have a rendezvous with Sylvie at 4 o'clock.

Rereading it now (p. 43) I see that the author wrote 'Pierre', but I am sure that I *read* 'Sylvie'. And, look, this was surely my café too, 'replete with customers, tables, booths, mirrors, light, smoky atmosphere, the sound of voices, the clinking of saucers, footsteps'. All in all, yes, 'a plenitude of being'. That was the *mot juste*. And yet, when he looks for the face of Pierre/Sylvie and doesn't find it, 'absence haunts the café'. Sartre's nothingness was my nothingness. All this sound, the people, the food, the coffee: it was all subtly permeated, perfumed, with the vacancy, the lack, that was Sylvie. And her absence was in some way a commentary on his. It was obvious that the relationship with Sylvie was not going to work out too well, but if I didn't have Sylvie at least I had Sartre. Maybe he was more my type anyway. He made a life that was – broadly – stupid, meaningless and futile, somehow *philosophical*. Philosophy was not a remote and arid discipline; it was an inherent part of everyday life, so self-evidently there – you just didn't notice it most of the time, like air.

This book had found its ideal reader: I had found *my* book. Its strangeness was my strangeness. And if I had had any sense or regard for morality I would have duly saved up and bought it. But – and this is not an excuse, only a description of what it felt like – I could feel this big book in my hand urging me on to do something reckless and illicit. An *acte gratuit*. The book *made* me do it. When I went up the stairs and crept past the bookseller and the till, where I did not stop to pay, I was sure that it was making an enormous guilty hump in my coat. But I kept on going regardless, out the door, and down the street, expecting alarm bells at any moment, the scream of sirens, pursuit by high-speed police cars, a dragnet closing in on the perpetrator. I was ready to face the consequences, whatever they may be. I would *assume responsibility*.

I didn't think my parents or teachers or twin brother would understand, but the book would. The author would. I was at large in the world, on the run, a fugitive from justice, on my own – except for the book.

So this was what it felt like to be alive. I existed – for the first time. The book-thief was escaping on a bus and he was reading Jean-Paul Sartre's *Being and Nothingness*. I see now, of course, that he (my younger, more felonious self) was not escaping at all: he was hooked, on a bus driving him deeper and deeper into addiction. Sartre had taken the place of Sylvie in my heart. Here was the pre-eminent philosopher of the blues. Feeling bad had never felt so good. Worse was better. 'The emptiness of all plenitude'. As time went on, nothing could brighten my day more than the thought that 'Every existent is born for no reason, prolongs itself out of weakness, and dies by chance.' I carried the book around with me in the way an apprentice gangster stuffs a gun into his belt. On the very rare opportunities that arose to declare my philosophical allegiance, I started – very tentatively – to call myself an *existentialist*. It was just as well not too many people asked me what I meant by it. But then the difficulty of defining it was part of its charm, like an Impressionist painting.

Although, technically, had anyone taken the slightest interest, I could presumably have been thrown into jail (or at least some fearsome youth-rehabilitation facility) on this account, I had the odd feeling that the book guaranteed my immunity from prosecution and allowed me to get away with just about anything. Naturally when I set off not long after for St Tropez, in search of Brigitte Bardot, I took Sartre with me, as a good luck charm. And if I failed then so be it: was everything not 'doomed to failure' anyway? I became a paragon, an evangelist, of *negative* thinking. One thing I knew for sure about being an existentialist: it didn't mean you were necessarily pro-existence.

Which explains why I was instantly seduced by the first sentence of *The Myth of Sisyphus* by Albert Camus.

There is only one really serious philosophical problem: suicide.

My best friend, Bruno (a dog), had died in a road accident not long before and I (a) was initially crushed, but then (b) retaliated by experimenting with improvisatory forms of Russian roulette (I didn't have a gun, but cars and people would definitely do). I hadn't dared go back to the bookshop for a while. This was a book I picked up, quite legally and much less dramatically, from a shelf in the local library (I borrowed it and – a reformed character – took it back again). This might have had something to do with Wendy, who worked in the library on Saturdays and went to the nearby girls' grammar school.

I was starting to read Camus in the sixth form, but it wasn't till I came across that resounding opening sentence – as arresting as the opening chords of Beethoven's Fifth Symphony or Richard Strauss's *Also sprach Zarathustra* – that I felt a real connection. It was *déjà vu* all over again. I had already thought something like this, but I hadn't realized that I thought it. Now I knew. The surprising thing about both Sartre and Camus was that the darker and bleaker their pronouncements, the more life seemed worth living – or, if not entirely worthwhile, then at least intriguing in its very insignificance, or what I learned to call its *absurdity*. (Meaning what exactly? Only to stop worrying about exact meaning.)

For one long hot summer, I *was* Meursault. Like the protagonist of *The Outsider*, I too would go swimming (that was the easy part), have sex (harder), kill someone randomly on the beach (the thought was there), go on trial, get executed, and so on – and keep a diary of my experiences. I adopted the cool, casual, laconic, rather detached way Camus had of speaking of all of this, almost as if it was happening to someone else.

'Do you love me?'

Wendy (unlike Meursault's girlfriend) never did ask such an obviously idiotic question, and vowed instead to study art history, become a prostitute, and write her first novel in French, finally running off with a welder from Bristol. But, had anyone asked, I was ready with my Meursault-style answer: 'That means nothing to me, but probably not.'

Qui perd gagne. Loser wins. It was a perplexing phrase I came across in the stolen book. There was a dash of death-wish about it. And it resonated with the idea of the 'moral victory' we always spoke of after losing a football match (which seemed to happen a lot). I felt sure that the image that Camus conjured up of Sisyphus sweatily shoving his great rock up a hill and yet being at the same time 'happy' with his lot expressed a similar thought. Sartre and Camus became my philosophical guardian angels: minders and bodyguards. I learned from them that no one ever really slotted perfectly and painlessly into the group (family, school, country). Everyone, at some level, no matter how seemingly well-adjusted, was a lonely, anomic wanderer. The world, as Baudelaire said, is a vast hospital in which all the patients want to change beds. Through these two thinkers I learned to love other beings – or hate them, as the case may be, but at least I acknowledged their independent and finally unfathomable existence. I understood that they were just as weird – like refugees from a country that did not exist – as I was. They were outsiders too. It was a beginning. Sartre and Camus provided a self-help (or potentially self-harm) manual for day-to-day existence. They were clearly (so I thought) brothers-in-arms, comrades, intellectual *compadres*.

For some time I tended to mix them up and think of them as one epic writer – Sartre/Camus. Their books – from *Nausea* to *The Plague* – nestled harmoniously together on the shelf, like a vast collaborative exercise. Maybe that wasn't entirely wrongheaded and farfetched. Were all writers not part of some vaster, indeterminate uber-text that shaded off into infinity around the edges? And then they had in common what was perhaps the crux of all existential thinking: a dangerous chemistry between life and literature, ideas and existence. But I should have realized that these two would never be able to fit together into any mutually respectful collective – the duo – for very long. In fact it came as a shock when I discovered that my supposed dream team had morphed into sworn enemies, duellists who feuded over every inch of intellectual territory. It was as bad, in its way, as the Beatles splitting up. Their whole relationship had been more like a collision, a slow-motion car crash, than a collaboration. Half-bromance, half-war of words. Their split marked not just a fault line in the history of the twentieth century, but also a rift in the psyche.

In truth, Sartre and Camus now seem to me like the heavy hitters of a philosophy fight club, exemplifying the clash between the savage and the symbolic. But their schism reflects a duality that goes to the core of what we are and defines what it feels like to be alive. Contemporary insights in cognitive psychology suggest that we are always in two minds. Remixing both Sartre and Camus, existentialism and the absurd, I call it *X-theory*. Each one of us is already double, divided, conflicted. It was something they both realized – that human beings are inherently ironic and philosophers, above all, somewhere between comic and tragic: riven by prehistorical, prelinguistic, preliterate habits and traditions and our more literate or postliterate tendencies, poised between past and future, associative and analytic. Socratic savages, hairless apes with pen and paper – or iPads – in our hands, we cannot live without telling stories about our lives. But what first drew the two men together was bound, equally, to tear them apart. The precarious friendship between the two writers was, as Sartre put it in his uncompromising way, 'a binary praxis of antagonistic reciprocity'. Friend *and* foe. In philosophy, as in football, 'everything is always complicated by the presence of the opposing team'.

Sartre scorned the idea of guilt. It's done: you can't rewind and do it differently. Assume responsibility, be a man. Regret nothing. *I must be without remorse or regrets.* It was Camus who persuaded me to take the book back. Camus had more of a conscience than Sartre; he knew what it was like to be penitent. But really Sartre should have understood: having a conscience was nothing other than having multiple, fragmented selves, slightly out of kilter.

The book-thief's life of crime was over. I had kept well away from the place for a long while in case they had a 'wanted dead or alive' picture of me nailed to the wall. Finally, driven by remorse and the 103 bus, I went back to that undeservingly ripped-off bookshop, book in hand, with some vague notion of confessing or paying up or doing penance. Or perhaps returning the stolen goods (although my copy was now anything but pristine: grubby, torn, battered and littered with delirious marginalia and exclamation marks). In some symbolic way effecting a rectification. And, at some level, I really wanted to ditch the Sartre once and for all. To state the obvious: it wasn't a clear, carefully worked-out plan.

This is what the bookshop looked like when I went back:

It was finally replaced by an estate agent.

The pile of rubble formerly known as 'The Bookshop'

This time I really did feel *responsible*, as if I had personally caused the downfall of a once-mighty edifice by running off with the one book that served as its foundation. I had singlehandedly, unintentionally, deconstructed an entire shopful of books. There was no confession. I could not be forgiven or punished or redeemed or rehabilitated. No one could absolve me of anything. But perhaps it is not too late to atone for that original sin and give back the book I stole. Even if it is warped and mangled and scribbled on.

2

THINK COFFEE

I AM SITTING IN A CAFÉ in New York, on the corner of 4th Street and Mercer, called Think Coffee. This is the capital of the kingdom of outsiders – 'striped', as Sartre once wrote of the city, 'with parallel (but not interconnecting) meanings'. I'm not waiting for anyone in particular any more, neither Sylvie nor Pierre, but I am surrounded – sitting at the counter – by NYU students tapping away on their laptops. What is it about the café that makes it such a natural venue for thinking, the habitat of the philosopher and the writer? The idea is that coffee is good for the brain, an intellectual stimulant. I drink therefore I am. Add to the caffeinated café, if we rewind a few decades, the nicotine factor. The smoke from cigarettes and pipes was like clouds of pure thought wafting towards the ceiling, just as in jazz clubs of the era it seemed like the visual equivalent of improvised music. The true thinker needed not just strong coffee placed nearby but a half-burned cigarette between his fingers.

But there is a more obvious answer. The café is somewhere to sit and talk, somewhere we go to meet other people. The café is a public house, a form of *agora* – the ancient market-place that evolved into the academy: the realm of the inter-subjective, the

point where the parallel lives finally intersect. The seats, as Sartre put it, are owned by everyone and no one. And the café is somewhere, sheltered from the elements, to write in. They rarely throw you out, no matter how long you take over the coffee. Writing, for both Sartre and Camus, was the continuation of a conversation. Their work, even when not explicitly in the form of a play or a novel, has the feeling of a dialogue. Philosophy resides in a relationship or set of relationships, in the resonances and, above all, the intermittences or 'cognitive dissonance' – or flat-out disagreements. The café is also, philosophically, a battlefield, a place where verbal wars – the *agon* – can be fought out in metaphysical combat.

Sartre – after a spell in a German Stalag – wrote most of *Being and Nothingness* in the Café de Flore on the Boulevard Saint-Germain during 1942. He liked to sit near the wood stove (coal was in short supply). He was good at blocking out the noise, the

Nazis, and the distractions, and staying focused. But the café nevertheless seeps into the philosophy, even becomes philosophical. Consider the waiter, for example.

The Flore had no shortage of *garçons*. Perhaps if it had been a fast-food joint the idea would never have occurred to Sartre. Sartre spent hours there every day. He and Simone de Beauvoir had two main working shifts, before and after lunch (for which, ironically, they went elsewhere, to keep costs down). Sartre had his pen, his bottle of ink, and a thick wad of paper all lined up, and a pile of books, spread out on the table, like cards from the pack. He went to one end of the café, Beauvoir to the other. The waiter was the link between them, their go-between. Others would come and go, but the waiter was a constant. Sartre would sit and watch him, going through the same motions, again and again, day after day, until he realized that the waiter embodied

The Café de Flore on the eve of World War Two

something fundamental about human beings generally. He was in a rut and he needed to get out of it.

Sartre, observing the garçon closely, had the impression that he was overdoing it – overacting. He picked up his pen and jotted down the following analysis:

> He has brisk and emphatic gestures, in fact he comes towards the customers a little too briskly, and he bows a little too eagerly, his voice and his eyes express a level of interest in the customer's order that is too full of solicitude. Finally he returns, trying to imitate in his gait the inflexible rigour of an automaton, all the while carrying his tray with the temerity of a tightrope walker, maintaining it in a perpetually unstable equilibrium, perpetually destabilized, and perpetually re-established with only the slightest movement of the arm and hand. His entire conduct seems to us like a game.

So what if the garçon's movements and gestures are a little theatrical? Perhaps all he wants is to make sure he gets a decent tip? No, it's more than that: 'he is playing at being a waiter'. He is *pretending* to be a waiter. But – hold on – surely he *is* a waiter (in the same way, a tailor is a tailor, says Sartre, and a grocer is a grocer), so is that not reasonable? True, but to the extent that he thinks of himself as a waiter, to the degree that he has consciously adopted the role of waiter and made it into his identity, then he is committing the sin of 'bad faith' by excluding at any moment the multiple alternatives, as a free human being, that could be available to him. He is a fake, a phoney.

The garçon is wearing his distinctive black waistcoat, the bowtie, the white apron. But he is, after all, another human being. What if the customers are a little like the waiter? Are they phoneys too? Maybe at some level we – NYU students, professors, baristas, writers, footballers, builders, tree surgeons – are all as guilty as the waiter, by pretending to be what we are when we could just as well be what we are not. That is our rut. But it is a rut of our own making. Beyond the rut lies the land of freedom, at once enticing and frightening. On the upside, we have 'an infinite horizon of possibilities'. On the downside, we will never coincide perfectly with ourselves, 'sincerity is a metaphysical impossibility', and cracks and fissures start to open up in the surface of everyday life, revealing great voids beneath. The waiter is also, Sartre suggests, a *tightrope walker*; his equilibrium is unstable. He could easily fall off his tight, rigid rope, tip one way or another – and become something other than a waiter: a Resistance hero, for example, or, by the same token, a collaborator, a spy, a traitor. Perhaps – secretly – he is already leading these other lives.

Sartre, persisting with his Socratic café dialectic, tried hard to explain his paradoxical point. Perhaps even to convert the garçon into a fully-fledged existentialist freedom-lover.

And look, what have we over here?

I don't see anything, Monsieur, could you be more specific?

But what you have just said confirms the very point I wish to make.

What do you mean?

You used a negative, did you not?

Did I?

You said, 'I do *not* . . .'

Well, yes, but . . .

And where do you think this negative comes from? The power, the possibility, of negation?

I don't know. Oh sorry, there I go again . . .

You see. Contained within all your negatives, like a germ at the heart of a grain of wheat, like an embryo, but more like the opposite of an embryo, must be the possibility of nothingness itself.

I don't get it. I mean, explain further.

All right, let me simplify. Look at this coffee cup, for example.

I see it.

You perceive the coffee cup. You have consciousness of the coffee cup. But *are* you the coffee cup?

No, obviously I am *not* a coffee cup.

There, now you see: consciousness is always consciousness *of* something. But *you* are defined by negation. You know what you are not. You are not a coffee cup – or anything else in particular for that matter. You have a clear sense of what you are *not*. But, let me ask you: do you have an equally clear sense of what you *are*?

Hmm, let me think about that ... Maybe *not*.

I am not an inkwell, nor a glass, adds Sartre in *Being and Nothingness*, looking around his immediate environment. So simple, so obvious, this not-being-something, that we forget it. It is not just that Pierre or Sylvie, by their absence, haunt the café: it is rather that – perpetually – 'nothingness haunts being'. Whatever I am, I am is 'in the mode of not-being', in the same way that an actor is (and is not) Hamlet. To be *and* not to be: there is no 'or' about it.

Thinking and conversation: as integral to the café as cups and saucers. The very sounds and sights of the café illustrate philosophical arguments. The café is shot through in its every atom with the themes of being and nothingness. Like the milk in a good *café au lait*. Like the butter in a croissant. There is nothing that is not philosophical (Sartre was inspired to go to Berlin to study by the suggestion that it was possible to make philosophy out of an apricot cocktail). In fact nothing is – mysteriously – the philosophical subject par excellence. Which is why Camus' parody of a philosopher (in a play he will write some time after meeting Sartre) is known as 'Monsieur Nothingness'.

Jean-Paul Sartre and Albert Camus first met in the summer of 1943 at the opening of Sartre's edgy and provocative new play, *The Flies*, which reworked the myth of Orestes into an anti-Nazi allegory, just subtle enough to get past the censors. The theatre was once called the Sarah Bernhardt, but her all-too-Jewish name had been erased and it was now Théâtre de la Cité. Camus saw Sartre in the lobby of the theatre and went up and introduced himself. Towards the end of 1943, Sartre, Camus, and Simone de Beauvoir met up in the Café de Flore, the very café where Sartre had waited for Pierre, where the clatter of crockery and silverware and the buzz of conversation gave him a sense of 'plenitude'. Camus had already written *The Outsider*. In many ways, in Paris at least, he *was* the 'outsider', having been born and brought up in Algeria, then a French colony. He was the son of an illiterate charlady. Now, having recently turned thirty, he had an office at Gallimard, the publishers, where he had become an editor or 'reader'. Sartre, aged thirty-eight, was the already established author of *Nausea*, short stories, and a play or two. His monumental *Being and Nothingness* had just come out, weighing in at around a kilo and several hundred pages, his 'essay on phenomenological ontology', which shins up the mighty tree of philosophy, clambers bravely out on a high branch and proceeds to saw it off – and is miraculously suspended by the invisible wires of nothingness (while the rest of the tree falls over). Beauvoir, having been dismissed from her teaching job on a charge of 'corrupting a minor' (she had picked up a habit of seducing her students), had recently published *She Came to Stay* (*L'Invitée*) with Gallimard.

Sartre and Camus had so many things in common: neither man growing up had known his father; both had notched up significant literary and philosophical achievements; both were (in their different ways) serial womanizers. Both preferred to be known by their last name. Both had a notion of giving expression to what it feels like to be alive. Both had a powerful sense of humans as divided, contradictory beings, unable to decide between the savage and the symbolic, or mind and body: 'I am not what I am' (Sartre); 'I am a stranger to myself' (Camus). Each man held out the promise of secular transcendence. Camus even wrote a 'defence' of Sartre when he got into trouble with the censors ('when you see who is against him, you have to be with him'. But there were obvious differences. They were, in Bloom's terms, the 'precursor' and the 'ephebe'. Camus, even though a literary sensation, was still very much the new kid on the block.

They ordered coffee and made it last, even though it was not particularly good coffee. When Camus discovered that the waiter's name was Pascal, he started calling him 'Descartes' instead. An absurd joke, but perhaps it made the point about everyone being a philosopher, potentially.

Occupied Paris: a place of fear, torture, and terror. 'A vast Stalag,' said Beauvoir. Wherever they went, Beauvoir, Camus, Sartre, to cafés or the theatre, Nazis and SS officers would go there too. There was no escape. This was post-*Casablanca*. The last train to freedom had left the station long ago. The SS had its headquarters around the corner from the Hôtel Mercure, where Camus was staying. Paris was plastered with Nazi posters ('No Jews Allowed'). As the three of them sat at the Deux Magots or the Flore, German cars cruised by outside and German troops ordered Schnapps at the bar. They were right there all the time, in your face. Which was the whole idea.

At different times and in different ways Camus, Sartre and Beauvoir participated in the Resistance, certainly at an intellectual level. Sartre accepted that he was more one of the 'writers who resist' than the 'Resisters who write'. Occasionally they risked their lives. Being alive always implied the risk of death, but now more than ever. People they knew were being arrested and killed. Others were collaborating. Thousands of Jews were being routinely rounded up and shipped off to die in the camps. This was the high tide of the Holocaust. It is odd then that, as Sartre put it in an essay written some time later, 'we were never so free as under the German Occupation'.

To understand this point of view, it is necessary to forget that the Liberation of Paris took place in 1944 or that the Second World War came to an end in 1945 with the death of Hitler and the final defeat of Germany and the Axis. In other words, we have to give up any idea of history. In 1943, 1943 is anything other than history. It is still happening. Rommel has surrendered North Africa. The Allies have landed in Italy. The Soviets are punishing Germany in the East. But in the middle of 1943 it is still possible for the war to go either way. Or in any one of several different ways. If you are alive in 1943, whichever side you are fighting on, you can have no real confidence in the final outcome. You might hope, pray, scheme, plan, struggle, make confident statements and prophecies, and so on, but you can have no clear knowledge about how all the forces in play will ultimately shake out. Who, for example, will put any money on the subsequent Cold War, or the rise and fall of the Berlin Wall? And what will the role of America be post-World War Two?

In *The Man in the High Castle* (1962), Philip K. Dick describes an America that has been taken over and divided up by Imperial Japan and Nazi Germany. This is now seen as an 'alternate history', a story of what might have been had things gone differently. In *Fatherland* (1992), Robert Harris evokes a Germany where the Nazis are still in power and the Final Solution is still on the agenda. Historians call these hypothetical scenarios 'counterfactual'. In 1943, they are not counterfactual. These outcomes are not only imaginable; they must also seem plausible or even likely.

In one future, Hitler dies and the Nazis are defeated.

In another, there is no D-Day, the Axis nations roll back any

Springtime for Hitler

adversaries and fascism gradually encircles the world. George Orwell's vision of a boot stamping on your face *forever* comes true.

These are possible futures. Nothing is inevitable. Maybe the world comes to an end. Maybe it doesn't.

Paris, now part of Nazi Europe, nominally ruled by Vichy but still looking towards de Gaulle, the Resistance, and the Allies, was a divided city. It was a place of bifurcating paths leading in radically opposed directions. If you were alive in 1943, it would be reasonable for you to feel that whatever you decided to do next could well make a difference to the shape and fate of the world. You would be personally responsible (in no matter how small a way) for the future. You would make a difference; what you chose to do would have serious consequences. You could be a traitor, a hero, a fascist, or a freedom fighter. Whether or not you were a waiter. All this is true at any time – it is still true – but it was especially and graphically true in the middle of 1943 in the middle of a war in France and beyond. 'I have to choose between making a bomb and concentrating on philosophy,' Camus wrote (rather riskily) from the mountains of the Massif Central. 'This is a cruel uncertainty.'

In the midst of the war he was trying to write a book about the war, *The Plague*, in which invading rats cause an epidemic of the bubonic plague in an Algerian town. But he had no idea how it was all going to turn out, the war or the book. He often felt like a failure. He lacked an ending. Maybe this was what made it so hard to write. He came up with a threshold ending, open-ended, in which he admits all this or something like it could happen again, at any time. 'The plague bacillus never dies or disappears.' Still he had doubts about the allegorical approach. 'I do not think that the war is finished,' he wrote to his friend and mentor Jean Grenier, 'and in any case the worst of it is yet to come.' This state of not-knowing was part of what he had a habit of calling the 'Absurd'. We want to get everything clear, says Camus, to understand, to know – to live a life as if it were already history – but demand outstrips supply. Life is absurd, nothing is fixed; there are alternative outcomes. It is like being in a room and there are a number of different doors and depending on which door you open you end up in an entirely different world.

Or doors that somebody else opens for you; doors you would rather remain closed.

Towards midnight one heard the sound in the street of late passers-by hurrying to get home before the curfew, and then there was silence. And we knew that the only footsteps clacking past outside were *their* steps. It is difficult to give the impression that this deserted city could give, this *no-man's land* plastered against our windows and which they alone inhabited. The houses were never exactly a protection. The Gestapo often performed their arrests between midnight and five in the morning. It felt at each moment as if the door could open, letting in a cold blast, a bit of night, and three affable Germans armed with revolvers. Even when we did not talk about them, even when we did not think about them, their presence was among us.

So Sartre wrote in 'Under the Occupation', evoking not just a historical episode but also a mood of existential uncertainty. 'Being is discovered as *fragile*', as he puts it in *Being and Nothingness*. Friends and acquaintances would simply disappear in the night. But it didn't take a war to persuade him of this feeling of not knowing what happens next. Rather the war came as a confirmation of his preliminary intuitions. '*I am* this war', he wrote. In his first novel, *Nausea*, written in the 1930s while he was teaching in Le Havre, the hero, Antoine Roquentin, is trying to write the biography of an obscure eighteenth-century nobleman, and failing miserably. Eventually he decides to give up when he realizes that there is something dubious about all history and in fact all stories. His main example is Balzac, the great nineteenth-century novelist, who wrote in a quasi-historical way about people who were no longer alive (even assuming they ever had been in the first place). Not so different, in other words, from what Roquentin is trying to do.

But, concludes Roquentin, it can't be done. Every story, every history (in French – *histoire* – the distinction disappears) is a lie, an obvious falsification of real experience. A fake. Here is the fundamental problem: if you are telling a story (as opposed to hearing it, or reading it) you already know the outcome. You have a punchline. You have the sense of an ending or a *telos*; hence the whole story is teleological, end-oriented, even from the very beginning. There is a feeling of inevitability. But there shouldn't be, since this is just what is missing from our lives. The novel, or biography, is the narrative equivalent of the waiter who is overdoing it – fakes or phoneys. For the fictional hero, the end is there from the very beginning; everything is 'radiant with the light of future passions'. In everyday life, in contrast, it's all the other way around. We have no idea where to begin because we don't know where it's all going to end either. This is the advantage of apocalyptic thinking, 'The End is Nigh', for example, or 'The world will come to an end tomorrow': when you know how it's going to turn out everything makes some kind of sense (however dark). This, says Sartre, is like 'trying to catch time by the tail'.

In the present, the future has by definition not yet taken place. No end, no beginning, and not too much sense either.

Take away the narrative structure and things quickly fall apart. The present is precarious. This, Sartre implies, is why we make up stories in the first place: to try to hold it all together. We invent narrative in order to rectify our sense of lack or foreboding. But then, in telling the tale, we cannot possibly be speaking the truth. But what if we give up stories, relinquish our tenuous hold on structure and closure, what then? The answer is: we don't know, not really, we are not sure, because we live in a state of ignorance about the future. What Camus called the absurd, Sartre – borrowing from Hegel – calls *contingency*. Their common thrust is that '*anything, anything* could happen', nothing is foreclosed. Narrative has an end, a point; life doesn't, it's pointless. 'You have to choose,' Roquentin/Sartre writes. 'To live or to tell stories.' I am not my narrative.

Stories are told backwards, life is lived forwards. A tale told by an idiot, perhaps, full of sound and fury, signifying nothing. 'Case closed' is written, explicitly or implicitly, at the end of every good detective story. The problem is solved, all the absurdity and contingency are erased. But life isn't like that. The case is not closed. Life is open. Everyone is a writer; you can keep on changing the script, again and again. And that is part of the problem: there are too many writers out there, each with his or her own plot, with quite distinct endings in view, or none at all. We are self-created, self-authored. 'Freedom and creation are one' (as Sartre put it in his essay on 'Cartesian Liberty'). We cannot choose: we have to live *and* tell stories about it. There is no 'or', neither for Roquentin nor the rest of us. Philosophy is nothing more than a meditation on the *and*, the frontier between the physical and the metaphysical.

The trouble with the Nazis was not that they killed people, Sartre reckoned, it was *how* they killed them. Sartre, like Philip K. Dick, was a quantum thinker: he imagined parallel worlds, he saw the Real as a giant acceleration chamber in which particles collided with unpredictable results. The Nazis, in contrast, were monists, not pluralists: they wanted to control what the particles were doing. They hated unpredictability. They were attacking the future, the very possibility of there being a future. 'They stole our future [...] the Occupation stripped people of their future [...] we had no more destiny than a nail or a doorhandle.' The Resistance was a way of 'recovering a future'. Or futures.

It is something Sartre complained about, obliquely, in the essay he wrote in February 1939, before war broke out, on the highly respected Catholic novelist François Mauriac: he cannot be a serious novelist, argues Sartre, because his characters are not unpredictable enough. He is like a fascistic puppet-master pulling their strings (and using terms like 'fate' and 'destiny'). Whereas, even in a novel, you shouldn't know how it is all going to work out. 'The theory of relativity applies fully to the novelistic universe. There is no place for a privileged observer in the true novel any more than in the world of Einstein.' He finishes the essay with a scathing put-down: Mauriac has tried to make himself into some kind of fake god, equipped with pseudo-omniscience, but 'God is not an artist; and neither is Mauriac.' (Curiously, Camus thought that God, if only he existed, would make a decent artist – a novelist of the realist tendency, to be specific, with a solid grasp of the omniscient narrative.)

Sartre would have said something similar about the Nazis: that they were like bad artists, trying to impose their own narrative, to be surrogate gods. They were trying to control and dictate the real, abolishing the virtual. Under the Reich there would be no parallel worlds, only one world and that world was Nazi. That is what totalitarianism is like. You have to fit in: there is no room for misfits and outsiders: no self-authoring. For them, there is no alternative. Alternatives get arrested, tortured, and sent to the gas chambers.

Sartre, in contrast, was the supreme advocate of virtual realities. For Sartre, the virtual was real. The real was virtual. Nothing was set in stone. There was no past and no future: nothing that could not be rewritten. I think that is why, even in the middle of 1943, surrounded by Nazis and the forces of Vichy France, it was possible to feel 'free', which is to say having no idea how it was all going to turn out. The writer is not God. A book is only a patchwork of guesses, gaps, and interpretations ('a book exists *against* its author' Sartre wrote. No one should be quite sure how the story ends, or even if it ends. In some way it is still happening. The bacillus will return.

Sartre and Camus in 1943: this could be the beginning of a beautiful friendship. Or, of course, not.

3

THE INVITATION

B EAUVOIR WAS STRUCK first of all by the differences between
the two men, in terms of physique, physiognomy, accent,
bearing. On the one hand (as Arthur Koestler describes
the pair), the 'malevolent goblin or gargoyle' (Sartre), on the
other the 'young Apollo' (Camus). Beauty and the Beast. Shrek
and Bogart (Camus deliberately cultivated a trenchcoat, with the
collar turned up). The Nordic philosopher (in Camus' terms)
and the sensual man of the south. It seemed more like a collision of worlds than a meeting. But the two men soon found
common ground in their enthusiasm for the prose poetry of
Francis Ponge, *Le Parti pris des choses* (*The Voice of Things*), which
brings out the strangeness and complexity of everyday things:
snails, pebbles, butterflies, an orange (and which Ponge himself
called 'failures of description'). They talked theatre. In Algiers,
Camus had been the leader of an amateur theatrical troupe.
At a certain point in their conversation, Sartre and Beauvoir
invited him up to Beauvoir's hotel room to try out *No Exit* (*Huis
clos*, literally *Closed Doors*), the new play Sartre had been writing.
Maybe he would like to play the part of Garcin, how would that
be? He could even be director.

Camus hesitated. An invitation from Sartre. He could say yes or he could say no. All he had to do was look at his watch and claim a pressing engagement. There were certainly a lot of other things he could be doing. The future was 'not there yet' (as Sartre puts it in *Nausea*). He didn't want to be boxed in. Least of all become an add-on or accomplice to Sartre-Beauvoir (like the garçon?)

And, to be honest, he could readily think of a lot of good reasons for saying no. *Look at what happened to Xavière.* The *Invitée*. Admittedly, she was only a fictional character, but it didn't feel like fiction. Camus had only skimmed Beauvoir's *She Came to Stay*, her novel about what happens when she moves a friend into her hotel (someone at Gallimard put it on his desk). It wasn't so much the fact (if you could call it a fact) that she is murdered on the last page that lingered in his mind. It was more the first page.

He had been surprised that it took so long to bump off the Xavière character. She was set up as potential victim almost from the beginning. In his own novel, it took only about a hundred pages or so to shoot the Arab on the beach (the rest was all different takes on what had happened). Beauvoir span it out to more than 400. Not that there weren't things in it to savour and admire. On the contrary. Look, for example, at her simple description of having breakfast. 'Françoise picked up a piece of toast; it was all crusty on the surface and yielding inside; she coated it with butter and filled the bowls with café au lait.' Camus noticed how good she was on the texture of everyday life; it gave a kind of authenticity and anchorage to everything she wrote, no matter how strange and perturbing.

Or, again, towards the end of the book, on that camping holiday with the young Gerbert, how she twists and turns – will she, won't she (an uncertainty that starts around page two)? – before finally getting up the courage to ask him, lying there in the straw in some barn deep in the countryside, 'I was wondering what you would say if I were to say to you, "Would you sleep with me?"' Camus could just imagine her saying that, in its contorted, prolix way. And still they had to have a longwinded conversation before anything really happened. And they both use the formal *vous* throughout (as Sartre and Beauvoir do), before, during, and afterwards, as if they had only just met, and everyone had to be madly polite, even though naked in a barn. Yet, at the same time, this was the frankest depiction of feminine desire that he had yet come across. For a moment he could almost – the effect was spooky – feel himself inside her body, having all those sensations but *as a woman*: 'Hesitantly, incredulously, she caressed the surface of this hard, smooth young body, that had seemed to her for so long untouchable.' Almost like the toast. Firm at first and then yielding. He could taste it, feel it in his hands, on his lips. Maybe that was the point of fiction, after all, to *be* someone else. Something else. To experiment with identity and gender. Sometimes Camus would grow tired of the immense effort of virility: 'It is not always easy to be a man, and even less so to be a pure man.'

There was no question about it, she could write. Gallimard were fortunate to have her on their list. Maybe, in some ways, she was even a better writer than Sartre. But sometimes she wrote like an academic, determined to prove a point, burying the argument in footnotes. If I'd been writing it, Camus considered, sipping at his coffee, I'd have cut it in half and made it twice the book. It was something he thought about when he'd been reading Sartre's *Nausea*, back in Algiers. Camus loved philosophy, but he thought it was possible to have too many words. Sometimes you had to bypass all the 'what would you do if I were to say to you . . .?' stuff and just get on with it. He wanted to be seduced by language (almost as if it were not language at all), not persuaded rhetorically, beaten over the head with it, doing philosophy (as Nietzsche would say) with a hammer.

Camus inspected Beauvoir intently. She could hardly present more of a contrast to Sartre. He was like a flyweight boxer who has taken a few knocks and doesn't care. She was more like . . . a mannequin. That smooth, perfect skin, the sort of turban or headscarf – *hijab*, they would call it in Algeria – that she wore around her hair, the well-pressed clothes, elegant, so demure. High-class. Hard to believe she could be capable of murder? No, that would be to underestimate her. Everybody was capable of killing, in certain circumstances. Camus himself for one. Which is why he wrote about it in *The Outsider* (at heart, he was anything but a pacifist). But few would do it as neatly as Beauvoir – or, at any rate, her protagonist, Françoise. The perfect crime. Françoise made his own Meursault look like a naïve, blundering fool. He blew the guy's brains out right there on the beach in broad daylight. Crudely, brazenly, without thinking about it. Naturally he didn't expect to get away with it. Fully expected to be executed from that point on. Whereas she, on the other hand, so clever, so cunning, switches off the gas at the main, turns on the ring in her victim's room, without her noticing, then slips back to switch the gas supply back on, just as soon as Xavière has knocked herself out with sleeping pills. It would be seen as either suicide or accident. Very neat, no loose ends. The door is even conveniently bolted on the inside. No one, not even Agatha Christie or Sam Spade, would suspect her of murder. And yet – this was her essentially philosophical point – they really ought to. Don't be fooled by the looks. Beware the hammer.

Maybe it is not so surprising that Camus was slightly scared of Beauvoir.

*

She had first heard about Camus on the train. Or overheard. People were discussing *The Outsider* and were actually comparing it to *Nausea*. Despite her irritation, it was obvious she would have to read it in the end.

She had to admit that she liked his face. There was something so frank and open about it. Spontaneous and unconsidered. His face (you could say) abolished the duality of the real and the apparent. For once, she felt, appearances really could be trusted. He smiled and laughed easily (mostly at Sartre's jokes). His mouth was slightly lopsided with the half-smoked cigarette permanently stuck to his lower lip in that man-of-the-people way of his. He put her in mind of Jean Gabin, the great French movie star of the era. Except that Gabin was always so tragic (look at *Le jour se lève*, for example, where he commits suicide at the end, and which some said had contributed to the downfall of France). And Camus, on the other hand, seemed like the exact opposite of tragic. Humorous, yes, but not exactly comic either. Perhaps more like one of those American actors, a cowboy or a gangster. No hubris, no hamartia, no fissure or fatal flaw of character. He seemed so reassuringly solid and present.

Unlike Sartre, of course, where one was practically obliged to look beyond the surface, not into the 'soul' of course, but rather outwards at a horizon of infinite possibilities. There was no point denying it: she could feel a definite sexual tug in his direction (which she could choose to ignore or not). Maybe he wasn't really her type – supposing she had a 'type' – but she couldn't help wondering what Sartre would say if she were to end up sleeping with Camus. It would be an interesting experiment. He might even be jealous for once. That would be a change. Sex and death: these were the core phenomena, she felt sure, that defined you as a human being. What attitude did you take up towards them? You had to be *unafraid*.

Meursault, his fictional hero, was unafraid of dying. Camus, she suspected, was the same way. She couldn't find any real philosophical justification for it (that wasn't quite true, she could find a philosophical justification for anything), but she had an instinctive horror of cowardice. Everyone should really be ready to die at any moment and any other attitude was simply a pathetic overestimation of self-worth. This is how she saw it. Narcissism: Camus seemed to be devoid of it. No, not *devoid* (obviously there was a hint of Rastignac about him) but not consumed by it either. Perhaps it was a kind of bond between them: they had both been murderers, through their fictional personae. He was the outsider, certainly, a *pied noir* among Parisians, but she had a sudden presentiment that he could easily become an insider, one of the inner circle, part of *la famille*.

Perhaps even – yes, she might as well admit it straight out, the idea occurred to her almost instantly – become part of a brand new type of *trio*. Look at *No Exit*, for example: it was another variation on the *ménage à trois*. One man, two women. Not a bad deal for the guy all in all (and yet still Sartre has the audacity to call it 'hell'!). But did it always have to be that way around?

She would always grow tired of these young girls (Olga, for example) before Sartre did; she couldn't help it, that was just the way she was. She liked to get rid of, he liked to collect, hated to let go. Sex was like a statement, a proposition – how often could you keep repeating yourself? In a sense, Sartre was doing her a favour by relieving her of the burden. She was (suddenly seeing herself as some kind of Olympic athlete) passing on the baton, so to speak, and having a quiet breather. Still, all the same, no doubt about it, going purely by the numbers, Sartre was getting the better part of the deal. He, after all, had two women constantly vying for his attention (at least two, she should add –

there was nothing to stop him acquiring a whole harem at the current rate).

Whereas she, conversely . . . Wouldn't it turn things around dramatically – level the playing field – for there to be two *men* in the trio and let them compete over her for a change? How would that be? Wouldn't it be . . . fair? Just? A small victory for women, or at least *a* woman. What was sauce for the gander . . .

It was the kind of thing you could read about in romantic novels from Jane Austen on, Madame de Staël, Colette, but come to think of it she had never before really experienced it at close quarters, the threesome, at least not involving two men whom she actively wanted to pursue her, fight over her, ultimately – and it didn't take long to start thinking the ultimate – kill for the right, the privilege, to plant their flag in her body. Perhaps, who knew, Sartre might even consider . . .

*

Camus was not exactly anti-Hegel, but he was not pro-Hegel either. Maybe that was what reading Hegel's dialectic did to you: you could never quite make your mind up for ever after. He'd never really taken to it, though, not in the way Sartre clearly had. Maybe, in fact, he really did hate it. And Beauvoir's Hegelian epigraph was possibly the most intimidating and off-putting epigraph he had ever read – unless perhaps it was the exact opposite and that was precisely what sucked him, in some perverse way, into the book. It was the darkest possible view of human instincts. '*Chaque conscience poursuit la mort de l'autre.*' Each of us seeks the death of the other. The philosophy of either/or, what Hegel called the 'master-slave relationship'. If you weren't Napoleon, then you were condemned to be the victim of other Napoleons; kill or be killed. Such were the options. In a time of war, it made a lot of sense. How could one think in any other terms? And it fitted the book to perfection – he had to admit that much.

Camus saw Beauvoir's book as something like a room, or a black box, or possibly like light entering the retina: you go in one way, and you come out again completely turned around, inverted, transformed. It began with one absurdity and ended with another. Solipsism: me, myself, and I, maybe all human beings were a little like this. A natural self-protective instinct that got out of hand, a principle of extreme selfishness taken to its logical conclusion. Perhaps writers in particular, with their fondness – their need – for solitude, were this way inclined. Hadn't the Irish philosopher Bishop Berkeley based his whole philosophy on the idea? It was a surrealist metamorphosis of empiricism, inflating sense data into the building bricks of reality. He held that when you left the room, everyone else in it either ceased to exist or fell into a kind of slumber from which they would awake only when you walked back in. And what happened when you fell asleep? Did the whole world collapse in on itself for want of an observer to perceive it and thus conjure it up out of his 'impressions'? Fortunately for the bishop, God was somewhere in the wings, keeping an eye on things, ensuring its continued existence. But what if . . .

Beauvoir put it so much better, he thought. With her it was a form of realistic solipsism, an everyday solipsism, the kind that people really suffered from. Especially at night, in a theatre, when all the actors and the crowds had gone home.

When she was not there, this scent of dust, this penumbra, this desolate solitude, none of it existed, not for anyone. But now she was there, and a red glow rose up out of the carpet and penetrated the darkness like a timid nightlight. She alone had this power: her very presence snatched things out of their state of unconsciousness, their inexistence, she invested them with colour, with smell. She went down a floor and pushed open the door to the auditorium. It was like a mission that had been entrusted to her: to take this whole vast empty space, this void, a thing of the night, and make it exist.

Beauvoir's Genesis – almost as if she were giving birth. Let there be light – or at least an eerie red glow. He had experienced something like it himself, back in Algiers, at the university (like another world! A lost paradise!) with his own theatre group, after the theatre itself emptied out, when everything that had taken place on stage, or off it, came to seem increasingly like an illusion, a fantasy, a bubble blown through a pipe on the surface of which, if you looked closely enough, you could see your own reflection. The point, though, surely, was to burst the bubble, to remember always that there are other beings out there, just like you, other solipsists, thinking similar thoughts. As there were in this café, right now.

'It is impossible to conceive that other people are conscious beings too, aware of their own existence just as I am of mine [. . .] Nothing was real but her own life.' Camus understood Beauvoir's view – he even considered it seriously – but rejected it as a mistake. Alone in a theatre at night, you could entertain the idea, but here, now, sitting in a café, surrounded by autonomous beings with plans of their own, in broad daylight, it became practically inconceivable. So it was in the novel: other people, so unpredictable, so *other*, with their own ideas and feelings, start getting in the way and spoiling the comforting illusion of omniscience. It was obvious that, in the end, if you felt this way strongly enough, and held to it and privileged the self above others, you would have to murder somebody, perhaps everybody. Or possibly have sex with them.

The murder scene struck him as an allegory of the sexual act itself: a slightly more extreme way of giving vent to and quelling all those chaotic desires. That could be the secret power of

Beauvoir's work, Camus hypothesized: she wouldn't come out and say so explicitly, but amid all the talk and bravado and actual liaisons, it was clear (to him at least) that what she (or Françoise) really wanted was to have sex with Xavière herself, another woman. To 'possess' her, body and soul. That was the great *unsaid* of the book, the repressed, lesbian undercurrent. He couldn't help wondering why she didn't just come right out and say it. All women were potential lesbians after all. Just as all men were inverts, at one time or another, in theory at least. The Greeks were perfectly explicit about it.

Except that there it was, even before page one, right up front, even before Hegel, in the dedication itself: 'To Olga Kosakievicz'. Maybe it meant nothing, but philosophically speaking, if you insisted on being a serious solipsist in daylight hours, either you had to have sex with other people and they became an extension of your own desires, yielding and surrendering; or you had to kill them. Possess the body entirely – or eradicate it.

That was the simple choice that Beauvoir, looking at him steadily across the table, seemed to offer: sex or death.

*

And then there were his stupid jokes. Camus made you laugh. Calling the garçon 'Descartes', for example, when his real name was Pascal. As if, at some level, everyone was truly a philosopher. Which in fact they were – just not necessarily very good philosophers. Mostly they couldn't think their way out of a paper bag.

That, Beauvoir reflected, was surely Sartre's point about the garçon in *Being and Nothingness*. Everyone was pretending to be something. A waiter, for example. But this waiter took himself too seriously; he was guilty of bad faith. Let him play at being a waiter. But he didn't seem to realize he could be anything he pleased or, at least, *not* a garçon, the domain of not-waiter appeared unintelligible to him. This was his big mistake.

Garçon: Pascal or Descartes. Waiter or . . . boy. A male. Why not *garçonne*? The word contained *garce* (bitch), after all. Yes, a point that really should have occurred to Sartre, but one that eluded him somehow. Boys were being boys all the time in some bad-faith way, like John Wayne, a man's gotta do what a man's gotta do, and nothing else. But couldn't girls be boys too? And boys could be girls, surely . . .

But no: impossible. Sartre told her flat-out. He admitted he couldn't justify it philosophically. He simply preferred the company of women. Funny really. On the one hand, he was possibly the most radical man in the world, anti-everything, he could dazzle and burn a hole right through any argument with the sheer lens of his intellect. But in some respects he was endearingly old-fashioned and conventional. Straight as a die. Not a warped or queer or inverted bone in his whole damn body. He could write about inverts only from the outside. Although he had no objection to her own Sapphic exploits, thank goodness.

On the contrary, he took pleasure in hearing all about them, in the most intimate detail possible. It was as if he was there himself, he would say, living through her. But how would he feel about *her* fucking another *guy*? Maybe, with his marked preferences, he would be simply indifferent? Unless of course he were to become obsessed, jealous, moody, and decided to murder both of them in a fit of passion. It was a classic scene; it happened every day of the week, the *crime passionnel*. Always in the newspapers. Sartre, on the face of it, seemed like an improbable candidate for murderer, but on a horizon of infinite possibility all scenarios were equally likely and unlikely.

On the other hand, yes, she could readily imagine Camus killing somebody. He would have no compunction in pulling the trigger. Sartre would probably stand there thinking about it too much and dithering, like Hamlet. Whereas once he, Camus, *l'étranger*, the strange one, had made up his mind then you were as good as dead. She liked that about him. Direct, decisive. More a man of action than a philosopher.

He reminded her of that character in Malraux's *La Condition humaine* (*The Human Condition*), the Chinese assassin, the 'terrorist', who gets a great buzz out of it, actually enjoys sticking the knife in and driving it down and twisting it around, ripping the flesh and tearing into some vital organs and feeling the body give way, limply, beneath him. It was a feeling of power, obviously, the same feeling that went through her when she imagined Françoise gassing Xavière. It was a good feeling. She had long wanted to kill off that character, almost from the moment she had invented her (if she had invented her), so naturally she would get her protagonist to do the job for her. She often thought about killing people who annoyed her and whom she was simply tired of (the entire German army would be top of the list, of course, but it was a long, long list). Just as she often thought about having sex with others. Camus, for example.

But then what if he was an invert? Surely not. He seemed straight enough. But who could tell? It would certainly explain a lot about *The Outsider*. All that *misterioso*, the ellipsis, the enigma. What if it was just a code for homosexual desire? Meursault, who we knew enjoyed the company of men – all that naked swimming, very Greek – and felt uncomfortable or inadequate in the company of women, has to kill the Arab to cover up his perverted lust. Is that it? He would rather kill somebody, anybody, than admit to being gay. This, after all, is what she had had in mind when she used that line from Hegel as the epigraph to her own novel: everyone seeks the death of the Other, obviously, but above all of the Other that is the secret self, that which cannot be admitted openly. Which we would do anything – including murder – rather than own up to. And the gun going off, pulling the trigger,

New York Times

Camus

the sun beating down, the heavy breathing, all that: an obvious allegory of the sexual act itself. She determined to reread the book with this in mind. It was certainly something that Sartre had missed in his review, all that obsessing over tenses and style. Perhaps he had a blind spot as regards the *repressed*.

Which did she think of more often? Sex or death? It was an intriguing question. It would provide a kind of barometer of human emotions, and she was going to have to monitor her thoughts more closely and try to keep count if at all possible (she suspected it would come out around equal – *égalité*, deuce, as they say in tennis). That was the silver lining of Occupied Paris, with Nazis marching right down the boulevard and Resistance burrowing in every alley and dark corner, she thought: sex or death or some lethal combination of the two always seemed imminent. No, not just imminent – present, right here, now, in the very air you breathed, inescapable, inexhaustible.

It was odd, almost a paradox: it used to be, before the war, that life was utterly pointless, futile, worthless – that was a given; now, in the midst of war, life was worth infinitely less than ever before, it could be sacrificed in an instant many times over, for no reason – and yet, on that account, the rather high probability of being extinguished at any moment, the mere fact of being alive felt rather more valuable and desirable than before. The *Blitz mentality*, as she had heard it referred to. Pleasure amid the bombs, dancing on the edge of your own grave – with or without a Blitz. Well, then, let us dance!

*

*I can have sex with you, or I can kill yo*u. Camus could see something of all this in Beauvoir's flawless, almost Oriental face. Not so inscrutable. *I haven't quite made my mind up yet, so you'd better behav*e. It was at once seductive and intimidating. Maybe sex *an*d death. All sex was a form of suicide, after all.

There was one other thing that stuck in his mind from reading that novel. Something he couldn't quite manage to unstick. A mere detail, almost nothing really, a trick of style. Maybe he was imagining the whole thing, and yet it had made a powerful impression at the time. It was there and it was not there. And yet now, as he looked from Beauvoir to Sartre, it came back to him again, in an almost physical, visceral way. Only two letters, but still . . .

Once Camus had started noticing it, he could hardly stop, so that the whole novel seemed to be permeated, underpinned, undermined by it, like a worm or a mole tunnelling through the soil. It gave the whole thing the feeling of an un-novel, an anti-text. He picked it up only around halfway through, but he was willing to bet that, if he went right back to the beginning, he would find it there too: all those verbs, apparently so different, and yet really only variations on a theme of *un*doing: dé*commander* (cancel) *un rendezvous*, décontenancé (discomfited), décomposé (distorted), dé*visager* (stare at someone's face), dé*concertée* (disconcerted), and so on. On just about every page. Even the Sartre/Pierre character is described as having '*dis*orderly' or '*dis*organized' (or 'irregular') features [*traits désordonnés*]. Fair comment (especially those crazy eyes!). But, still, it struck him as a mysterious, subterranean leitmotif, seeping into and subverting just about everything, tearing it all apart, dis-arranging or un-creating, abolishing and wiping out the very thing that has just been forced into existence by the act of writing. Like Penelope – so loyal to Odysseus – unpicking her sewing during the night. A grammatical form of murder. An assassin among prefixes.

To Camus, this single syllable, in its microscopic, quantum way, confirmed what the rest of the novel seemed to say, that the idea of the trio, the three-way relationship, even the three-way conversation, stands no chance of ever succeeding. Beauvoir, Olga, Sartre. Sartre, Beauvoir, Camus. One way or another, the trio would always fall apart, dis-integrate, de-cohere, come unstuck. Everything would always fall apart. *Dé* – a die. Another throw and everything would be changed. Beauvoir, the dice-woman. Or *un*-woman. Simone *dé* Beauvoir.

*

He looked at Camus, fixing him with his gaze, and Camus looked right back at him, frankly, giving him a disarming grin. Like Chaplin almost. So cheerful, so cheeky. He really was perfect for the part of Garcin. A tough guy, not bad-looking, who starts off optimistically enough – well, this place isn't so bad! – and yet he was surely doomed to be beaten down in the end, consumed by the hell of it all.

Garcin: how odd, he'd only just noticed, the merest difference from *garçon*, as if he were some exemplary male figure, or perhaps not so different from a waiter after all. Perhaps deep down he had had that in mind all along. Sartre struck a match and relit his pipe and sucked on the stem and let a great cloud of smoke billow out of the corner of his mouth. The smoke floated between them like a veil.

It was something Sartre had first noticed at school, this mystery of the gaze. It prompted what was one of his earliest properly philosophical inquiries. He must have been aged around ten or eleven; even then, he couldn't understand why he hadn't thought of it before. It was obvious really. Everything really important always was obvious – it just needed a little spelling out sometimes, that was all. He was conscious, first of all, of the Thing. And, at the same time, the *No*-thing (that was himself) being conscious of the Thing. The Thing was obviously real, there was no doubt about that. Solid and imperturbable. Whereas he, the *No-thing*, was he real? In other words, there was a necessary antithesis between sentient and non-sentient being. Take, for example, this book. No, too easy – obviously that was just reading. Take, then, this pen. The one he used every day for

Sartre doing his Maigret impersonation

writing in his exercise books, dipping it in ink, then scrawling on the paper with it, filling page after page, like some kind of machine, recording the pulse of the world, or his own, signals of some kind, incomprehensible but inexhaustible.

He held the pen in his hand now; he glanced at it for an instant only, but inspecting it closely. Nothing in the least bit disturbing about it, nor exciting either, just a length of matter (deeply eroded and gnawed-at here and there) with a metal device on one end (the nib). He could look at it all day, he supposed, except it would become very boring. Come to think of it, at a stretch, it could be used to stab someone, but he didn't think it would be very effective. You would have to stab something very vulnerable and exposed. Like the eye, for example.

Which was the point that had originally preoccupied him, precisely. Why would you even want to stab someone, especially through the eye? Yet there it was, the thought was there. It had announced itself, as he knew it would. A mini-epiphany of sorts. Like the scene with the scalpel at the beginning of *Un Chien Andalou*. And the reason for that thought seemed to have something to do with the eye itself.

For when he tried to look directly into the eye of another, one of his schoolmates, François or Léon, for example, then it was incomparably different to the experience of looking at the pen. For one thing, François would look right back at him, returning his gaze, as if in a game of tennis, putting extra power or swerve into it, trying to get past his defences. The pen did not look back, could not return the gaze; it just sat there inert. Tranquil, indifferent, devoid of anxiety. Easy to control, relatively speaking.

Whereas François and he: they had pens, they owned them, but they were *not* and never could be pens. At some level it would be good to be just a pen, to be a pure pen, nothing other than a pen, for a change (God knows, he tried hard enough at just that!). But impossible of course. When he and François looked at one another, they knew all right: it was as if they were locked in combat, arm-wrestling, say, or in fact just plain wrestling (and sometimes they did that too but, fundamentally, it was always the gaze that decided it). It was *eye-wrestling*.

He used to love this game, in part because he would invariably win. The other *garçon* would eventually crack and shy away, or blink, or break into a smile, or let out a great cry and storm off in anguish. The young Sartre could last longer than any of his schoolmates, could sustain the agonizing, inquiring stare of the scruffy urchin on the opposite side of the desk. Eyeball to eyeball. Nose to nose. He could take it. He always would win – it was a foregone conclusion. He was class champion: he would take on all-comers, and conquer them. Then or now.

But that wasn't what interested him, philosophically speaking. Winning was nothing, or next to nothing. No, what really intrigued him was *why* it was so insanely difficult, to the point of delirium, for two human beings to look each other in the eye for much longer than a second or two. What was so hard about that? And yet even he, J-P Sartre, found it intensely uncomfortable, as if he would rather be anywhere other than here, doing anything other than gazing into the window of the soul, faced with 'the unbearable and obscene indiscretion of your gaze' (as Garcin says. But it was clearly worse for his miserable adversaries. Momentarily they would be driven mad or, to put it another way, would choose madness rather than continue to stare into the eye of the boy sitting opposite. As if it were some refined form of torture.

And yet there was no contact at all, so how could there be pain? Where were the rack and the pincers and the burning oil?

It made no sense. It was one of the presiding unanswered questions of his youth.

There was one answer, of course. An unpleasantly recurrent answer. They said it was because he was 'an ugly bastard' and they couldn't stand the sight of him for very long. As if he were some kind of bloodcurdling monster. They surely had a point there – he often thought he looked like something hanging off the outside of Notre Dame, the stuff of nightmares really, Frankenstein's monster on an off day, and he still remembered the day his mama came home and saw him with all his curls cut off and shrieked and ran upstairs sobbing – and yet it couldn't be the whole story.

Your eyes go off in different fucking directions, *petit con*! That is cheating! Also fair comment. His strabismus gave him an unfair advantage. He was really looking out of only one eye, but it was like he could choose to look left or right, depending. But then wasn't everyone a little like this? Left, right, in-between, both, neither – everything was possible, surely? Unless you were flat-out blind, of course.

And now ... sitting in this café on the Boulevard Saint-Germain, with the Nazis trundling by outside, he thought he had finally understood. He nodded benignly at Camus, smiling through the voluptuous smoke, or at least gripping the pipe visibly with his teeth. He, the great champion of eye-contact, felt fairly confident he could outstare Camus. Camus had switched his attention back to the Beaver, Beauvoir, *le Castor*, he noticed. Was that a kind of politeness and even-handedness, pure egalitarianism in action – or could it be, rather, a kind of weakness? Wasn't Camus in fact running away from Sartre, ophthalmically speaking?

Call it a truce, a *cessez-le-feu*. Like all truces, strictly temporary. A time-out.

Sartre swung his own gaze around, swivelling like the turret of a tank, towards the street outside the window. He inspected the scene, analysed it, weighed its metaphysical implications. It was a fine winter's day and there were a lot of pedestrians going by on the boulevard, some cars too. Every now and then a German officer, or soldiers in pairs, or a military vehicle. It was not that he wanted the Fritzes in Paris – far from it. But it didn't surprise him that they were there. Like beetles. He reckoned he could take on the whole lot of them in an eye-wrestling contest, combatting all-comers, and they would slink away defeated. Or perhaps they would have to kill him to stop him staring at them. Or he could challenge them to a philosophy contest. Sartre vs Heidegger. Or Hegel, or Husserl – no problem, he could easily out-think the lot of them stuck together. Germany provided him with the weapons, but now he could turn them around on the Germans themselves.

He noticed how smartly dressed they were, the Krauts, buttoned-up, brushed-up, combed and coiffed and perfumed, as if they had spent hours in front of a mirror and were going to a stylish dinner party or parading on a catwalk rather than fighting and holding a foreign land. All these handsome SS officers, standing up on their camouflaged cars: they resembled priests, executioners, martyrs, Martians, anything except men. They made him feel scruffy, and he intuited rather than saw his own patched trousers and frayed jacket: scruffiness, shabbiness, as a form of revolt, he told himself. They would probably pass a law against it soon enough, so you could be arrested and tortured for losing buttons on your shirt or having a hole in your sleeve. Or refusing to comb your hair or brush your teeth.

If not for this damn ersatz coffee, you could almost forget that there was a war on at all. But it was there all the same, *they* were there, the enemy, ever present. *Rats*, that was what Camus called them, and he could see where that came from: they were always scurrying around busily, up to no good, infiltrating, grabbing anything that was going, creeping up on you and – that is it, in the end – staring at you. Inspecting. Checking your papers. Giving you the once-over, the evil eye. Well, he was used to that. It seemed like just an extension of everyday life. And he, Sartre, the irrepressible schoolboy, would always look right back at them, unflinchingly. At last his ugliness had given him an edge. They didn't like to look at him too closely, he noticed. Maybe that explained how he managed to get out of the camp? He would never give way. They could rip his fingernails off and pull out all his teeth and still, he felt, he would always fix his gaze on them, until finally they surrendered.

But in truth no one really knew what was going to happen. Maybe the Third Reich really would last 1,000 years, or 2,000, or maybe the blessed de Gaulle would lead a heroic liberation army up the Champs-Elysées tomorrow, he didn't know, he really didn't have a clue, and the odd thing was he actually enjoyed not knowing, the feeling of profound uncertainty, this sense that the world – unscripted – was capable of turning out quite differently to anything you could reasonably . . .

*

She was talking, for no particular reason, about skiing and the mountains. It resonated for Camus, who had spent so long in the mountains himself, the *magic mountain*, in search of a cure. But, owing to some irrecoverable chain of associations, what Camus couldn't help wondering was what Beauvoir would be like in bed. Naturally. Why would he treat Beauvoir any differently to any other woman? To be fair, he tried hard to concentrate on what she was saying too. Something about Chamonix and an 'odourless, colourless, blindingly white landscape'. She had a kind of poetry, the Beaver. But that was

© Art Shay

Beauvoir: rear elevation

part of the problem, wouldn't you say? With the emphasis on *say*.

He had a suspicion that she would be like that in bed too, a real chatterbox. A classic intellectual who never knew when to shut up. It would almost be like going to bed with Sartre. Or at least having Sartre perched nearby watching everything, being a voyeur, because you knew for a fact that it would all get back to him and they would be comparing notes. Like being under a microscope, an insect being scrutinized by a couple of biologists in white coats. It would be like becoming part of the Sartre Beauvoir novel. They were living out their text, clearly. But to be written into their work, to become part of the marginalia . . . ?

To Camus' way of thinking, there was a time for words, and then there were other times . . . beyond words . . . or maybe before . . .

*

... predict. Whatever happened, the war, and especially the period of the Occupation – Occupied Paris! – confirmed what Sartre had long supposed: that terror was the secret factor in all human equations and encounters. Or rather, it used to be secret, but now it was right out there, in the open, and all secrecy had been relinquished. You had to hand it to the fascists: they were completely explicit about it, there was no beating about the bush, you knew exactly where you stood with them. Look at them sideways and you were a dead duck. They wanted to be looked at and admired, but they didn't like anybody staring at them for too long, inspecting them back again, eyeballing them, giving them the once-over as if searching for a weakness, the inevitable chink in the armour.

Sartre had a sudden realization. *They* are frightened of *us*.

*

He spent most of his days writing (why?), and would probably spend the rest of his days writing, one way or another. But at some level – Camus knew this much about himself – he was *not* a writer, not really; he was anything but a writer. (Sartre and Beauvoir – they were the *real* writers!) He wrote books for a living, he read them, day after day, book after book, all day long, morning, night, and noon. Like some kind of monk. At the same time, he wasn't quite sure he *loved* books. A mere stack of paper, after all, bound together with glue. Maybe, secretly, he hated them. He certainly hated some of them. Writing: it was like a war *against* language. A form of *revolt*, against itself. No wonder, then, that he was such a fucked-up sort of guy. At war with himself, another manifestation of the absurd. When I talk about the absurd, Camus reflected, I am only talking about *me*.

*

It was obvious to Sartre now – perhaps it always had been – that the gaze was nothing other than another form of warfare.

Mirrored in the eyes (in every move, in every word) was our inevitable struggle for survival and domination. For conquest. That was why François and Léon and the rest of them eventually yielded and admitted defeat: they had been overcome by superior forces. His own personal *blitzkrieg*. Punching a great gaping hole right through their pathetic little Maginot Line. *Seek the death of the other*, as the Beaver would say.

Or, to put it the other way round, war, all this immense mobilization of forces, this tremendous clash of flesh and hardware, was only, at bottom, an extension of the staring competitions at school, taken to their logical conclusion, with no quarter given. *War and Peace*? More like *War* followed by more *War*. The peace part of it was just war by another name. So this was the *Second* World War? He expected to be around for the third and the fourth (always assuming this one ever stopped). He was old enough to remember the *First* (one of his frenzied adolescent novels – unfinished – *The History of Private Perrin*, concerns a young soldier who sneaks across no-man's land, captures the Kaiser, challenges him to a fist fight and punches his lights out, thus winning the war). Somebody was always going to get hurt. Or a lot of bodies. No prisoners. I must conquer your consciousness or be conquered. Thus spake Hegel – and Beauvoir.

Anything could happen, that was the rule of *contingency*; truth was so much stranger than fiction, but at some level all the options seemed to boil down to two. Win or lose. Heads or tails. Sadism or masochism. Being and Nothingness.

He gazed one more time at the kid from Algiers. Whether humans faced each other across a table at a café or from behind their defences, armed to the teeth, staring out across the barbed wire and the dead bodies, there was always a battle for the soul going on. Of course there was no soul but there was certainly a battle for it all the same. A battle for something ... or no-thing.

He had only just written it, it was fresh out of the typewriter, could probably do with a bit of tightening up here and there. *Huis clos. No Exit.* His new play. The Beaver had copies in her room.

Why don't you come up? suggested Sartre. We can try it out, see what you think, you don't have to commit at this stage.

What's the basic idea? Camus wondered.

The idea is that everyone is already dead.

How many?

Three – and the *garçon*.

Do they know they are dead?

Not at the beginning.

So where are they?

They're in hell.

4

Lying in Bed
in the Afternoon,
Looking out of
the Window

TWO MEN, HAVING A CONVERSATION, mediated, encouraged, provoked by a woman. But how did Camus and Sartre come to be here, in Paris, in the middle of a war? The whole of the space-time continuum and a comprehensive history of philosophy might begin to explain the course of a single day in 1943. But one afternoon in January 1936, in Algiers, with Albert Camus lying in bed, not asleep and yet not entirely awake either, could help to elucidate a small part of it.

He was not being a slacker: this was not a siesta; he would rather be out playing football. But he had been hit by tuberculosis and, on this particular day, was finding it hard to breathe or move much. He was more or less forced to minimize his activity and fold in on himself. So there he was, lying in bed, alone, frustrated to be cooped up, on a sunny day in Algiers. It was from this platform that he began to explore the universe, intuitively, flying free of his physical constraints. He was twenty-two years old.

He began by thinking. Since he was a postgraduate student of philosophy (working on Plotinus and Saint Augustine) he thought naturally, first of all, of Plato's myth of the cave (in Book VII of *The Republic*) in which human beings, who are chained up inside, see only shadows projected on the wall and assume that this is all there is. Camus, similarly, saw shadows of leaves – 'the shadow of the world' – projected on the white curtains. In the distance he could see the walls of a walled garden. Camus clearly identified with the lone prisoner who manages to escape and sees that there is a wide world beyond the cave and brings back the news to the others inside, at the cost of his own life. He is the scapegoat who must be sacrificed to protect the community.

But then, in a second phase, Camus realized that in this very act of thinking he was still, in some sense, a prisoner. Was he not a prisoner, now, of Plato, of the idea of the philosopher, to some extent chained to these thoughts? He was a prisoner, for example, of the word *prisoner*. A strange thought – or not even a thought, but something more like the opposite of a thought. Camus had the realization, lying in bed, that if he wanted to be a philosopher – seriously – he had to break free of philosophy. He had to overcome thought itself, to somehow outwit and out-manoeuvre the forms of language he had worked so hard to acquire over many years. It could be called a 'philosophy of poverty' or perhaps an anti-philosophy. In England, around the same period, Wittgenstein said that if you wanted to be a philosopher you should become a car mechanic. For Camus this was too much like hard work and it was enough to just lie there. And light a cigarette.

He watched the smoke curling up towards the ceiling then

sliding out into the air, 'consuming itself'. His attention was drawn to the window, to the light. He watched the clouds drift lazily by. He could smell the air outside, full of the scents of the garden and a sense of 'jubilation'. There was a distant chill that the sun had yet to penetrate. It was, after all, an afternoon in January, in the northern hemisphere, and therefore technically winter, even in Algeria. Camus felt himself floating. He saw the foliage of a wisteria winding up the wall outside like a giant beanstalk, climbing up into the sky, towards the sun. A breeze blew through the window and caused the shadows on the curtain to dance.

Then all at once there was a flash of light as the sun broke through from behind a cloud and illuminated a yellow vase of mimosa in his room. And it was like a bolt of lightning striking the young Albert – a *coup de foudre*. Transforming him, as if in a magical metamorphosis. He was 'flooded with a confused and bewildering joy'. He became, for a moment, something other than he was.

I am the world.

Camus recorded the experience in his *carnet*, the school exercise book he had recently begun to use as a diary. He felt, as he did so, that there was something slightly dissonant involved in writing it down. He must be, in some sense, betraying the episode, falsifying it, even as he described it, since he was thereby re-entering the realm of language and thought – the symbolic – to report an event, if it was an event (possibly something more like a non-event, a pure state of being, or non-being), that seemed to him to go well beyond the boundaries of language and thought. Nevertheless he tried to get a fix on this 'happening' with a few loose, lyrical sentences. It was not an analysis, only an evocation. Camus made no attempt to understand, only to succumb to seduction. He didn't plan on this happening: it just happened.

> Who am I and what can I do other than enter into the patterns of the foliage and the light. To be this ray of light into which the smoke from my cigarette vanishes, this sweetness and this discreet passion that is like a breath in the air.

It was of course clinically inadvisable for Camus to be smoking. Even if his doctor did not tell him so, he probably appreciated that inhaling tobacco smoke was not the best treatment for lungs that had been afflicted by a virus. Perhaps this was why there was nothing about inhaling, only exhaling (at other times he tried giving up completely). He was fascinated by the ghostliness of smoke, its weightlessness and insubstantiality. And the smoke, as it drifted away from his cigarette, like music emanating from some wind instrument, provided a hazy bridge to the world outside, an implicit system of communication. In some strange way Camus was exhaling himself, wafting up towards the light with his smoke. He was becoming his own breath.

Another Albert, Albert Einstein, attributed the inspiration for his theory of relativity to a 'thought-experiment' (conducted around the age of sixteen) in which he imagines what it would be like to be riding around on the back of a ray of light and holding up a mirror to his face. He asks himself the question: will I still be able to see my image reflected back at me? He conjures up the idea of his face completely disappearing from the mirror, the light rays moving too fast to ever be recovered. But then he rejects the hypothesis: the reflection in the mirror will never be lost; it is saved thanks to a finite speed of light ('c') and the inertial frame of relativistic physics. Camus, on the other hand, dreams not of riding around on top of a beam of light but of dissolving into it.

The face in the mirror therefore disappears. There is no frame, no mirror and no face. Nothing but light. The observer, like smoke, has vanished into thin air. Extinguished, like a cigarette. But the self flickers back into life, catching fire again. 'If I try to attain myself, it is in the depths of this light.' You could call it a moment of 'enlightenment' for Camus, or *satori*.

Nothing dramatic had happened. Camus had still not stirred from his bed. If we discount the smoking, he had not moved an inch. He was unlikely to sell this experience as a novel or as a movie script (a non-motion picture perhaps). It was the opposite of a drama. And yet he had the sense of having discovered 'the secret of the world'. We can call the secret *a coefficient of relatedness*. But even *discovered* is too strong a word: it is not as though he was actively seeking anything; it just presented itself to him, like a gift. Suddenly, nothing else much seemed to matter. Matter did not matter. 'Am I going to wonder whether something is dying or people are suffering when everything is written in this window through which the sky pours forth its plenitude.' Where before there was nothing but spare parts, fragments of an unimaginable whole, now they had interlocked, fused, the human and the inhuman, and *tout* – everything – had become manifest. Even his own pain became a matter of indifference. 'This suffering dizzies me because it is nothing other than this sun and these shadows, this warmth and this chill that one can feel far away, in the depths of the air.'

It is curious that he uses the same word – *plénitude* – that Sartre will use, in *Being and Nothingness*, to describe his experience of the café. The same sense of profusion, albeit in a different key (that segues soon enough, in Sartre, into something like its exact opposite, nothingness, absence). But there is one other writer, not too removed from Camus in time or space, who conjures up a similar horizontal experience. Marcel Proust, even without suffering from TB, spent a lot of time lying in bed. The opening page of *In Search of Lost Time*, his vast, labyrinthine one-million-plus-word novel, published between 1913 and 1927, recalls how he would lie in bed in Paris in the darkness half-dreaming of the books he had been reading before the lights went out: 'It seemed to me that I was myself the very thing the book spoke of: a church, a quartet, the rivalry between François I and Charles V.' Perhaps the entire arc of the novel can be understood to be contained within the mind of the narrator or within his readerly dream.

Proust explicitly refers to the ancient idea of 'metempsychosis' or transmission of the soul (or 'psyche'), normally associated with death and reincarnation. But you don't have to die, says Proust. It is possible, even in life, in certain circumstances, to erase the distinction between a person (in this case, the narrator, Proust himself or his counterpart, 'Marcel') and such seemingly distinct phenomena as architecture, music, or other people. This dream-like state, suspending the divisions between self and non-self, becomes the core logic of the whole work, in which everything must be ultimately fused together in a transcendent network, more mental (or aesthetic) than social, looping across time and space. In the same way, we can find Camus' waking flash of pure luminosity radiating through his entire oeuvre. The dancing, dissolving smoke from his cigarette corresponds loosely to the transmission of a soul. Camus is going up in smoke, blowing himself out into the air. I *am* the smoke, I am the light. This was Camus' secular transcendence.

We know that Jean Grenier, his teacher, gave Camus a copy of Proust's novel in 1933. But there are significant differences between Camus and Proust. Perhaps, after all, it is not so difficult to iden-tify with churches or quartets or rivalries, since they all imply the involvement of other people. They are human constructs, like the novel itself. With Camus – who became dissatisfied with Proust and ultimately set it aside as only 'half-truth' – it is pure light, pure smoke, weightless, mass-less, liberated from the gravity of one's fellow beings, empty of any possibility of language. This helps to explain why, as Camus walked into a new apartment, he experimented with thinking in the opposite way to Proust and trying to imagine the future, 'set off in search of a time that has not yet come'.

Être la matière! Saint Anthony's aspiration, according to Flaubert in the climax to *The Temptation of Saint Anthony* – *be* matter, become one with nature, annihilate the ego. But Camus focused on the idea of the immaterial: that which is without mass, having the quality almost of a mathematical abstraction. It is not hard to find in his later writing a green Camus, environmentally conscious, intent on the conservation of living beings, but this persona is preceded, illuminated, by a more colourless Camus, devoid of self, an intimate of nothingness and transparency.

In any case, it is somehow misleading to come up with literary points of reference for an episode that is clearly not so much literary as more like the opposite of literature. Around the same time as he was lying in bed communing with the light and the leaves, he was making a pledge to scale down his demands where personal relationships were concerned.

> When I was younger, I used to demand more of other people than they could reasonably supply: a non-stop friendship, a permanent high. Now I know better and I ask of them less than they can give: a companionship without sentences.

Camus experimented with taking a vow of silence in his friendships, putting language to one side, as if it could be the origin of potential misunderstandings, and working with pure emotion and body language alone. *No sentences*: no chit-chat, no letters, no phone calls. No texting either, or emailing, or any other kind of verbal communication. A Trappist monk-style relationship, which would be strictly contemplative. He suspected it would be safer that way. He sought out the kinds of environment (the desert, for example, or here a beach in 'Summer in Algiers') that tend towards eclipsing or erasing all forms of the symbolic:

> Between this sky and these faces turned up towards it, there is nothing on which to hook mythology, literature, ethics or religion, only stones, flesh, stars and these truths that the hand can reach out and touch.

But he kept getting sucked back into the literary vortex, caught between the savage and the symbolic, the beach and religion.

In *Writing Degree Zero*, the literary theorist Roland Barthes held up Camus (and especially *The Outsider*) as an exemplar of a stripped-down kind of twentieth-century writing, a minimalist style, with all the flourishes and embellishments of overinflated nineteenth-century Romanticism shorn away. Camus as Bauhaus, with clean modernist lines and no fuss. More Zen, less ornate. I think the key to the Camusian degree zero is a resistance to literature itself; not just style but also attitude. His natural genre is the haiku. 'Everything is written in this window.' He is an anti-writer. The anti-Proust. A negative realist (to use a phrase of his own). '*The Outsider* is the zero point,' Camus writes, anticipating Barthes.

> The book falls open at a much thumbed page. How flat it seems today in the presence of the book of the world.

Lying in bed, looking out of the window, Camus was seduced by a degree zero of consciousness, a primordial state of mind, in which it is possible to extinguish or transcend or suspend the self and become *like* other entities or phenomena. To perceive secret affinities. It occurred to him, often enough, at odd moments, unbidden – whether lying in bed or going for a swim.

I am not in the least concerned to be happy, only to be conscious. We can feel cut off from the world, but it is enough to see an olive tree rising up out of the golden earth, or to be dazzled by beaches in the morning sun, for us to feel this resistance melting inside. So it is with me. Each minute of life has the worth of a miracle and the appearance of eternal youthfulness.

When he wrote, at the very beginning of *The Myth of Sisyphus*, that suicide was 'the only serious philosophical problem', I suspect that he may have been thinking above all of the kind of self-annihilation, going up in smoke, dissolving into the ocean or merging with a grain of sand on the beach, that occurred to him quite spontaneously: the savage state of degree zero – absolute simplicity. 'The death of myself to myself', as he wrote in his notebooks. Camus lived his own death: the 'happy death' (the title of his first, unpublished novel). Everything he wrote after that was a way of writing about what could not be written.

Technically a French colony, Algeria was geographically and culturally one of the great Mediterranean crossroads, poised between East and West, more a candidate for centre of the world than Paris. It was Jean Grenier, in the early thirties, who introduced Camus to non-Western ways of thinking, to Hinduism and to the Tao. Together they would have considered the opening of Lao-tzu's *Tao Te Ching*:

The Way that can be described is not the true Way.
The Name that can be named is not the constant Name.

It must have struck an echo in the student Camus, studying so many great works of literature and philosophy and yet looking back towards his preliterate past (and his illiterate mother), in love with the book and yet perfectly capable of floating out of his bedroom window on a ray of light. 'Innocence is never having to explain', he noted. He would have agreed that – in the words of the Zen slogan – he who speaks does not know and he who knows does not speak. Hence his fondness for silence: the silence of noon in the town square, the silence of the siesta time, the silence of summer evenings.

'Let me cut this minute out of the cloth of time', he wrote in his notebooks, 'in the same way that others press a flower between the pages of a book.' Perhaps he thought of writing in the same way, cutting out his experience and then pressing it into all the pages of his books.

When am I truer and more transparent than when I am the world?

If only it were that easy. Camus came to employ different words for referring back to this primal moment, his epiphany. 'Beauty' was one of them. Perhaps he was thinking of lying in bed and morphing into pure light when he wrote in his first notebook that 'Beauty is unbearable and drives us to despair. Like a flash of eternity in a minute that we would like to stretch out across the length of time.' Cutting it, pressing it, stretching it, Camus thought about different ways of getting the raw, non-verbal, peak experience of confusion and intensity into his work. But despair was inevitably mixed up in the process too. 'If anguish still has me in its grip, it is because of the sense of this impalpable instant slipping between my fingers, like beads of mercury.' Camus felt like a failure as a writer from the very beginning. He knew that something was lost at the same time that something was gained.

'The true work of art is the one that says less.' Camus dreamed of the book without words and the friendship without sentences. It was probable, perhaps inevitable, that he was going to run into trouble. Certainly the friendship with Sartre was a friendship *with* sentences. It was almost nothing but sentences. Existentialism meets the philosophy of the absurd. On Camus' own assessment, there was always a high probability of misunderstanding.

5

BAD HAIR DAY

M Y EARLIEST ENCOUNTER with Beauty took place one day in the late sixties in a barbershop. The men's magazine I found there displayed a stack of books on the cover, artistically arranged, looking rather precarious, with one – by François Mauriac, the French novelist – left tantalizingly, teasingly open. Mauriac did not detain me long, for inside Simone de Beauvoir had written an essay in praise of Bardot, 'Brigitte Bardot and the Lolita Syndrome'.

This was Beauvoir:

This was Bardot:

In this context it was easy to confuse the two. I assumed that philosophy had something to do with beautiful people or that philosophy – like a barbershop – could make you more beautiful.

Many years later, while writing this book, I was back in Cambridge and Luigi gave me a haircut. I was starting to look like a mad professor (or like Doc in *Back to the Future*). So Luigi took his scissors out and tried to fix me up. Except, and this is the point that occurred to me as I inspected the hair in the bathroom mirror the next morning, he didn't really take enough off. He had enhanced the style, true, but there was a big floppy fringe that was starting to annoy me. And it was hot out. So I opened up the clipper attachment on the razor and hacked away at it for a while. When I finally emerged there was a general consensus that I looked like a particularly disreputable scarecrow. In the end I went to another barbershop (I didn't dare show Luigi my handiwork) and had it all sheared off. For a while I looked like a cross between Britney Spears and Michel Foucault.

In short, it was a typical bad-hair day. Everyone has them. I am going to hold back on my follicular study of the whole of western philosophy (Nietzsche – the will-to-power-eternal-recurrence moustache; the workers-of-the-world-unite Marxian beard), but I think it has to be said that a haircut can have significant philosophical consequences. Jean-Paul Sartre, for one, had a particularly traumatic tonsorial experience when he was only seven.

Up to that point he had had a glittering career as a crowd-pleaser. Sartre was a blond to begin with. Visitors to the household, coming to contemplate the phenomenon like wise

A place of learning

men, agreed, 'He really is an angel!' It is hard to imagine, with so many photographs of a man in glasses, often with a pipe, sitting in cafés. But there was a time before all that, when Sartre was not yet Sartre. He was not even Jean-Paul. He was Poulou. He of the long blond curly hair. And everybody loved him. It was like being in heaven. Nothing but applause and admiration. Then came the day that Poulou was brought down to earth, the day Sartre was finally born and released into the real world.

Poulou had no idea that he owed his sublime success to the gorgeous head of long blond locks. Not until the day he lost them. He had no father – his father died when he was only a year old – but he had no need of a father. He saw himself through the gaze of his adoring family. When he looked in the mirror he saw a beautiful face. What he didn't realize was that all the beauty inhered in the hair, shedding a kind of heavenly light over him, like a halo.

One fine day in 1912 (Camus was not yet born), at 1 Rue le Goff in Paris, Sartre's grandfather, Karl, took it into his head that the time had come for a haircut. He feared that the boy was starting to look like a girl. 'You're going to make a girl out of him!' he reproached his daughter. The hair, it was true, was lovely, but it was possible to have too much of a good thing. He was a boy, after all; he was not supposed to be *too* lovely anyway. It was time for him to become a little man, instead of a 'wimp' (*une poule mouillée*, literally a wet chicken). There was a suspicion that the mother really would have preferred a girl anyway, and was trying to reconfigure Sartre to fit. The very idea of being an 'angel' was probably some kind of compromise, gender indeterminate but 'feminine around the edges'. So it happened that, when his mother was out, the grandfather took young Poulou off to a nearby barbershop. It was almost as if he had been waiting for the mother to go out, so he could get it over with. The coast was clear! Like some kind of military manoeuvre behind enemy lines.

At first it was just: We're going out for a walk. But very soon it was: We're going into this barbershop right here. 'We are going to give your mother a surprise!' Poulou willingly joined in the game. He loved surprises. Unexpected presents, secrets and revelations. Don't hold back! Grandfather told the barber. Take it all off. We don't want to have to come again tomorrow or the next day, do we? Poulou agreed with everything he said. He agreed with the barber. He collaborated and cooperated. There had never been any significant division or difference of opinion between him and the big people all around him. They were of like mind. Up until this day he referred to his mother and grandfather with a single collective term, 'Karlémami'. How could anything his grandfather recommended possibly be bad? Or in conflict with his mother?

Poulou watched all those blond, girly curls rolling down the white towel around his neck and falling on the floor of the barbershop, 'inexplicably faded', as if the light – and the life – had gone out of them. All that white stuff on the rough brown wood. Like sawdust or fallen leaves. Was this himself, or a part of him, lying there on the ground? He was aware that hair was something separate, or potentially separate, from the rest of the body. One moment it was there, on top of your head, the next it was gone, sheared off, swept up and binned. And you were radically changed. Forever. There was something here – beyond the hair itself – that would never grow back.

They returned to the family home together, grandfather and grandson. Perhaps, after all, nothing had fundamentally changed. Was he not approximately the same boy he was when he went out? Was he not still an angel? He felt 'glorious and shorn', a hero of the haircut. No cause for anxiety or alarm. Not, that is, until his mother returned home.

With no husband, but a strong father figure – in fact her father – running the household, she had reverted to childhood. She was relying on her beautiful boy to fix her own life for her. And then, as she came through the door, she caught sight of Poulou, lying in wait for her, expecting admiration as usual, actually drawing attention to all the missing hair. Madame Sartre was stunned. She looked at her son but had no words for him. She felt betrayed. Forsaken. Did she not tell her father not to touch the hair, ever? She should never have trusted him. She would have got the task done in the end, made some minor adjustments, a subtle cut so that people would hardly even notice a change. Now he was virtually bald, like an old man. So long as he had the hair, she could convince herself he really was as she thought he ought to be, perfect, without flaw, a gift of God. And now . . . 'her little girl had been switched for a little boy'. She was the little girl; Poulou had suddenly grown up. He expected hugs, but she bolted up the stairs and into her bedroom, where she threw herself on the bed and collapsed, convulsed by sobbing.

Her carefully *combed* universe had just been torn down, like a Hollywood set being broken down and reassembled for some quite different movie, rather harsher, darker, less romantic and devoid of semi-divine beings, gender indeterminate. For Sartre – and he was now Sartre, no longer Poulou – there is surely some parallel with the story of Samson. Having all his hair cut off had brought about some unanticipated catastrophe. He had lost his mysterious power. But it was not in fact the loss of the hair in itself that caused his personal temple to collapse all around him. The effects were held in suspension – like a cartoon figure running over a cliff but still hanging in mid-air – until the point at which his mother returned home and turned her eyes on him for the first time. Or what felt like the first time. And then the crash could finally occur.

He had become an object of the gaze. It was as if he had been branded – stigmatized. He could no longer look in the mirror with the same calm self-oblivion. Since the haircut, he had become fully self-conscious and realized, obscurely, that there was a possibility of not loving, and not being loved. More distantly, that it must also be possible to hate and be hated. A degree of uncertainty had been planted in his mind. Did he even love himself any more? At the very moment that the question is asked, the answer becomes unclear. It is the moment at which Sartre becomes a philosopher. And it coincides with the shocking revelation of his own ugliness.

The idea that 'hell is other people' starts here.

So long as 'the beautiful ringlets' remained intact, embellishing his head in a heavenly haze, his mother could sustain the fiction of the angel. Now that he was virtually bald she could no longer conceal this terrible truth from herself. He really was *ugly*. There were no ugly angels. The mother had been shaken to the core, the coiffed-up scaffolding of her world collapsing all about her. Worse, from Sartre's point of view – and it still comes as an unexpected twist in the tale: *even the grandfather was shocked*. Karl, the tough guy, the German teacher, even he was *interdit*: speechless, flabbergasted. Maybe he should have left well enough alone. The kid was better off the way he was. But there was no reversing the haircut and sticking it all back on and restoring the lost original. The illusion had been definitively shattered and there was no way back. For the grandfather, it was the opposite of a fairy tale. The idea was to take a wet chicken and turn him into a man. Instead of that he took out a prince and 'brought home a toad'.

It is not so surprising that, at the same time he ceased to be an angel, Sartre/Poulou lost any confidence in the existence of a wise and benevolent God. How could anyone wise and benevolent pull this sort of trick? Later, when he came across anyone speaking of God he often felt like an ex-lover bumping into an old flame and thinking, *Who knows what might have been.* 'Fifty years ago, without this misunderstanding, without this mistake, without the accident that tore us apart, there could have been something between us.' The *accident* was the haircut and the discovery of ugliness and disability.

The ugliness became a barely suppressed leitmotif of his writing. Sartre wore it like a badge of honour. *Nausea* was the extrapolation of a mirror crisis:

> The grey thing has just appeared in the mirror. I go over and look at it, I can no longer move away. It is the reflection of my face [...] I can understand nothing about this face. Other people's faces have a meaning. Not mine [...] When I was small, my aunt Bigeois used to tell me: 'If you look at yourself too long in the mirror, you'll see a monkey looking back at you.' [...] What I can see is far below the monkey, on the edge of the vegetable world, at the polyp level [...] the eyes in particular, seen at such close quarters, are horrible. They are glassy, soft, blind, and red-rimmed; anyone would think they were fish-scales [...] the eyes, the nose, the mouth disappear: nothing human is left.

Mirror, mirror on the wall, who is the *ugliest* of them all? The experience is somewhere near the origin of his future career: 'I was born from writing: before that there was only a reflection in a mirror.' Simone de Beauvoir refused to overlook Sartre's ugliness. He was, she observed, unflinchingly, 'the dirtiest, worst dressed, and also, I think, the ugliest' of all the students at the École Normale Supérieure. The novelist Michel Houellebecq has one of his characters being 'underwhelmed by the work of the philosopher, but impressed by how ugly he was, bordering on disabled'. It is fair comment. But who, after all, has not felt – at least occasionally – at the level of the polyp? Perhaps (the episode of the bad-hair day further suggests) ugliness is indispensable to philosophy. Thinking, serious, sustained questioning arises out of – or perhaps at the same time as – a consciousness of one's own ugliness. Sartre's mission was to make the world safe for ugly people. In Sartre, ugly is the new beautiful.

It doesn't matter if you are an ugly bastard. As an existentialist you can still score. Sartre, so far as I know, never actually said it flat-out. And yet it is there in almost everything he ever wrote. It is there, for example, in his account of how he fell in love with a little blonde girl, Lisette, the daughter of a ship's chandler, when he was only eleven – in his post-barbershop phase, in La Rochelle. He dreamed of her and tried to attract her attention by spinning around her one day on his bike but succeeded only in eliciting her laughter and the crushing put-down, 'Who is this bum with one eye that says *merde* to the other?' Philosophy offered a get-out-of-jail card. An ironic comeback. It was a form of retaliation against the beautiful people and their archetypes. Poulou's revenge. Beauty is a *thing*, just as ugliness is a thing (social facts are things, Émile Durkheim said). Whereas, Sartre and Beauvoir argued, I am no-thing. Which explains why I can never be truly beautiful – even if it doesn't stop me wanting to be. Beauvoir's *Second Sex*, that great foundational work of twentieth-century feminism, written after the war, is another indictment of the tyranny of Beauty: the requirement of women to fit into a particular concept of being. The point of existential thinking was to revolt against the normative, whether masculine or feminine. Weren't all these categories just another constraint on freedom?

My plans to be some*thing* – to make something of myself – will always fail. The words '*voué à l'échec*' – doomed to failure – echo through *Being and Nothingness*. Desire, for example, 'is itself doomed to failure'. Everybody always fails at everything. But alongside this inevitable catalogue of failure is a compensatory sense of unlimited possibilities. Loser wins. Loser takes all. I am nothing, or nothingness. Like a ghost or a phantasm. I cannot be pinned down to a mere incarnation or perception of ugliness. I disassociate myself from the world, from others, quite naturally, in order to be what I am; but I also disassociate myself from myself, in order to be what I am not. I am split apart. I contain multitudes. I am nothing and I am everything. A 21st century schizoid (wo)man. Be against everything, but first of all against yourself. I-theory morphs into X-theory.

Sartre discovered *a coefficient of un-relatedness*. Which was also his take on the secular transcendent

The ugly little boy is not an ugly little boy.

The wet chicken is not a wet chicken.

The waiter is not a waiter.

A man is not a man ('human reality is what it is not and is not what it is'.

A woman is not a woman ('I am not born a woman,' says Beauvoir. 'I become one' – just as Sartre could say, 'I am not born ugly: I become ugly').

No more archetypes. No more norms. No more predictives.

Human 'nature': a contradiction in terms, for human beings are the opposite of natural.

Everyone has avatars, alternate personae, alter egos. Popeye says, I am what I am and what's all what I am. Poulou says, I am what I am not.

But even if I cannot know my 'self' (any notion of *authenticity* – I want to be myself – is therefore rendered eternally elusive), nevertheless I am always conscious of myself: unlike Camus, I cannot turn into a beam of light or float away in a cloud of smoke. Some time after the war, when they were out drinking in a bar, Sartre told Camus he was going to give a lecture at UNESCO the following morning. 'You'll be speaking without me, then,' Camus muttered, not much liking the sound of it. 'I wish I could speak without *moi*,' Sartre replied.

If Beauvoir is the un-woman, then Sartre is the un-man. Or *ex*-man. This is the core of 'existentialism': he defines himself by the refusal of all definition. The 'divided self' was R. D. Laing's take on the existential soul: it would be truer to say that the young Sartre was not so much divided as at war, with himself and other people, permanently conflicted.

6

Fight Club

'I FOUGHT CONSTANTLY,' Sartre said, recalling his school-days in La Rochelle. He wasn't exaggerating. Sartre was always a fighter. Even if he shied away from self-definition, he still explicitly refers to himself in his letters to the Beaver as 'the boxer'.

He often got into trouble for fighting with other kids. He was small (technically, a featherweight) but touchy and he could punch above his weight. In his mind, he was tall and good-looking and adept with fists, sword and pistol. He was – in this parallel universe – Pardaillan, a Zorro-like figure (who originally appears in the works of Michel Zevaco), a masked musketeer with a habit of saving damsels in distress and over-coming ridiculous odds. Whereas Dumas' heroes signed up to the slogan 'All for One and One for All', Pardaillan is an anarchist who believes in 'One against All' (and presumably 'All against One'). Just as he derived his invincible alter ego from novels, so Sartre projected his imaginary body into his own early writing, dreaming up lofty, powerful heroes who nevertheless come to grief one way or another. Behind them was a writer who liked to think of the pen as a sword (which might explain why he never really took to the typewriter). 'I unloaded on to the writer the sacred powers of the hero,' Sartre recalled.

And there are echoes and reminiscences of the action-hero and the epic even in the more mature fiction. In *Nausea*, Roquentin grabs an aggressive 'little Corsican' (a librarian) by the neck and lifts him off the ground, so that he is wriggling, unable to breathe, in his vice-like grip. The Corsican's arms are too short even to reach his captor. 'I could easily have smashed him on the table,' Roquentin writes in his diary, or knocked his teeth out. If he doesn't exactly win these encounters, at least the Sartrean scrapper goes down fighting, in a blaze of glory, like Mathieu in *The Roads to Freedom*, taking on the might of the German army. This heroic conception of writing might help to explain why it is that Sartre could never stop: he had 'an epic cast of mind', and the epic is a never-ending story – because there are always more potential villains to overcome, not to mention damsels in distress.

When he became a teacher of philosophy, in Le Havre in the thirties, Sartre took to sparring with his students in the most literal way. With Europe rumbling relentlessly towards another war, three of his colleagues at the Lycée François 1er – Classics, English, and Physical Education, all of them keen boxers – introduced him to the Charles Porta gym. The classicist, who would be selected to represent France at the Olympics, gave tips on technique. 'He taught me how to box,' Sartre would recall, 'and I got to be pretty good.' Boxing was all the rage in Le Havre where local boy Le Person had become the French bantamweight champion and national icon. For Sartre, philosophy (like just about everything) was a form of pugilism, a martial art. So it was only logical that he should bring his students along to the gym too and put them in the ring, teaching them the art of the uppercut and the right hook, training them up with the skipping rope and the punch-bag, and flooring one of them – even though he was bigger than Sartre – in a straight fight. It seemed to him like a natural extension of the Socratic dialogue. The better you could box the better philosopher you would be. The primary question (as Bertrand Russell put it) was, 'Can I take him or can he take me?'

In the ring, Sartre was able to become Pardaillan again, mystifying and laying out his enemies. His main advantage: he was already so ugly it was hard to make him look any worse. Disadvantage: having to take his specs off. Regardless of which, he took on all-comers, and no matter the result (some of his students gave him a good thumping), his fantasy of being 'someone who could fight anyone and win' never left him. He even got into a fist-fight with one of his fellow teachers back in Paris over some sarcastic remark. Like Ernest Hemingway, like Norman Mailer after the war, Sartre took boxing to be a reliable allegory of mankind or capitalism and the violence inherent in human relations. In the *Critique of Dialectical Reason* (written towards the end of the fifties) boxing – or as Sartre defines it in his late style, 'a binary praxis of antagonistic reciprocity' – becomes the exemplary form of all human struggle. The public, formal bout is only 'the incarnation of a pre-existing violence'.

The two boxers gather within themselves, and re-exteriorize by the punches they swap, the ensemble of tensions and open or masked struggles that characterize the regime under which we live – and have made us violent even in the least of our desires, even in the gentlest of our caresses.

It was his highly combative version of X-theory. Even when Sartre ventured beyond the ring it was as if he was still inside it and everyone else was caught up in an immense interminable fight, 'the original struggle': 'the fight is everywhere, omnipresent war wheels about'. At this stage Sartre tended to look on himself as more of a 'spectator' at a boxing match, but he could never really give up on being a fighter: '[there are] no witnesses to violence, only participants.' Non-violence is an illusion. We can never fully make sense of the agon, Sartre argues: the clash of conflicting subjectivities – of points of view – resists intelligibility (for none of us is above conflict). But the struggle against an adversary remains the norm: 'even if Engels was right, even if this unity [of society] did exist in the golden age of unrecorded History, it disintegrated so long ago that we should waste our time if we sought to relate the divisions of all History to that lost paradise of intelligible unities.' The 'totalization' or resolution of conflict promised by dialectical history – the 'synthesis' – always falls short of its target. Boxing is a way of 'detotalizing' your opponent. Hence that awkward and yet resonant phrase that recurs in his late phase, the 'detotalized totalization'. Which seems to mean: keep on fighting, keep on struggling, any notion of harmony is just a dream.

Locked up in a prisoner-of-war camp in 1940, eager to be fighting someone, anyone, Sartre ('proud of his boxing skills' according to Father Perrin, the camp priest) kept in shape by getting back in the ring with Gaillot, a young printer from the provinces. They agreed on two rounds. Sartre easily took the first, but couldn't finish off his opponent, and lost the second as he ran out of steam, and a draw was declared. It may have been his last official bout but he never really resigned from the fight club. He was always ready to put the gloves back on and replay 'this absolute, useless adventure of two men'.

Camus got into his fair share of fist fights. His avatar, Jacques, bests a bigger kid (Muñoz) in a schoolyard showdown in *The First Man* (the semi-autobiographical novel he was working on when he died), for example. But the grown-up Camus took a dim view of boxing. He went along, purely as a spectator, almost out of a sense of duty, to Le Central Sporting Club in Oran, but found the mindset too 'Manichean' for his taste. He never fully embraced the binary praxis of antagonistic reciprocity. He was always more of a footballer at heart.

There is an urban myth to the effect that Camus once played in goal for Algeria. He certainly played in goal *in* Algeria. Sartre thought of football as a form of mass boxing, yet more antagonistic reciprocity. Whereas for Camus football was more an exercise in morality and solidarity: 'After many years during which I saw many things, what I know most surely about morality and the duties of men [...] I learned from [football].' In *The First Man* he writes, 'football was [my] kingdom'. He was an adept dribbler of the ball and could as easily play striker as keeper, but he was more or less obliged to stay in goal in the end on account of his poverty. His tyrannical grandmother prohibited him from playing football at school altogether because they played on cement and she didn't want him wearing his shoes out – they couldn't afford a new pair. She used to hammer metal studs into the soles not to help him keep his grip while going on a mazy run, or to inflict serious damage on the shins of the opposition, but only to make them last longer. And she would inspect them when he came home at night, with Camus lifting up the underside of his feet like a horse being shod. Woe betide him if she found the studs worn smooth. His early life turned into a perpetual battle of wits with that unsympathetic grandmother (a form of binary praxis, Sartre would have said). Thus he learned his sense of immorality from football too.

In order to travel secretly to one football match, Camus pocketed a two-franc coin (worth only a few pennies), claiming that it had disappeared down their 'Turkish toilet' when he pulled his trousers down. Suspicious of the tale, the grandmother rolled up her sleeve and stuck her arm down the cloaca and, finding nothing of significance, branded him a liar. Football was always an illicit pleasure. Playing in goal was a kind of compromise. Even so Camus still had to rub his shoes in wet earth to deceive her. She knew he was up to no good even when she couldn't prove it and gave him occasional random whacks just to be on the safe side. It was quite possibly the origin of his creativity – having to lie to his grandma on a regular basis.

He started playing for the junior side of the RUA, Racing Universitaire Algérois, the Algerian university team, in 1928, when he was only fifteen. He trained on Thursdays, played on Sundays, and soon acquired a reputation as one of their toughest and most consistent players. 'Camus gave a splendid exhibition', raved the university sports magazine, which rated him as their best player. There is something about the goalkeeper, however, that makes him more, or perhaps less, than a team player. Except

The young goalkeeper, c. 1930, kitted out in hat and team scarf

on rare (usually desperate) occasions, the goalkeeper does not roam around the field of play occupied by all the other players but is locked into his own 'box' (the penalty area); by way of compensation he is the only player allowed to make use of his hands. He yearns to be part of the team but can't be, not fully. The goalkeeper, then, technically playing for his team or his country, at the same time wears a different kind of shirt and is branded an outsider. 'Standing sentinel in goal,' the journalist Jim White observed, 'Camus had plenty of time to reflect on the absurdist nature of his position.'

In 1930 he was still playing for RUA juniors when he started spitting blood and was diagnosed with tuberculosis. Camus blamed it on 'too much sport'. His team-mates linked the condition to a specific match when he blocked a shot with his chest and passed out between the posts, or to another when they played in torrential rain throughout. Camus called it a 'metaphysical illness', perhaps because he found the contemplative life thrust upon him. Forced into early retirement from football, exchanging the savage for the symbolic, he tried to discover something of the same intensity and comradeship, in philosophy, politics, theatre, writing, that he knew on the field. He was always ready for a casual kick-about if anyone had a ball; and if not, coming out of a political meeting, he would turn up an empty shoe-polish tin on the pavement and kick that around instead. But he was haunted by the sense of having lost (or been forced to abandon) something fundamental. When his friend Charles Poncet asked him, 'Which would you have chosen, given the chance – football or theatre?' he replied, 'Football, without hesitation.'

The Plague, in the midst of a holocaust, still lingers on this personal nostalgia for a lost paradise:

the once familiar smell of embrocation in the dressing-rooms, the crumbling terraces, the brightly coloured shirts of the players that contrasted with the brown pitch, the half-time lemons or lemonade that stung their parched throats with a thousand refreshing needles [. . .] As they walked the broken suburban streets, the player kicked around any pebbles he came across. He was trying to shoot them straight into the mouths of the gutters, and whenever he succeeded, he would shout, 'One-nil!' When he finished a cigarette, he would spit out the butt in front of him and try to catch it on his toe before it hit the ground. Some children were playing near the stadium, and when one of them sent a ball towards the three men, Gonzales went out of his way to curl it back to them with a perfectly weighted pass.

Death is described in footballing terms as 'losing the match'.

If Camus had, like Sartre with Pardaillan, an imaginary alter ego, it was the Goalkeeper: the lonely last line of defence, someone whose job was to *save* not just the ball but his whole team from defeat. At the same time he carried around with him a persistent guilt that he had already *missed* it, that he was always missing something (thereby suffering the kind of angst dramatized in Peter Handke's *The Goalkeeper's Fear of the Penalty*). He certainly missed keeping goal and sought out alternative ways of making saves.

The one sporting activity that Camus was able to carry over from childhood into his adult life was swimming. He was forever on the lookout for opportunities (not so much in Paris) to strip off and get wet. In Algiers, when he was not at school, or training or playing football, he and his mates would go off swimming in the Mediterranean.

In a few seconds they were naked, in the next instant they dived in, swimming energetically and clumsily, making a great din, dribbling and spitting, challenging one another to dive down and see who could stay longest underwater. The sea was balmy, warm, the sun now gentle on the dripping heads, and the glory of the light filled these young bodies with a joy that made them yell out ceaselessly [...] They reigned over life and the sea, and they immoderately gobbled up all the sumptuousness of the world, like lords assured of their irreplaceable riches.

That too was prohibited or at least disapproved of by the great matriarch, who would punish him again for coming home late from the beach. Again it didn't stop him. The epiphany of lying in bed and dissolving into the light has already been anticipated in the episode of diving into the Mediterranean, and trying to become one with the water, kissed by the sun as they surface, and experiencing the same 'joy' Camus attained as he floated away into space with his tobacco smoke. The idea of the 'glory of light' suggests a mingling of the two moments in Camus' mind.

The First Man – the last work – is a recollection of such primal experiences. But swimming bubbles up throughout his work. All his heroes are swimmers. Meursault goes swimming in *The Outsider*, as does Rieux in *The Plague*, and it is the failure to dive into the Seine to save a drowning woman that torments Clamence in his late novel *The Fall*. Camus even equates writing with swimming: 'I have to write in the same way that I have to swim, because my body demands it.' The first of his notebooks contains a detailed evocation of going night-swimming in August 1937. By this time he was twenty-three, had left university to go and work for the *Alger Républicain* newspaper and had begun writing the novel that would eventually become *The Outsider*.

And he went into the water and he washed off the dark and contorted images that the world had left there. Suddenly, the rhythm of his muscles brought back to life the smell of his own skin. Perhaps never before had he been so aware of the harmony between himself and the world, the sense that his movements were in tune with the daily course of the sun. Now, when night was overflowing with stars, his gestures stood out against the sky's immense and silent face. By moving his arm, he can stretch out the space between this bright star and its flickering, intermittent neighbour, carrying with him the sheaves of stars and trails of clouds. So he scoops up great armfuls of the sky, while the town lies around him like a cloak of glittering shells.

It is a kind of post-SOS message: swimming can save your soul. The purifying water, blanking out the dispiriting sense-data of dry land, offers a form of baptism or metamorphosis to the swimmer. Swimming is tantamount to magic or miracle. But the key word in this passage, Camus' favourite word I suspect, is *like*. A principle of analogy – comparability and resemblance and correspondence – holds the world together. It is one of his key arguments in *Sisyphus*: the important thing is not the individual terms but the comparison. At some level, amid all the myriad differences, everything is fundamentally the same: the water, the earth, the swimmer and the stars, swimming and writing, smoke and light and the vanishing self, they are all connected by a network of 'likes'. Thus the swimmer becomes linked with the universe. Everything is linked. Everything *flows*. It is a pre-Socratic vision of the world in which the many are fused into one or a quasi-Buddhist perception of a secret underlying unity (Camus kept a Buddha statue from Cambodia on his desk). The swimmer, as he cuts simultaneously through the sea and the stars, has achieved the state of *satori*, or enlightenment, or possibly grace. This time he is crowned by the glory of light from other suns. This is Camus' 'starry night', like those paintings of Van Gogh's in which the stars – like spinning footballs – seem close enough that you can reach out and touch them.

In *The Outsider* all could have been well if only there had been more swimming. Meursault is fine so long as he is swimming with his girlfriend; it's only when he comes back to the beach that it goes horribly wrong. It's hard to shoot somebody while swimming. *The Plague* is explicit in its critique of Algeria: the 'soulless' city of Oran 'turns its back on the bay, with the result that it is impossible to see the sea', closing itself off from grace. But there are moments, like the passage in his notebooks, where this can be reversed and the city is temporarily turned around to face the sea again. When he wants to get away from the plague, the doctor narrator goes swimming with a friend. More night-swimming – now felt as a liberation and a communion in the midst of collective suffering. Tarrou and Rieux, carving through the water and scooping up armfuls of stars, share 'this same happiness' and swim 'with the same rhythm [...] with the same cadence and the same vigour'. Camus brings in the word 'same' here several times as if to erase or suspend the very idea of difference. Camus often laments how arid the business of writing is, but – as in these exceptional, lyrical episodes, the peak experiences – he seems to accept writing when it can be experienced as a kind of swimming, an immersion in the oceanic feeling.

Sartre was a quantum thinker: for him everything was nothingness with a few isolated, random particles scattered about, and flying apart (*Being and Nothingness* explicitly invokes Heisenberg's uncertainty principle). For Camus, everything was waves, not particles. Everything and everyone was connected in a network. In his post-war essay, 'Return to Tipasa', a version of paradise lost, and to some extent regained, Camus was content to hear rather than see, tuning into birdsong, the wind sighing, the vibrations of trees. 'I was hearing all that, and at the same time I was listening to the waves of happiness rising up in me.' The mountain hanging over the bay – that too was a wave, 'an immense and motionless wave'. The wave, semi-miraculously, would always save him, he thought: 'If I were to die, in the midst of the cold mountains, unknown to the world, cast off by my own people, my strength at last exhausted, the sea would at the final moment flood into my cell, come to raise me above myself and help me die without hatred.' The idea of swimming, and the sea, and waves echoing around the universe, gave Camus the sense of a vast, all-inclusive continuum, what the physicists would call a *unified field theory*. 'What else can I desire other than to exclude nothing?' This gives us a clearer sense of what the 'absurd' meant to Camus (in *The Myth of Sisyphus* and beyond). The clash of rationalism and the irrational is under-pinned by a big evolutionary picture: the sea-creature crawls up on dry land and becomes a philosopher ('a whole race, born of the sun and the sea, vibrant and salty, striding the beach') but always with a lingering sense that he was better off in the water than spouting theory. Camus, whether lying in bed or keeping goal or swimming under the stars, can find ways of accessing the great totality that is prohibited to the 'detotalized' Sartre. He is able to call up the memory of some primordial perception that is never entirely lost. 'In the midst of winter, I at last realized that there was in me an invincible summer.'

Sartre was a good, strong swimmer, when he had to be, but he always feared the ocean. Often he would sprint back to shore in a panic. He always expected some monster to pop up out

Antanas Sutkus, 2012

Collection Christiane Galindo

Sartre on the beach   Camus (and friends) on the beach

of the depths and drag him down (specifically, as he told the Beaver, one with twenty-four legs and huge crab-like pincers). In *Nausea*, the nausea begins when the hero picks up a pebble on the beach, still glistening with water. Whenever Roquentin looks out at the sea, he can't help but wonder: what is lurking there, *beneath* the surface? The *thing*? He was bound to head for high land.

In the winter of 1934-35, against the background of the irresistible rise of fascism and the looming Spanish Civil War, Beauvoir persuaded Sartre to go for ten days' skiing in the Alps, near Chamonix (she invited Camus too, later, and they talked about it but he never went). Sartre was struggling with the third draft of *Nausea* (then still called variously *Melancholia* or *The Adventures of Antoine de Roquentin*) and was glad to get away from it all for a while. Beauvoir, in her memoirs, *The Prime of Life*, says that 'I had never before experienced anything like this odourless, colourless, blindingly white landscape, its surface iridescent in the sunlight'. She presents an idyllic picture of a negative universe, the opposite of the Boulevard Saint-Germain, and therefore in some sense harmonious. She returns to skiing in *The Second Sex*, in the chapter on the formative years of the young girl, as a great gender-equalizer: 'the featherweight boxing champion is as much a champion as is the heavyweight; the woman skiing champion is not the inferior of the faster male champion'. Despite the Occupation, she continued to go skiing through much of the Second World War. The fact is, she was a better skier than Sartre. For Sartre, the sense of a struggle persisted.

The experience leaves its imprint, like tracks in the snow, in a passage that reads like a microcosm of his philosophical work. *Skiing and Nothingness* – the chilly mini-book within the book – it should be stressed, offers anything other than a useful practical manual on 'how' to ski. Whereas Beauvoir sees skiing as an opportunity to transcend conflict, for Sartre skiing replicates the notion of 'antagonistic reciprocity'. Me against the mountain. Skiing – like all sports in Sartre – comes out sounding like boxing or war or sex or art, or all of them combined. 'Conquest' is key.

Sartre begins by asking the broadly semiotic question: 'What is the meaning of skiing?' Obviously, says Sartre, the snow-field is like the body of a woman. I want to take possession of it. I want to dominate it. The snow melts by virtue of my pressure upon it and enables me to glide across its face. *I*, the skier, am an agent, I have intentions, therefore I represent consciousness, the 'for-itself' (*pour-soi*). I am a virtual being, with unlimited alternatives. The mountain, on the other hand, is never anything but a mountain. This is the 'in-itself' (*en-soi*) par excellence, nothing but matter, unambiguous and undivided, incapable of conscious thought or intentionality. If we could imagine the mountain – for a moment – being capable of self-consciousness, it would still think of itself, unimaginatively, only as a regular mountain, nothing else. My problem, reckons Sartre, thinking back to his own experiences in the Alps, is that I want to be so good at skiing that I am a skier in the way that the mountain is a mountain (or the way that the waiter serving in the Café de Flore wants to be a waiter, the whole waiter, and nothing but the waiter). In other words, I don't want to be a virtual no-thing any more: I want to be a thing. Not just a skier but *the* Skier, like a Platonic Idea, an archetype. I want to switch ontological categories and metamorphose (as in a fairy tale or science-fiction parable) from the status of conscious being to an unconscious *it*. At the same time, I would retain my conscious awareness, thus becoming the paradoxical 'for-itself-in-itself' or God. At least *a* god: the god of the mountain. Sartre probably saw something of this in Beauvoir, the sense of effortless domination and power (he calls her 'my little skier').

And it is possible that he too really has this sensation, for short periods, that he is talking about himself, at points when he was really skiing well and felt dominant and all-powerful – the Pardaillan of the piste. But he has to concede: I'm not going to be able to keep this image up forever; I am not really this quasi-thing I was pretending to be. My pseudo-divine status is bound to be compromised in the end. If I fall or I smash into a tree, for example. Or, less dramatically, if I start thinking about something other than skiing (philosophy, say). This is like a micro-version of the Nietzschean death of God, happening again and again right there on the slopes. And any notion of grace or harmony or effortless supremacy explodes in his face. Or melts, like a snowman.

There is a manic-depressive curve to Sartre's writing. It is as if he is taking a potential 'peak' experience and trying to demonstrate that the whole thing is a fallacy. I am going to go as high as you can physically go, and then at the same time still show you why it is about as low, metaphysically speaking, as you can go. Everything is in meltdown, flying apart, not converging into an oceanic continuum. The totality remains detotalized. We are confronted by the gulf between the mountain over there, in all its massive and effortless solidity, and our own more complicated consciousness that I-am-not-the-mountain, in fact I am not anything, I am not even *me*, let alone some dazzling archetype. Everything else is bad faith and self-delusion.

Sartre seems to hanker after something that is not really skiing any more. Skiing would be better 'if the snow were to reform after I have passed'. In a slightly paranoid way Sartre fears to leave any tracks behind him – as if he could be followed, like a fugitive – and is driven to argue that 'the ideal form of sliding would therefore be one that leaves no trace: that is, sliding over water.' It is characteristic of Sartre to suppose, even while doing one thing, that some other thing could, conceivably, be the 'ideal'. But this is not an invitation to go night-swimming: he is gliding *over* the surface of the water, not *in* it or *through* it. He doesn't want to leave any tracks for the police to follow, but he doesn't want to immerse himself in the water either (for fear of what lies beneath the surface). There is no record that Sartre ever water-skied or surfed but it is hard to resist the image of him – perhaps in his Pardaillan persona – poised on board or ski and carving up the face of one of Camus' cosmic waves.

But, finally, when he speaks of 'this slight sense of disappointment that never fails to come over us when we look back at the tracks we have left behind', this is surely Sartre the writer looking back over what he has written, and perversely driven to go on writing more and more in search of some impossible perfection. To be *the* Writer, not just *a* writer.

7

PEN ENVY

HELL IS OTHER PEOPLE'S BOOKS. Every serious book reviewer hates the books he reviews. Either they are sad and pathetic and abominable; or, what is really annoying, they are outstanding works of unsurpassable genius. Before the war, Sartre and Camus clashed from afar, sending one another distant smoke signals. Half love-letters, half shadow-boxing. First Camus (in 1938), reading Sartre, and later Sartre reading Camus (in 1942), had parallel experiences and both published reviews that, while broadly favourable and enthusiastic, were also subtly sceptical, shrewdly subversive.

Camus was, from the outset, the 'outsider', marginal, non-metropolitan, *pied noir*. Sartre always occupied the centre, embodied to a high degree the establishment culture of his age, even when – especially when – he was most militantly opposing it. Camus was, chronologically and intellectually, the junior partner; geographically and politically, he was out on the periphery. It was natural that Camus should have to acknowledge the existence of Sartre first. And to imitate his precursor.

Sartre published his first novel first (with Gallimard) and his collection of stories, *Le Mur*. Camus was a twenty-something journalist, writing the 'Reading Room' column for the daily newspaper *Alger Républicain*, based in what was then the French *département* of Algeria in October 1938, when he reviewed Sartre's *Nausea*. War was on the horizon. The whole point of the Reading Room was to keep track, in far-off Algiers – on another continent, after all, whatever the political affiliations – of what was being published in Paris. And at the same time manifest 'its respect for this dignity so peculiar to mankind, which is artistic creation'. Camus read and reported on Gide, Nizan, Huxley. He had a way of writing that suggested that he was the equal of these authors. There was no false deference. But the review of *Nausea* struck a new note of sympathetic engagement. Months before, in July, Camus was already telling his friend Lucette Meurer he had been reading it for weeks and had 'thought a lot about this book' and 'would have a lot to say about it': 'it is too close to a certain part of me for me not to fall for its charms'. He soon found himself thinking like Roquentin and living out his sense of estrangement from humanity at large. 'Since your friend the Tahitian woman knows Sartre,' he wrote to Lucette, 'I'd be pleased to have some details about him as a man.' Sartre became an inspiration. He had shown the way, written a novel about everyday experience that was also philosophically literate.

Some of the original passion and admiration for Sartre survives on the page, however pared down. Sartre's writing is 'seduction' in book form and Camus allows himself to be seduced: there is enough here to 'love' Sartre (or perhaps 'like' – the verb *'aimer'* leaves it open – but the feeling seems stronger than that). It's a *coup de foudre*, love at first reading. 'The natural suppleness in the way he explores the extremes of conscious thought, his lacerating lucidity, reveal limitless gifts.' Every chapter 'attains a kind of perfection of bitterness and truth'. Existence in Bouville is depicted 'with a sureness of touch and a lucidity that leaves no room for hope'. Camus compares Sartre to Franz Kafka for his sense of absurdity and alienation. Surely it must be possible to do something similar, but transposed from the mythical Bouville to Algeria? After all, he and Sartre seem to share so much – 'this feeling is common to us' – almost as if they were already collaborators or old comrades. And so, following in his tracks, the younger man begins writing – right here in the review, as if by way of homage – a synopsis of his own first mini-novel:

> Even in the most well-constructed lives, there always arrives a moment in which all the facades collapse. Why this or that, this woman, this job, and this appetite for the future? And, in any case, why this feverish determination to live on in this body that is doomed to rot? [...] As a result of going against the tide, a sense of loathing, a feeling of revolt, takes possession of our entire being, and the revolt of the body is what we call nausea.

But he cannot just go ahead and copy Sartre, obviously. The whole point of 'going against the tide' (*à contre-courant*) is to go *against*. 'I have to react *contre*' Sartre, he tells his friend Lucette, precisely because he loves him (again he uses the verb *aimer*). Sartre with that lacerating lucidity of his must be resisted. Camus has to deviate and oppose, not let himself be bewitched and bedazzled. From the very beginning, Camus is forced to position himself as not just an admirer of Sartre's, but equally – or more so – an adversary. Reading is anything other than a passive, deferential experience, but rather a form of struggle against possible domination and the anxiety of influence. The agon – the binary praxis of antagonistic reciprocity, the 'total activity' – has already begun, long before the two men meet in person.

The praise, not surprisingly, is not unstinting. Is there not a sense in which *Nausea* is, itself, nauseating? Camus never says it flat-out – he is too polite here – but the thought is there, all the same. Just as Roquentin revolts against the elusive Marquis de Rollebon and the novels of Balzac, so too the reader is likely to find something objectionable in the novel. Camus has to admit, sadly, that he is a little disappointed, in the end, by what seemed so promising. *Could do better.* Sartre's 'remarkable fictional gifts and the play of the toughest and the most lucid mind are both lavished and squandered.' *Nausea* suffers from philosophical overload, as if the author is showing off. Sartre has read too much philosophy and most of it ends up being regurgitated in his writing. And the ending! That makes no sense; it just contradicts everything that has gone before. And amid so much that is repugnant – all that ugliness! – Sartre has omitted all sense of 'love' and 'beauty' and 'danger'. As if all that heavy-duty philosophy has squeezed out the potential for poetry. 'A novel is nothing but philosophy put into images', but the point is to absorb the philosophy, to live it, to show it, not to quote it, and leave indigestible chunks of it (Kierkegaard and Heidegger, for example) lying about the place at random. Too much 'theory' has eclipsed 'life'. This is not 'a work of art', it is not a novel; it is more like a dissertation. An academic trying to be a novelist.

'Some indefinable obstacle prevents the reader from participating and holds him back when he is on the very threshold of consent.' A few months later we find Camus reviewing *The Wall*, Sartre's collection of short stories, and paying tribute to his 'profound mastery', 'the greatness and truth of his work'. He is on the verge of consenting again. What holds him back this time? Only the 'obscenity' – the 'explicit sexual descriptions' that seem 'often gratuitous', not to mention the 'taste for impotence'. Sartre has become a *voyeur*.

None of which stops Camus borrowing *Nausea*'s first-person

diary form for *The Outsider*, marking a decisive break with the third-person narrative of *La Mort Hereuse*.

Perhaps Sartre took it as a kind of *homage*. When he wrote his review of *The Outsider*, in September 1942, he had recently finished *Being and Nothingness* and was busy with *The Roads to Freedom*, his trilogy of wartime novels. And he was working on plays. But this still didn't stop him dedicating a full twenty pages to this first novel by a young writer. And he brings into it *The Myth of Sisyphus*, in which he finds Camus referring to him – refusing to name him – only as 'a writer of today' with his theory of nausea (which is the absurd by another name, says Camus). Was that a snub? A gesture of dismissal? Sartre found himself depicted as a kind of comrade figure, not a precursor, not someone who can conceivably exert any influence over Camus therefore, but just one among many.

The Writer of Today argues that the Outsider hasn't done his homework properly: 'M. Camus has the affectation of quoting the works of Jaspers, Heidegger, Kierkegaard, without, however, fully understanding them.' A B+, at best, for Modern Philosophy (Sartre had, after all, graduated at the top of his class at the strangely named Superior Normal School – one year precisely after coming bottom! – and gone to lectures by Husserl, and always assumed professorial superiority). But Sartre rather approves of the idea of Meursault – the novel's hero – shooting an Arab on the beach and being condemned to death. That is just the way things are. Just as Camus tried to keep Sartre at arm's length, so too here Sartre is concerned to place Camus; to categorize and defuse his writing even as he admires it. It is a strategy of containment. Camus' sentences are like Hemingway's, and the novel as a whole has the feel of one of Voltaire's fables, so Meursault is an updated Candide, an innocent abroad, almost an idiot. But more than anything Sartre can't help finding Sartrean elements in Camus. The best bits in Camus, Sartre argues, are when he is most like Sartre.

It is characteristic of Sartre that he takes Camus to pieces – reverse engineering his sentences, like a car mechanic taking an engine to bits – to see how his text works. In particular, the thing he homes in on is the use of the '*passé-composé*'. *The Outsider*, emulating *Nausea*'s diary style, privileges the relatively informal perfect tense. It's the closest, Sartre notes, that Camus can get to being silent while still using words. And the fact that the 'composed past', consisting of an auxiliary (either *être* or *avoir*) plus a past participle, can, in effect, be de-composed, seen as a bundle of disconnected pieces, appears to Sartre as the key to understanding the book: the world is just like that, a miscellaneous collection of things that don't really fit together to make anything meaningful – it is not a 'plenitude' but a constellation of gaps, holes, and voids. 'Every sentence of *The Outsider* is an island.' Camus, reading Sartre, asks himself: what does Sartre have in mind, and – by extension – what do we all have in mind, 'at the limits of conscious thought'; and where is beauty anyway? Sartre, on the other hand, asks himself: what tense is he using? Sartre sees the writer as a kind of stage magician and he needs to know how the trick is done.

Sartre welcomes Camus to the brotherhood of existential writers, but under certain provisos. You have to tick the box accepting terms and conditions. Sartre invokes the 'analytic' mentality: everything can and should be taken apart, undone. And the fundamental difference is this: between self and others, of course, but more generally between human beings and the non-human. It is the definition of absurdity. Sartre sums it up in a word he finds in Camus: 'divorce' (even without there having been any kind of marriage in the first place). This is what absurdity is like: the opposite of lying in bed and flying away on a magic carpet of smoke; it is the lack of an epiphany. The insurmountable dualism of mind and matter. We are here, *on* earth, but we are not *of* earth. We inhabit these bodies but we are not reducible to mere physicality. In one aspect, we are lost; in another, more upbeat way, we are transcendent beings. 'Alienation' simply means we are alien beings who have landed on this planet, marooned here, but never really belonging. We *are* the body-snatchers.

Camus, we know, read Sartre's commentary on Camus (which appeared in February 1943). 'Most of his criticisms are fair,' he wrote, 'but why that acid tone?' Both Camus and Sartre would continue obsessively reading and commenting on one another's work for the rest of their days. Each would define himself increasingly in opposition to the other. But Sartre in particular, for all his robust tough-guy talk, suffered bursts of 'pen envy': not just an extreme fascination with what other writers are up to, but also a suspicion that one way or another they may have been better endowed than he was. It was already there in *Nausea*.

Roquentin can't get the jazz song 'Some of These Days' out of his mind and he has to listen to the recording of it again and again. At first it seems as if it is the music and the singer that he is bewitched by, but it finally becomes clear that he is obsessing about the composer – i.e. another writer. The end of the novel has Roquentin taking off to try to do something similar in novel form. Camus finds 'hope' in the ending: that of 'the creator who finds deliverance in writing'. It is probable that Sartre was more preoccupied by Proust than by any other writer as he was writing *Nausea*, and he was confident that he was better than Proust. But the final chapter of the book, with Roquentin still in his hotel in Bouville, listening for one last time to the song, strikes an authentic note of Sartrean envy.

'I am thinking about a clean-shaven American, with thick

black eyebrows, in stifling heat, on the twentieth storey of a New York apartment building. Sartre imagines the composer, Shelton Brooks, as a New York Jew, whereas he was in fact a black Canadian. The facts were not uppermost in Sartre's mind ('It happened like that. Like that or some other way, it doesn't matter'). Brooks is not so much a myth; more he's any possible writer, anywhere, any time. '*Et pourquoi pas moi?*' he asks. *Why not me?* He wants to be *this other writer*, whoever he is. Play it for me, he says, to Madeleine – like Bogart in *Casablanca* – play it for me. Before he gets on the last train out of Bouville, before the Nazis arrive. It is an almost Camusian moment of self-detachment. Roquentin can feel himself morphing into Brooks:

> I am no longer thinking of me. I am thinking of this guy over there, the one who composed this tune, one day in July, in the black heat of his room. I am trying to think of him *through* the melody, through the clean, acid notes of the saxophone. He made that.

Sartre loves the acid notes. There is no question of the author being dead, even if he really is. He is flamingly alive and present in every note. The idea that the creative process could be something neutral and impersonal is far from his mind. It is this *other writer* who has what he, Sartre, lacks.

> I would be happy if I were in his place. I envy him.

Sartre suspects that happiness is out there somewhere, being enjoyed by writers other than him.

They began by sparring at a distance, but it was not long before Sartre and Camus had the opportunity to meet in the great jousting arena – the Coliseum – that was Paris. They both had a taste for physical confrontation. Sartre makes it explicit, the need to get in close, physically, to make it personal. And make precise comparisons, measurements. And then impose himself.

> He loved the big body of that stooping athlete. The sight of it made him shiver with ecstasy at the prospect of their future combats. The body was always there: he would have liked to rub up against it as if it were a wall, but, particularly, he would have liked to fight with it, to clasp it with all his might and try to throw it down.

The writer is also, in Sartre's thinking, a wrestler:

> His muscles, the muscles of a wrestler, felt a relentless need to fight, to crush. The joys and sufferings of his huge organism were in a constant, extraordinary state of frenzy. While writing, he would grip his penholder so hard it would almost crack. There isn't a single sentence in his books [. . .] that did not bear the full weight of his abandon.

Perhaps because he already felt mortally wounded by tuberculosis, only marginally pre-posthumous, Camus had no particular fear of combat. He feared only the symbolic. Which explains, I think, why he needed to become a writer while, at the same time, doing his best to be the exact opposite, to write *against* writing, to find a way of erasing mythology, literature, ethics and religion.

For Sartre, meaning is always already out there, 'contemporary philosophy has established that meanings [*significations*] are immediate givens'. But they are not given to Meursault in *The Outsider*. He doesn't really get it when his girlfriend asks him if he loves her. The word 'love' doesn't make a lot of sense to him. (He doesn't bother with any false politeness in his reply either: 'he supposed not'). He feels the same way, at the very opening of the book, about the telegram from the old people's home informing him of his mother's death: 'that means nothing'. (Later he reiterates: 'Doubtless, I really loved Ma, but that meant nothing.') Nor can he make a lot of sense out of murdering the Arab on the beach, even though he clearly did it. What he resents, above all, in the second part of the book, is the mighty judicial apparatus – the ultimate symbolic power – imposing its own interpretation, passing its own 'sentence' on him and his apparent lack of feeling. 'I didn't understand too well what he [the judge] meant by that so I said nothing [. . .] I could barely follow his reasoning.' Everything happens twice in *The Outsider*, as in dual-process cognition: the first time, in its primal, savage, spontaneous form, as real; the second time around, reconstructed, interpreted, infiltrated, transposed, translated. But Meursault feels as if everyone around him is speaking gibberish. Philosophically, he is closest in spirit to Wittgenstein: 'We tend to take the speech of a Chinese for inarticulate gurgling. Someone who understands Chinese will recognize *language* in what he hears. Similarly I often cannot recognize the *humanity* of another human being.' To Meursault, everyone around him seems to be speaking Chinese. Psychologically, he seems to be a classic Asperger's case, better off with systems (like light, the wakes of ships, the sea) than fellow humans. He is 'mindblind'. The thing he says most often is, 'I said nothing.' After being found guilty (of what it is not entirely clear), when he considers at least making some kind of statement: 'on second thought, I had nothing to say'. Finally, after the sentence – to be beheaded in a public place in the name of the French people – is read out, he is asked if he has anything to say. 'No,' is all he manages. If he enthusiastically embraces his death sentence at the very end of the book, it is because a public execution seems so meaningless that it makes the case for him. His death is a form of protest against symbolic power.

One way or another, sooner or later, Camus always expected to be locked up and ritually slaughtered. When he identified so passionately with the condemned in his essay 'Reflections on the Guillotine' it is because he felt he too had his head on the block.

8

HELL IS OTHER PEOPLE

I WAS IN SING SING PENITENTIARY not long ago and I
happened to cite Sartre's most quoted one-liner, perhaps
the most resonant proposition of twentieth-century philosophy:

Hell is other people.

A young black convict serving twenty years for murder came up
and said he'd had that phrase rattling around in his head for a
long while and was grateful to me for clarifying the source. I
wondered if it would help him to exorcize the line, to get over
it finally, now we had established its genealogy. He said, no, he
was still broadly in agreement with the idea. 'Especially in Sing
Sing.' It seemed to provide a measure of consolation. Something
similar could be said of the whole of *Being and Nothingness*: it's
a philosophy of the prison-house; it's for people who feel
trapped. Perhaps it's even an escape plan.

L'enfer, c'est les autres. In English, with just the slightest tweak,
it turns into its opposite:

Health is other people.

In some parallel world, we can imagine Sartre – another Sartre – coming out with that. It doesn't quite work in French, but the thought is nevertheless there, in one form or another. There has to be scope for *collaboration*. Even in Sing Sing. When I was there, the convicts were putting on a play, a dramatization of Steinbeck's *Of Mice and Men*, written in the 1930s; a story of explosive tension, adulterous sex, friendship and murder. Sartre's play *No Exit* – in which the line first appears, towards the end, like a summation – is like this, except that nothing happens. Nothing can happen any more. We are no longer in the realm of happening, of the event. It is a non-event. A 'one-act' play technically, but you could just as easily call it a no-act play. Three people in a room, talking of sex a lot but not doing anything much about it. The opposite of an orgy. There is a clumsy attempt at murder, too, and it appears that each would like to kill one or more of the others at various times, but again, in this world, blades and bullets can have no impact. It is more the aftermath of a massacre. A growth in awareness, bitterness, and mutual hostility, is about the only difference between the end and the beginning.

Camus was one of the first, perhaps the first, other than Sartre, to utter the immortal line about hell. After a lot of hesitation, sitting in the Café de Flore in the Paris of 1943, Camus agreed to go with Sartre and Beauvoir, and audition – in effect – for *No Exit*. Ironically, he is the writer in French who comes closest to implying that *health* is (or *could* or *should* be) other people. Where Sartre was arguing forcibly that being with others is some kind of torture, Camus was by this stage hard at work on a book that tends to suggest that being without them is. After the absurdist self-contradiction of *The Myth of Sisyphus* and the self-destructive alienation of *The Outsider*, in *The Plague* it is the collective teamwork of the good doctor and all his comrades that keeps the rats at bay. Camus articulates the ethic of Resistance.

Many fledgling moralists in those days were going about our town proclaiming there was nothing to be done about it and we should bow to the inevitable. And Tarrou, Rieux, and their friends might give one answer or another, but its conclusion was always the same, their certitude that a fight must be put up, in this way or that, and there must be no bowing down [. . .] There was nothing admirable about this attitude; it was merely logical.

In fact even Camus – the philosopher of 'hope' – found it a hard case to make and confided to his notebooks, like a lapsed solipsist, that 'the real tragedy is not being alone, it is *not* being alone'. But he wrote this only after meeting Sartre.

Sartre, Beauvoir, and Camus went up to Beauvoir's room in the Hôtel la Louisiane just around the corner on the Rue de Seine, founded in the early nineteenth century by a former colonel in Napoleon's Grande Armée. Number 36 was reasonably spacious, comfortable, with a view over the rooftops and its own small kitchen, like an apartment. Larger and more welcoming than Sartre's rather austere quarters down the corridor. For Beauvoir it was a big improvement on her old place, a hovel on the Rue Vavin. This was the closest she had yet come, she said, to the 'place of my dreams' and she fully expected to stay there 'till the end of my days'. In the evening she liked to go up on the roof and read. She had pale skin, as thin as rice paper, and didn't like to expose it to too much sunlight during the day.

It was something she noticed about Camus from the first time they met in the theatre back in the summer. He had brown skin. Not olive but actually brown. A serious suntan, even in winter. A real outdoorsy Mediterranean look. He made Sartre look like a lily, by comparison. And he was a lot taller of course. He towered over Sartre. Nearly everyone towered over Sartre. Beauvoir herself was a few centimetres taller.

The trio again. It struck Camus as soon as he picked up the page with the dramatis personae on it. As if there could be something magical about the number three. Three pigs, three bears, the trinity, the triad. One man, two women. Sartre's *Huis clos* was clearly a variation on Beauvoir's *L'Invitée*. Which in turn was a variation on their actual lives. The funny thing was that Sartre and Beauvoir weren't even discreet about it: they liked to boast of their conquests, assumed it was part of their philosophical duty to inspect their sexual history, lay it all open for public consumption, revisit it like a dog following a scent, and analyse it down to its metaphysical essentials, like detectives searching for clues or fingerprints. The Saint-Germain *quartier*, Camus realized, was like a provincial village in the middle of Paris where everyone knew everyone else's business – and Sartre and Beauvoir really *wanted* you to know.

Olga was a student of Beauvoir's, Camus knew this much. It was an open secret. Then somehow she became a student of Sartre's. Sartre, Beauvoir, Olga. In *L'Invitée* they became Pierre (the theatre director, a barely disguised take on Jean-Paul), Françoise (Beauvoir), Xavière (who gets gassed). Sartre plus two. Now, in *No Exit*, it was Garcin, Estelle, Inez. Sartre and the Beaver, endlessly replaying their experiences, inviting commentary, as if this was the whole point of existence: to tell stories about it. To *be* the story. To get their version out there and pre-empt what other people said about them.

There were only two copies, so Sartre and Beauvoir shared, sitting on the sofa, while Camus sat at the table. He was Garcin, the 'man of letters', shot for desertion, who fears he is guilty of cowardice. Beauvoir played Inez, the uncompromising lesbian. Sartre had to be Estelle, the straight woman, so concerned with good manners, who murders her own child. He started off treating it as a joke, putting on a high-pitched voice, feminizing himself, but settled down and got into the part. There was one more bit-part, that of the *Garçon*, the insider, the doorman and master of ceremonies, who knows everything but says very little. Sartre doubled up and got to steer Camus/Garcin around the room and show him around his new habitat. Which was exactly what he was doing anyway.

A strange congruence. Perhaps the play began as art imitating life, dancing around the idea of the threesome. Now it began to morph into life imitating art. *No Exit* seemed like an anticipation of this very moment, as the three of them read their lines. It hit each one of them, in different ways and at different times, during the course of the reading, that here they were, three people in a room, rehearsing a play about ... three people in a room. In the play, the three are supposedly dead and in hell and doomed to be tormented for ever by one another. Camus, Sartre, and Beauvoir were fairly sure they were still alive. But the play was unsettling all the same – were they perhaps equally condemned to torture one another, whether they wanted to or not? For Sartre and Beauvoir, the answer was: of course (*Being and Nothingness* is quite explicit about it).

For Camus, it was different. *No need for the fire. Hell is other people.* He delivered the line as if he had always known this to be true. It was something he was forever drumming into the student actors in Algiers. It is necessary to *be* the *other*. You cannot be half-hearted about this. You have to quell your own voice and adopt someone else's. You have no voice of your own any more, no ego, no I. A strange alchemy: I am he and he is me. Transmission, transference, transcendence. It echoed some of his earliest experiences. Which is what made him feel that *Hell is other people* could not be quite right. At the same time, Camus was shrewd enough to realize that, if he was thinking something different to Garcin (or Sartre, for that matter), then, to some extent, this proved that there really was a divide – a *divorce*. Maybe not an amicable one either. I cannot be Garcin. Not completely. I cannot be Sartre or Beauvoir. I am – we are – defined by our differences. The old feeling of absurdity swept over him.

Easy enough for Sartre to say, that hell is other people. But then he had Beauvoir and an indeterminate network of others to gather around and support him, to cushion him, a whole vast duvet of friends – a cast of hundreds perhaps in Paris – to keep him afloat, like salt in the sea. Whereas he, Camus, was if not sinking then at least cast adrift in a boat. 'Separation is the master theme', he wrote to Jean Grenier, thinking about his novel of the war, *The Plague*. He had been banished by his doctor to a sanitarium in the mountains of the Massif Central. Initially his wife Francine accompanied him there (the old hotel belonged to relatives of hers), but she had to go back to Algeria. He reckoned on joining her, but then he was cut off from home and family as the front line swept south in the early months of '43. He could take only so much isolation and snow and cold air. So he went north to Paris, coming down from the mountain into the realm of the literary, to Gallimard and Sartre and Beauvoir: from contemplation to – in theory – active Resistance. Far from home, Camus dreamed of solidarity; intimately connected to the Parisian intelligentsia, Sartre and Beauvoir could assert their extreme solitude.

They were the establishment and at some level Camus wanted to do what they did, be what they were. But while they were like fish in the sea, he was beset by an overriding sense of being in exile, torn away from everything he knew, and writing long letters back to Francine in Algiers, speaking of a 'universe of love' even in the midst of the 'plague' years. So it was that Sartre, completely surrounded and buoyed up by his symbolic *famille*, his little army, the whole of Paris, playing on his home turf, could allow himself the luxury of heaping scorn on everyone else and declaring that hell is other people, knowing all along that he had friends and comrades and lovers on every side in abundance. Whereas he, Camus, the 'away' team, who felt genuinely alienated and alone and bereft, suffering a kind of hell, was condemned to dream of and seek out love and affection wherever he could find it.

Camus had developed techniques for forgetting himself. And yet, as he read and recited his lines, breathing life (or possibly death?) into the figure of Garcin, there remained a part of him – detached and analytical – that discerned a couple of obsessive themes in Sartre's writing. For one thing, he wanted to be watched. Maybe all dramatists were naturally that way inclined. Of course they wanted their plays to be watched. But Sartre was in love with the idea of the voyeur. It came up in *Being and Nothingness*: 'I am bent over, peering through the keyhole. Suddenly I hear steps behind me. I am all at once seized by a sense of shame. Somebody has seen me.' The voyeur had another voyeur behind him, watching him. Everyone was perpetually under surveillance (as if in Sing Sing) and therefore paranoid – but, at least in part, they secretly enjoyed being watched. It was one of Sartre and Beauvoir's most influential insights: nobody was just alive any more, they were alive *for others*: brought up on film as much as literature and philosophy, they had realized that reality was a form of reality TV in which everyone was a minor celebrity, acting out their lives for the pleasure of an audience. That, in other words, we were dependent on others to reassure us about our own existence – and there was no longer any escape from the arrangement. From now on, life is lived inside out: no need for psychoanalysis (Sartre was anti-Freud) — the psyche is right out there, on the surface; it is visible, as if on a screen, not sunk in a well; there are no hidden depths, no id or unconscious.

I need a mirror, says Estelle/Sartre, where are all the mirrors? Let me be your mirror, says Beauvoir/Inez, the lesbian, I will look at you and reflect you back to your own eyes so you will know you exist. You can fix your lipstick and your eyeliner by looking into my eyes. But Estelle rejects her and insists on monopolizing the gaze of the man. But Garcin, in turn, is trapped: he would like to lose himself in Estelle, but he is more concerned to gain the approval of Inez. She denounces him as a coward, a deserter in the hour of war. If only he can convince her that he is a misunderstood pacifist, then he will have saved himself in some way. The three characters constitute a vicious triangle, each one needing the other two at the same time as they loathe and resent them. There is a great, climactic moment in the play when Garcin has been hammering on the door (of hell) to get out — and then finally, mysteriously, it opens. But Garcin stays put. Everybody stays put. Nobody leaves. Each of them has a reason to stay. It is a kind of climax, even though absolutely nothing happens.

For Camus it became clear that the idea of Sartrean existentialism as a form of rugged individualism, the lonely anomic soul wandering through a solipsistic universe, was radically wrong. It was almost the opposite: everyone was tightly locked into everyone else like the instruments of an orchestra. The opportunities for solos were strictly limited. Perhaps this was the meaning of Garcin's most poignant line: 'I wanted to be a man. A tough guy.' But he never can be quite man enough.

And then it was clear too that Sartre was haunted by language. How could he not be as the writer of a play (not to mention novels, short stories, philosophical tomes, etc., etc.)? And yet Sartre seemed at once pathologically alert to the words of others and unable quite to hear them or work out what they are saying precisely. His dead people could tune into the living, and Garcin, in particular, tracked his old colleagues relentlessly, examining their statements for their true thoughts – but only half hearing, losing the thread, only ever gathering tantalizing fragments, devoid of meaning. He feared what others might be saying about him behind his back – or to his face – and at the same time he had no confidence in whatever he could say to defend himself and put his case. He was on trial but – like Meursault – felt that only the prosecution could come up with anything like a coherent and compelling case. The whole point about being locked up in a room – whether the door was open or closed – seemed to be to dramatize this sense of being shut up in some kind of prison, a cave, an inferno made up of the half-heard and the half-expressed. A limbo of language. This is the ultimate punishment: to have people talking about you and to be unable to control what they say. But that wasn't hell – that was just life. Maybe that was why Garcin – obsessed, oppressed by words, to the point of delirium – hated everyone.

One thing Sartre was really quite pleased with in this play. It was a small thing, but it was a small play (call it *compact* and *claustrophobic*) and so nothing in it was really insignificant. The toothbrush. Hey, what happened to my toothbrush? complains Garcin ('with sudden violence'). You won't be needing one here, explains the *Garçon*. Good, he says, I didn't much like 'em anyway. To hell with toothbrushes! Camus grinned as he delivered this line, seeing the humour of it, dropping out of character for a moment. But the funny part of it was – yes, it was pure Poulou that line. He really resented the time taken brushing his teeth (and anything else to do with personal hygiene for that matter). Were you to add it all up it would have to be days that he had wasted shoving a brush around his gums when he could be doing something useful with his time, like writing. He wondered how Camus felt about the toothbrushing business. Probably similar. It was one of the advantages of being dead, he thought: not having to bother brushing your teeth, that is. It was the upside of the downside.

He had to explain to Camus how the play came about. It all started with Marc Barbézat, the chemical manufacturer, not to mention publisher of *L'Arbalète*, and him wanting a play for his wife to star in. It was a commission and he couldn't afford to turn it down. He played around with a few characters. The lesbian to start with, and then the straight guy who can't get away from her. Why not? Obviously because they are fighting over the same woman. That would be the part for Madame Barbézat – the one woman everyone desires. What if they were in prison together, locked up in a cell? That was his first idea. Didn't make a lot of sense, though – why men and women together? How about an air-raid shelter? But what if they were all executed and came back to haunt one another? Now that was more promising ...

It almost wrote itself in a few days. Every writer's dream – the painless creation. Painless for him, but not for *them*. No, he could see that now. He had realized something about himself that he would hardly have believed or guessed at not so long ago. He was essentially a *sadistic* writer. He liked to see his characters suffer, all wriggling on the hook of some terrible dilemma. The image that kept going around his head was of Harry Houdini, the great American escapologist. Houdini succeeded in escaping from great vats, even though tied up in knots and encumbered with chains and padlocks, swimming up again out of frozen rivers and the like. The ultimate nightmare. Holding his breath for impossible periods of time, then popping up and taking in great lungfuls of air, and bowing to the adoring crowd. But what if you tied someone up with ropes and chains but they couldn't escape – what then? Then you had a real drama. No Houdinis in Sartre. No loopholes and secret exits. No way out. No salvation.

Curious, he had to admit, when the whole thrust of his philosophy lay in the direction of 'freedom'. *Liberté* – probably about the most frequent word in the whole of *Being and Nothingness*. Yet freedom was really only interesting when it kept on bumping its nose right up against a wall. Drowning in chains. Then it became dramatic. The unstoppable force and the immovable object. He knew from first-hand experience what it was like to be cooped up, held prisoner. Really it was some kind of miracle he ever got out of that prisoner-of-war camp. A 'fluke' he liked to call it. Plenty of poor devils who didn't make it. And then there were all the Jews being rounded up and shipped off to die. But the case he always had uppermost in his mind was that of the Resistance fighter, betrayed, arrested, manacled, locked in a cell, subjected to torture, made to talk – and yet, still (this was his way of fighting back philosophically against the Fritzes), he retained some shred of freedom. No matter how metaphysical. That could never be taken away from him. There had to be a level at which the prisoner and the torture victim could be said to retain their irreducible liberty. At the level of the gaze and the imagination. Bodies could be tied up in knots, but consciousness, that was another matter – or, rather, not matter at all, but pure transcendence. That which could never be contained or caged or locked up and weighed down with chains. No matter what.

There was a passage in Faulkner – the last pages of *Light in August* – he never managed to quite put it out of his head, like 'Some of These Days' in *Nausea*. Horrifying and yet strangely reassuring. The lynch mob track down the black fugitive, Joe Christmas. They don't really care whether he is innocent or guilty; he is black and that is enough, a sure sign of his guilt – or if not his then another's. There are many of them and only one of him. They have tormented him, tortured him, to within a millimetre of extinction. Castrated him. One of them is about to put a bullet through his brain. It is all over for Joe Christmas. And yet there is that beautiful moment, that cannot be erased, and that will continue to buzz around the brains of the white murderers long afterwards, like an irritating fly that they cannot manage to swat: the moment when the black man looks up at them, with his last remaining strength, and curses them with his gaze. They could not conquer *that*. *That* remained. It was how Sartre felt about the Nazis too: it was what would ultimately drive them to distraction and defeat. Even they cannot beat *that*.

Being and Nothingness – it was like a rewrite of his old Private Perrin tale. The soldier *tries* to kidnap the Kaiser, fails miserably, finds himself locked up, tortured for his troubles, and finally executed – no question of spiriting anyone away at the last moment, none of that heroic nonsense – and still, nevertheless, despite everything that is against him at that moment, with the squad of rifles aimed at his heart, he must have something which is his and his alone, even if only his own death. His defeat is a weird, ironic kind of victory. *Qui perd gagne*. Loser wins. That which does not kill me makes me stronger, said Nietzsche. Go ahead and kill me, Sartre wanted to say: it will only make me infinitely stronger.

It was this powerful premise – the twisted assumption that every failure was a demonic form of success – that enabled Sartre, without a care, to devise the most deterministic, doom-laden narratives. With a sense of inevitability, predestination, as in the tragedies of Racine, that is positively Jansenist. No exit. *Les jeux sont faits* was the inevitable sequel to *Huis clos*.

In this story, as Sartre saw it, Eve and Pierre had to die, if not in the first scene then soon. How to kill them off? A road accident perhaps? Simple and plausible enough. But no, it needed intentionality. It needed what we'll call 'evil', for the sake of argument; the bad guys – a story was nothing without them. Beauvoir had come up with the poison idea. The Beaver was good at murder. Eve's husband would be slowly poisoning her to death, so sorry she was feeling ill, and all the time slipping drops into her medicine. Perfect. Presumably after her money. Not to mention her younger, sexier sister. And what of Pierre, how was he supposed to go down? Something political perhaps? He could be a radical; his group – shadowy, of course – want to overthrow the regime, he could be planting a bomb, and then he is shot . . . No, too heroic. Too much like Private Perrin again. What if . . . yes, this was better, what if he wanted to be heroic, but was killed stupidly, by an idiot. A kid on a bike. Who pulls out a gun and fires. Genius.

Two dead people: one man, one woman; a romance and a ghost story. Neither of them knew they were dead, not at first. Then Eve catches her reflection in a mirror. Or rather doesn't. Nothing. No reflection. Goes back for a second look, like something out of the Marx Brothers. But still: she is not there. A woman looking for her own reflection in a mirror and not seeing it. Pierre should go off down the street whistling – silly bastard missed! Look at me, I'm unscathed. Not a scratch. But nobody responds when he calls out hi. And then he asks some old guy for the time or directions or something and he realizes the old-timer is just looking straight through him. As if he is not there. He goes back and finds his own dead body, lying there in the street, drilled with rather well-aimed bullets after all.

But at least they can see one another, Eve and Pierre, united by virtue of being dead. Let them go off to the afterlife together – a dash of *No Exit* here – but not hell (and not heaven either), staffed by some anonymous bureaucracy, just the same place as before but now populated by all the dead people. And – this was the joke (or tragedy?) – they fall in love. Of course they do; what could be more natural? After all, they have just had a nasty shock, what with dying and all. And now they can provide comfort and consolation. They start dancing – there is ghostly music coming from somewhere – he doesn't know how to dance of course, but she does and she gently leads him ...

BUT, hold on a minute, haven't we forgotten something here? It is one of the rules of the game (everybody knows this): *ghosts can't have sex.* They would like to. But the dancing is all pretend dancing. Each of them is dancing on his or her own. The romance is all pretend romance. Shadow-boxing, for ever and ever amen. Look but don't touch. How many times has that happened to every single one of us? Everybody will understand that, alive or dead.

It was an odd thing with Sartre: this sense of unreality that seeped into everyday life. The feeling of being, despite everything, a bit of a ghost. He – like his characters – half-expected not to see his image reflected back at him in mirrors. (Really, wouldn't it be better that way? No more monkey, no more polyp!) He expected, when someone reached out to hold him, for their arms to close around thin air. He had had the experience of walking down the street in broad daylight, saying hello to somebody, and ... nothing, no reply, they look right through him. Perhaps, the thought often occurred to him, it was because he did not exist. He was a phantom. Smoke. He had finally attained pure nothingness.

Les jeux sont faits. First twist: they're dead. Second twist: they get a second chance at life on earth. Sartre could just imagine the chat with the garçon in the Flore.

Monsieur Sartre, with all due respect, isn't *Huis clos* just a little ... how shall we say, *depressing*? You know, a bit grim and negative. Isn't everything bad enough already without you making it a damn sight worse? It's like wasps in a bottle, stinging one another to ... no, not death, but you know what I mean.

Yes, yes, I understand, Sartre would reply, nodding amiably, fair comment. But look, here is this follow-up; it's more cheerful and optimistic.

Really?

Oh yes, the dead get to live again.

You don't say.

They can try again.

To do what?

To find true love of course. Isn't that what it's all about really?

Well, I'm glad you've decided to lighten up a bit finally ...

Gotcha! Another of his traps. For the innocent and the optimists.

So Eve and Pierre have another go – at *being* rather than pure *nothingness*. This has to be a movie, surely? Because this is exactly like 'Take 2. And do it with feeling this time, will you'. The bureaucrat who runs the afterlife admits that an error has occurred. Terribly sorry. You two were supposed to be lovers and live happily ever after. According to Article 140. Clearly something went wrong. So you can go back to the real world and fix it. But ...

(There had to be some kind of constraint, obviously. You couldn't just have *carte blanche*, could you? That would really be cheating ...)

OK, yes, you can live again – Orpheus and Eurydice return! How beautiful is that – BUT you have only twenty-four hours to fix it. Surely that should suffice. You have a whole day to get your lives straightened out – or rather curved, shall we say – so that you meet and finally, GET IT ON! Well, good luck, farewell, and hurrah for true love.

Pierre and Eve duly promise to do everything differently the next time around. Like another world. So they return to earth; well, they already are on earth and they haven't gone anywhere, so let us say they are fully re-embodied. Reincarnation. The Buddhists say you have seven lives, don't they. Or is that cats? But . . .

What happens next? Do they blow it or don't they? To be or not to be, that was the question. Sartre hadn't quite figured it out yet. The idea for *Les jeux sont faits* came to him in 1943. But the script was not published until several years later, when it was finally made into a film. At the end of 1943, with *No Exit* getting underway, it was still work-in-progress. Sartre was not one of those writers who hides it all away. He loved to get it out there in the public gaze as soon as possible, even before it was ready. Everything had to be done in a frenetic hurry, as if there was never enough time. And it had to be discussed. What could have been more natural than to kick it around, while he was still right in the midst, with Camus and the Beaver? He would be interrupting the play, the read-through of *No Exit*, it is true, but they were nearly at the end and he had heard enough now to know that Camus was a fine actor and a decent human being as well. Maybe too decent to play Garcin? But either way he could definitely write. It would be interesting to get his take on the dilemma.

I imagine the dialogue might have gone like this:

BEAUVOIR: Sartre, you know what I think.
SARTRE: To be honest, I wasn't really asking you, Beaver, I was asking our friend Camus.

BEAUVOIR: They don't stand a chance; that is clear.

SARTRE: Are you against true love or what?

BEAUVOIR: It's a myth. A fairy tale. Some kind of hoax. The stuff of movies.

SARTRE: But, hold on, this *is* a movie.

BEAUVOIR: Yes, I know, but not a *bad* movie. Not a cheap, hollow, shallow, sentimental movie. We have to *demythify*, to make up for all the trash out there. All the stupid books in the world, all the films, the posters stuck up on the walls, the soap-powder advertising. You're not selling anyone anything.

SARTRE: I hope I get paid, though.

BEAUVOIR: It's obvious, isn't it? They go back and everything is just the way it was before.

SARTRE: It doesn't sound very … *existential*, does it? Can't they change their lives – just a little bit? Some kind of twist. A fresh start.

BEAUVOIR: Oh, you can build in a few minor modifications, I dare say. You can't have total, unswerving iteration. But still and all – the car crash is coming and cannot be avoided. The differences between your two leads just about guarantee that. She is basically a stuck-up bourgeoise. She has money after all. Meanwhile, your leading man Pierre: he is not exactly going to give up his politics, is he now, for the sake of what? A good fuck? Ha! Surely he is a bit more high-minded than that? He has a revolution to take care of. And then he is broke, practically penniless, a classic proud proletarian, too proud to go prostituting himself with a stuck-up bourgeoise moneybags. She is *de luxe*; he is basically stowaway class. It's never going to work out. Think about it for a moment – Adam and Eve, Romeo and

Juliet, Troilus and Cressida, Abelard and Heloise – all the best love stories end in death and destruction. Or at least castration. It's the opposite of the pleasure principle. You can't have art without it. No happy endings, please. That is strictly Hollywood. It's a joke. Opium for the masses. You've got a hundred writers sitting around swimming pools in Los Angeles tapping out stories like that.

SARTRE: I wonder what the weather is like in Los Angeles right now.

BEAUVOIR: Don't be weak and pathetic.

SARTRE: What do you say, Camus?

CAMUS: I'm here as actor and director. I don't want to have to write your damn play for you as well. I'm having trouble enough writing my own stuff.

SARTRE: It's not a play, *mon camarade*; it's a scenario. It's not even a scenario; it's just an idea at the moment. A sketch, a hypothesis. You won't be changing a thing. But still, go on, just supposing for a moment you were writing it. Or living it! How would you do it? It could go either way, surely: it could *be* or *not be*.

CAMUS: Yes, I see that; it's beautifully poised.

SARTRE: It's fucking poised all right. Think of Schrödinger's box – you know the one with the quantum cat in it? When you open up the box, finally, is the cat alive or dead? You say.

CAMUS: Or alive *and* dead? Isn't that what the physicists say? The states are superposed. It's like the absurd speaking.

SARTRE: Choose, you irritatingly handsome, absurd bastard, choose! What if you were Pierre, what then? Wouldn't you like to go to bed with a gorgeous piece of bourgeois ass – like the Beaver over here?

It was one of the things Camus found endearing about Sartre. He swore like a sailor. Like a peasant. Nothing la-di-dah about him at all. Beauvoir was different – more tightly wound, precise, choreographed. A little starchy and severe. And hard as nails, tougher than any tough guy. Eve and Pierre, Sartre and Beauvoir. The high-class girl and the stubbly subversive. The two of them seemed to rub along just fine. So perhaps that was the answer. Let Pierre and Eve go back and find common ground in ... philosophy. They both become philosophers and live happily ever after. That is what binds them together, Sartre and Beauvoir, schoolboy and schoolgirl, their heads always in a book. It is the book that brings them together. But what if you were illiterate (like his mother), what then? He could see what Beauvoir meant about the *happy ending*. You couldn't have the 'kindred spirits' story. That went out with Plato: two souls, sundered at birth, who must find one another and thereby achieve perfect harmony once more. Nice idea but it was not going to fly. Was that the only alternative? Heaven or hell: choose, you bastard!

Camus sensed that a trap had been sprung. *Les jeux sont faits*: it was like a syllogism; once the premises had been put in place, then the conclusion followed irrevocably. The whole play – the movie, the hypothesis! – was nothing but an argument, almost a tautology, a perfect machine whose final outcome was built into the opening lines. The kind of narrative that Sartre used to complain about in *Nausea* – and now he was embracing it. On the other hand, Camus didn't want to come across as a romantic dreamer. That was the only alternative the Beaver seemed to offer. But wasn't the question really whether life was ever like a syllogism? Logical, inescapable, like a trap snapping shut.

BEAUVOIR: What if ...?

SARTRE: What if what?

BEAUVOIR: What if Eve's husband were to be the secretary of the Militia – the very organization Pierre is planning to overthrow?

SARTRE: And that would make it tight as a nut. And it would crank up the opposition between them.

BEAUVOIR: [*turning triumphantly towards* CAMUS]: The fascist and the anti-fascist! Let's see if your *love* can overcome that!

CAMUS: And what about *hope*?

BEAUVOIR: Abandon hope all ye who enter here.

CAMUS: It sounds as if you are condemning everyone to hell, then, for ever and ever amen.

BEAUVOIR: So . . .?

SARTRE: Define *hope*.

[CAMUS *stands up and walks over to the window and gazes across the rooftops. The sun is going down and the sky is streaked with orange. Beyond those houses the Seine is still flowing, down to the sea. Further away there is the Mediterranean and the desert.*]

CAMUS: Hope is the opposite of hell. That is the one thing you don't have in hell. It's the absence of hope that drives you mad, not the absence of mirrors and toothbrushes.

SARTRE: You still haven't defined it. The word.

[CAMUS *can't help smiling at how persistent* SARTRE *is – like a demented schoolboy who keeps on asking the same question, over and over, to the point of delirium.*]

CAMUS: I will tell you what hope is. [*He has no idea what to say next. But now he is committed.* SARTRE *and* BEAUVOIR *are watching him, expecting him to fall flat on his face.*] Hope is . . . not knowing precisely. For example, what hope is. Or anything else for that matter. Ignorance, that is what hope is. Pure dumb stupidity. Not knowing what the future will bring. Maybe, as you say, it will be just the same, pure repetition, eternal recurrence. Maybe it won't. It will be different, in ways I cannot predict. My hope is that it will be better and not worse. Hope is the thing that cannot be said exactly.

SARTRE: You know, I think Camus may have a point. I may have to build hope into the script.

BEAUVOIR: In order to vanquish it more completely?

There are two elements in the script as we have it now that suggest that Sartre took some notice of Camus. Almost in a coda, he adds *another* couple of lovers or would-be lovers, impatient for their shot at returning to earth. They are incurable *hopers*. Trying to do things differently. Like Eve and Pierre, of course. And therefore one more ironic repetition added to a litany of iteration. But there must be at least the *possibility*, however remote, just this once, of changing the script. And Sartre builds in a more explicit reference to Camus. Spells it out, but in a very modest obscure way. When the secretary of the afterlife is going through the register, looking up names and destinies, she is trying to find 'Charlier' – Eve's last name: 'Camus, Carnet, Chalet . . .' Camus must have laughed at the line when he went to see the film, years later, after the war. A grudging, fleeting allusion. A reminiscence of their collaboration. But, on the other hand, Camus found himself on the register of deaths. Sartre had already written his obituary, killed him off in the script, relegated him to the guest-list of ghosts.

As Camus got up and put his coat on, getting ready to leave, Sartre, garçon-like, opened the door for him. He pulled it right open, so that they could see the corridor beyond, then sank back down on the sofa and quoted from *No Exit*:

'The door mysteriously opens. Garcin looks at it and does nothing.'

Voilà! You could refute the whole of *No Exit* just by walking out of the door. You will show we are not in hell after all. Sartre, chewing on his pipe, was seeing his own construct seeping back into reality, in the shape of doors opening and closing, so that the world was becoming just a little more Sartrean. Like a play he had scripted. Even if it continued to deviate (however slightly) from what he had written.

And then – and this Camus must have felt, like gravity weighing upon him – Sartre was *controlling* Camus. Camus wanted to walk out of the door; he was planning to go – he already had his trenchcoat on, he was putting his hat on. Oddly enough – did Sartre guess as much? – it was just what he was thinking, that he would somehow refute *No Exit* by going out of the exit. And now Sartre had, in his cunning way, managed to anticipate that move and throw him off. It was completely trivial, utterly meaningless at some level; and at another Camus felt as if he was acting on behalf of humanity (perhaps everyone always was), representing the world beyond Sartre and Beauvoir, and now he had been reeled back in. There was nothing he could say, nothing he could do that hadn't been foreseen and – at least in his head – scripted by Sartre. It was like a chess game with real people and Sartre was moving him around the board at will. He had become a plaything. He began to see that there could be drawbacks to directing Sartre's play: above all, that all along Sartre was directing him. Pulling his strings.

Camus hesitated again. He felt trapped. Whatever he did now, he had been *owned* by Sartre. He could hardly move, as if his shoes were nailed to the floor. Frozen like a single frame in a moving picture. He could hardly breathe.

WANDA [*entering through the open door*]: Hello. I'm Wanda. Who are you?

She had broken the spell Sartre had cast. Wanda Kosakiewicz – Olga's younger sister. Sartre and Beauvoir reacted as if she had a gun in her hand. They were both silent. This wasn't in the script. She was already becoming a problem, a cause of friction between them. She shouldn't even be here. Camus, in contrast, was instantly enchanted: he had never seen her before and she seemed to him like a solution. Like a saviour.

[CAMUS *takes a packet of cigarettes out of his coat pocket, offers her one. He has been released, almost magically, like Houdini.*]

CAMUS: There. *She* is my definition of hope.

WANDA: I'm supposed to be playing the part of Estelle.

CAMUS: That is fortunate. Sartre was terrible as a woman.

[WANDA *laughs.*]

9

AN OCTOPUS AND SOME TREES

'YOU ARE AN OCTOPUS!' Camus could hardly have kept a straight face trying to deliver this line, one of the oddest in *No Exit*. Garcin is addressing Estelle, who is trying to seduce him, and he is trying to keep his distance, and he finds it helps, up to a point, if he denounces her, as violently as possible (she is also compared to a quagmire). Just in case anybody misses the point, Sartre drives metaphor to the point of madness: 'You are all sticky, you are soft! You're an octopus, you're a swamp!'

Sartre, who devoured the works of Jules Verne as a child in his grandfather's library in Meudon, was probably recalling the great scene in *Twenty Thousand Leagues Under the Sea* in which a giant squid tries to swallow an entire submarine, the *Nautilus,* and must be fought off by the heroic Ned Land, who takes an axe to those killer tentacles. Or, perhaps, the parallel scene in Victor Hugo's *Toilers of the Sea* – written in 1866, a few years before Verne – in which his hero Gilliat also has to scrap with an octopus (*pieuvre*: Hugo imported the word from the Channel Islands). Where rampant nature was concerned Sartre had the classic nineteenth-century mentality: it was us or them. Rather like Verne himself, who frequently fantasized about cannibalism, Sartre's anxiety often took the shape of a fear of being eaten alive – absorbed, ingested, assimilated into another being. And thereby deprived of his original difference.

Sartre had to disassociate or distance himself at all costs from other things. From nature, generally: all the things that threatened to suck him in and seduce him into being another thing along with all the other things in the world. Things, in other words, gave him nightmares. He feared being swallowed up by mere thinginess – reified, *chosifié*.

When Sartre was looking for a way of describing the feeling of losing friends and acquaintances who had been carried off in the night under the Occupation, he resorted to a trusty metaphor: 'I would willingly compare it to an octopus.' The 'it' was the enemy ('the most detestable of all') without a face. It could be anyone, not just Germans. But whoever or whatever it was, it seemed as if 'there were silent swallowings-up all around us'. The enemy 'had crushed us and was sticking its suckers to our skin.'

The nightmare returned at least once more in Sartre's writing, at the beginning of the last volume of *Roads to Freedom*:

> An octopus? He grabbed his knife, opened his eyes – it was only a dream. But no. The octopus was there all right, sucking the life out of him with its suckers. That was what the heat felt like [. . .]

A woman; the heat in New York. It seems as practically anything is capable of sucking him down to his doom. 'Outside, the octopus [. . .]' (later in the same book). To Sartre's tentacular mind there is always an octopus waiting outside. Or inside. Perhaps this biophobic tendency helps to explain why practically the whole of the first volume of the series, *The Age of Reason*, is devoted to the search for a decent abortionist. Such is his disgust or horror in the face of raw existence in all its squelchiness and 'viscosity' (sliminess, stickiness), he gives the impression he would like to abort it all. Especially, retrospectively, himself.

Sartre studied at the École Normale Supérieure on the Rue d'Ulm, in the Quartier Latin of Paris (where I followed in his footsteps, sixty-odd years later, as a *pensionnaire étranger*). He qualified as a teacher of philosophy and, in his late twenties, went to Le Havre, on the Atlantic coast of France, to teach. Le Havre mutates into Bouville – literally, Mud City – in *Nausea*. Some of his experiences filter into his writing. At one point Roquentin/Sartre is standing on the harbour wall, looking down into the water. He observes with a degree of grim satisfaction all the debris floating by, old bottles and assorted trash. There is an oily iridescence on the surface of the water, reflecting back a weak sun. Is he concerned with pollution? No: what he is really worried about is what lies beneath the surface. What is 'under the water', deep down, in the darkness, lurking, lying in wait just for him, to suck him down to sleep with the fishes? When he contemplates any expanse of water Sartre always naturally assumes that the sea is *after* him. The sea is populated by hungry sea-monsters, of course, but the sea *itself* is a monster, always liable to rise up and overflow and carry him off.

Roquentin's diary begins with a queasy episode in which some kids are skimming stones and he, following their lead, picks up a pebble from the beach to throw into the sea – but then something (he can't quite work out what exactly, 'a feeling of fear or something of this kind') stops him in his tracks. The beach is a frontier zone in which it is easy (and plausible) to anticipate drowning. But this characteristic paranoia extends to dry land too. One day Roquentin is wandering in the park (the *jardin public*) when he comes across a spreading chestnut tree.

Back in the hills of Algeria (in the area known as Kabylia, to the north, on the edge of the Mediterranean), around the same time, we find Camus saluting olive trees, fig, carob, jujube, contemplating them, trying to *be* a tree, and writing short, lyrical tree-inspired rhapsodies. 'Between the man and the tree, the gesture and the mountain, there arises a sort of consent and acceptance which is at once poignant and joyful.' Camus notes, 'nature = equivalence': we see, if we look properly, that there are all kinds of connections between us and everything else out there that is not us. It is not implausible for a man to know what it feels like to be a tree, or a mountain. There are equals signs all around, metaphors, analogies, 'this link that goes from the world to me, this two-way reflection [...] from the world to me and me to the world'. It is a mistake to think of ourselves as set apart in some way, cut off from the rest of the world when we are, in reality, in the midst of this secret network of liaisons. And it is this sense of connectedness that is indispensable to well-being and happiness.

Sartre's poem of the tree in *Nausea*, in contrast, is something like the opposite of an homage to nature. There is no passionate tree-hugging. But, amid all the primal terror of the biosphere, there is a moment when he sounds an almost Camusian note of ecstasy:

I *was* the root of the chestnut tree.

The roots, in particular, fascinate (but also repel) Roquentin. Their attraction (and their quality of repulsion) lies in the fact that the tree is not floating in mid-air but is anchored to the ground and that the roots disappear into the earth. They are, in effect, swallowed up by the earth. The tree willingly allows itself

to be swallowed, it is an accomplice in its own partial consumption, purely by virtue of existing. At the same time,
Roquentin begins to suspect that he too could be swallowed up,
like a stone skimming across the surface of the sea then, eventually, inescapably, sinking down into the depths. By virtue of
existing. This is what existence is like. Being in the *jardin public*,
Roquentin writes in his journal, is exactly like 'walking by the
edge of the sea.' The root is a claw. A tentacle. A hoover (*pompe
aspirante*), sucking stuff up. It is eating all the time. Roquentin
has only just realized. Everything is always eating. *Or being eaten.*
The tree, as if intermediate between land and sea, seems to him
to overflow its boundaries; it becomes viscous, flowing out
towards him, like a squid, an octopus, capable of digesting him.

The tree is another body-snatcher. 'Even now I am afraid that
it will grab me by the back of the head and lift me up and carry
me off, like a giant wave.' *It* is just about anything. It is being
alive. To exist is to be swallowed up by existence (if you're not
careful). There is a premonition of the *jardin public* episode in
a typically biophobic story ('A Defeat') he wrote while still at the
École Normale. A prince on a mad horseride is trying to escape
from life itself:

> [...] everything seemed alive with a dark, angry life – which
> made him feel sick – a life reaching out to meet his own. He
> felt as if he were in the midst of an immense world, which
> was observing him. He was being watched by the brooks and
> the puddles on his path. Everything was alive, and filled with
> thought. And suddenly he looked at his horse: it too was
> living, thinking [...] Barely able to hold on to his saddle, the
> Prince kept staring at the trees, these dark, huge beings, which
> he had thought he knew so well and now seemed to him
> monstrous apparitions. He started screaming.

Everything is ganging up on him, including trees, horses, and puddles – even the grass! 'What shiver was passing through the grass like a soul? What obscure life moved within it? The idea filled him with an immense disgust.' A puddle is a small sea, blades of grass the beginnings of a jungle. The symbolic is his way of fighting back and holding the savage at bay.

Is it wild nature, red in tooth and claw, that Sartre fears? Perhaps, in part, but there is more to it than this. The simplest example that Sartre gives of this phenomenon – what we can call (awkwardly, I admit) the disassociator's fear of association – comes on the very first page of Roquentin's journal. Here is a cardboard box containing my bottle of ink, he writes. Innocent enough, on the face of it. What could possibly be the problem? Does the writer fear ink? Does the ink make him think of the giant squid enveloping the unwary diver in its dark cloud? No, the issue is rather one of *containment* itself. He is looking at something that is capable of containing something else. The ink can absorb the nib. The box contains the bottle. By the same token, can he too not be *contained* or consumed in some way? Every box is, potentially, a coffin. Every human being is potentially an octopus.

But there was one in particular, recorded in *Words*, who was Sartre's worst nightmare:

> *It* [. . .] – an octopus with fiery eyes, a twenty-ton crustacean, a giant talking-spider – it was myself, a childish monster, it was my boredom with life, my fear of death, my greyness and my perversity.

The octopus was Sartre.

Sartre's mirror problem

I O

THE X OF SEX

SARTRE OBSESSED FOR YEARS about Olga. Then Wanda, her sister, took her place in his affections. But Wanda had no notion of being absorbed into another ménage à trois. She contemplated an alternative trio: with Sartre and Camus. It wasn't premeditated, it just happened that way. When she walked into Beauvoir's hotel room to rehearse *No Exit* she didn't even know Camus would be there. But as soon as she saw him, standing by the door, with Sartre and Beauvoir sitting together, a look of consternation on their faces, the idea began to take shape. In a sense it was already right out there. It was just as Sartre said: thoughts are not internal they are external; they manifest themselves in the world. The vision of the three-way affair was right there in the hotel room, fully formed from the very beginning. Especially when she saw the way Camus' eyes lit up.

It was the closest that Sartre and Camus came to getting into bed together: sharing the same girlfriend for a while. Sartre never really forgave Camus. According to Sartre's *Sketch for a Theory of the Emotions* (written before the war, in 1936), no one *has* to be jealous. All emotions are 'magical': I adopt an emotion – be it jealousy or anger or fear – as a subjective form of retaliation against certain objective realities. This is its function. Emotion is a way out of an impasse (I might faint, for example, in terror at the sight of a face at the window). Thus we have to say that Sartre *chose* to be jealous of Camus over Wanda (and not only Wanda). It was the magical equivalent of boxing, attacking Camus mentally, putting the voodoo on him. And, to some extent on her: as Sartre wrote to his chief confidante, the Beaver, at the beginning of 1944: 'What did Wanda think she was doing, running after Camus? What did she want from him? Wasn't I so much better? And so kind to her. She should watch out.'

Sartre's affair with Wanda had not begun well, that was clear. He thought she had 'the mental faculties of a dragonfly' and told her so. She didn't care. She was an artist, not a philosopher. She admitted to him that she didn't know what sensuality was, but suspected that she needed to know in order to make any headway in the arts. Sartre offered to educate her; he thought he knew quite a lot about sensuality, in a theoretical way. The first time he kissed her and held her down on her bed and made himself comfortable on top of her, aiming for something more practical, she managed to get away and hurried to the bathroom to throw up.

On the other hand, she didn't keep on running. There was something about Sartre that held her back. She felt obscurely that he could teach her something about life, like a high-speed university degree. When, at a hotel in Aigues-Mortes in the south of France, she finally underwent her 'de-virginization' (Sartre's word), she said afterwards, speaking quite frankly, that she 'hated' Sartre. We know this because Sartre duly wrote it all down and reported it immediately to Beauvoir. And he worried in case she could read, upside down, what he was writing. It is like the scene in *Les Liaisons Dangereuses* in which Valmont is writing to the Marquise de Merteuil using the naked backside of his new lover as a desk to write on. Except in Sartre's case it is reasonable to suspect that he was already crafting the sentences that he would write about this encounter even while it was still happening. Perhaps even beforehand, as if he was scripting it, like a playwright. To Sartre, a lover was like a twisting, snaking, erotic sentence.

He told Wanda that he loved her. And he was quick to reassure Beauvoir in a footnote that he was in fact faking it when he told her he loved her. But then he also became genuinely frantic when it looked as if he might lose Wanda, and dashed off rather sadistic letters to other rival women in order to please her. There were to be no more affairs. He even told her he would get rid of Beauvoir. 'You know quite well,' he wrote her from his wartime barracks on the frontier, 'that I'd trample on the whole world (including the Beaver) [...] in order to stay on good terms with you.'

In a panic, when she fell ill (could he be to blame?), he even volunteered to marry her. It was a serious offer, even if he also wrote to Beauvoir at the same time that the marriage would be 'purely symbolic'. Everything is always symbolic with Sartre. The wedding never happened, but he dedicated the *Roads to Freedom* trilogy to her. Back in Paris he also gave her a small part in *The Flies*. She performed well enough for her to be offered a part in *No Exit*. Which is how Camus came to be rehearsing with Wanda in Beauvoir's hotel room. We don't know if Camus knew from the outset that Wanda was already Sartre's lover. He must have known eventually, though. Perhaps it secretly pleased him to irk Sartre, to put one over on the older man: to steal his squeeze just as he had stolen *Nausea*'s diary style.

Naturally, Camus and Sartre would talk about women

together. They had literary locker-room conversations in many of the bars and nightclubs of Paris over the war years and beyond. The biographer Olivier Todd says that 'they spoke more about women than about philosophy'. But it's not as if there was any real polarity between women and philosophy: their relationships exemplified and clarified their divergent philosophical positions. It should also be added that they were of course boasting about their conquests and comparing notes. They even watched one another's seduction techniques at close quarters.

And Camus wasn't too impressed by Sartre's. One night in 1944, they were in a smoky dive on the Boulevard Saint Germain and Sartre was going into his routine. Giving a young woman rapt attention and flattering her wildly. She got up to go and speak to someone else. '*Pourquoi vous donnez-vous tant de mal?*' Camus asked, with a degree of condescension, head propped on one hand, cigarette in the corner of his mouth, looking at the older man with amusement. *Why are you going to so much trouble?* For Camus it was important to be effortless; his degree-zero aesthetics were applied to seduction. One must seduce without seeming to seduce. 'Don't seduce: surrender,' he wrote in his diary. From his point of view, Sartre was flirting too laboriously, lacking in style. It was like watching somebody swim who didn't know how to swim: a lot of splashing and heavy breathing and straining. The puritan work ethic applied to the realm of pleasure. Almost funny.

'*Vous avez vu ma gueule?*' (Have you seen this mug?) Sartre growled back at him, pointing at his own 'disorganized features' (as Beauvoir would say). I have to work to seduce women. I'm a writer, not a movie star. You try your effortless laidback charm with this little lot, *mon pote*, and see how you get on. Sartre could hardly stop drawing attention to his own looks, the mug, the ugliness, the disability, the impossibility of him ever being any kind of Greek god. It was almost like a trump card that he liked to smack down on the table, with a scent of victory. His ugliness, he explained elsewhere, was precisely why he became a good talker – he had to be, it was his only option.

Yes, Camus had seen that mug often enough. He was looking right at it. The smoke and the dim lighting probably helped, up to a point. But he understood that ugliness would always be a live issue with Sartre: disabled, physically, he was driven to exert himself, verbally, to overcome his disadvantage. Not so much the origin of philosophy, more the origin of language. But to Camus' eye, even so, he seemed to *over*compensate, to work too hard, to love to excess. But there was a more general question wrapped up inside his specific question to Sartre on that particular night. Why go to so much trouble? Why dedicate quite so much time to love? Could it be a compulsion, an obsession, a fatality – or were they still exercising free will?

It was around the same time – perhaps in just this kind of smoky, sexually amped-up bar – that Sartre said to Camus, 'I'm more intelligent than you.' Maybe Camus had been boasting about some affair, or – right in front of Sartre – he was effortlessly picking up some particularly beautiful woman. Sartre certainly saw it happen. Perhaps once too often for his liking (notably in the case of Wanda). He had to find some kind of riposte. It wasn't as if they had both been sitting an IQ test. It wasn't a cool, clinical assessment, more a sarcastic verbal jab, intended to provoke a reaction. We know what Sartre said; we don't know Camus' reply. Yet he must have said something – he couldn't just leave it at that. I would guess something like, 'You have the brains, I have the balls'. Or possibly, 'For an intelligent guy, you're an idiot.' Or, perhaps, on a more meditative note: 'You've just read more books and written more than I have. If that is a certain sign of intelligence, then I allow that, yes, you are more intelligent than I. And that is measurable. We can actually count the words. But you really ought to consider whether this is the only form of intelligence. There are other kinds of intelligence – emotional, for example – that you seem to lack. And talking of lack, the very assertion of just how intelligent you are is a sure sign that you are anxious about some possible inadequacy in this area. Not to mention jealous about some of my other achievements.' And if he didn't come right out and say it, he was certainly thinking it. Perhaps he gave him the silent stare and the sardonic smile and a puff of smoke in his eye, mocking Sartre's intellectual *de-haut-en-bas* style.

Often the pair of them would go out together with their women in tow, showing them off, each parading their amours in front of the other man. What do you think of her? Fabulous, what do you think of mine? Each man had a string of lovers, almost as if it was some kind of competition between them. If I can't beat you on quality, then I'll beat you on quantity. Sartre was always the more competitive of the two. If he couldn't achieve degree zero, then he would aim for the exact opposite – the maximum, not the minimum. It is hard to know exactly how many lovers Sartre had over his lifetime. Hazel Rowley's very thorough *Tête-à-Tête*, for example, suggests a figure of perhaps a couple of dozen. Even if we assume a number of unknowns and one-night stands that slipped through the net, we are still only looking at a grand total of around fifty or so, certainly under three figures. Well short of Georges Simenon's reputed 10,000 (Sartre galloped through many of Simenon's novels) or – venturing further afield – Warren Beatty's 12,775 (according to a recent estimate). The myth – to which Sartre himself generously contributed – comfortably outstrips reality. Perhaps it is because he often had several lovers simultaneously – a virtual harem – thus leading parallel sexual lives, that he has become notorious. On one philosophically-inclined website, bloggers even now post explanations of Sartre's mystifying sexual success (one has suggested that it was something to do with his pipe).

But it must be largely because he was so explicit about his exploits, so philosophical about being a lover, that something of a sexual legend has grown up around him. He had to keep telling everyone (or writing) about what he was doing – even while he was doing it. The Beaver was his chief confidante. They liked to say (borrowing from Hegel) that their quasi-marital relationship was 'necessary' while all the other countless love affairs they would have were 'contingent'. Each would be the other's '*pivotal(e)*' (taking this term from the utopian thinker Charles Fourier). I don't think either Simenon or Beatty wrote quite so many love letters – or *about-love* letters. Sartre's liaisons were always dangerously complicated, tangled: when the wires crossed, his lovers – or exes – were bound to denounce him. Which he accepted as fair. It is as if he expected and even wanted to be denounced (and he denounced himself often enough).

One small but scandalous example. Bianca Lamblin (née Bienenfeld), in her *Mémoires d'une jeune fille dérangée* (not published until 1993), tries to get even with both Sartre and Beauvoir, who undoubtedly used her and abused her (her psychoanalyst, Jacques Lacan, hypothesized that they assumed the position of symbolic parents, so were committing quasi-incest). Beauvoir (who seduced her intellectually and physically) first introduced Bianca to the great philosopher hero. He was, although immensely ugly, charming and witty and kind. Eventually, some time in the late 1930s, they went to Sartre's hotel to consummate this tentative affair. She was young, nervous, ambivalent, uncertain, mainly thinking of Beauvoir, not in love, and yet – possibly – willing to collaborate. It was the kind of episode that makes you think of Sartre's description of sex as 'consensual rape'. What did Sartre do on the way to the hotel? Did he put her at ease? Did he tell her how much he loved her? 'You know,' he said, as they approached the hotel, 'the chambermaid is liable to be rather surprised. Only the other day she found me taking the virginity of some other young girl.' Perhaps it was true. It certainly wasn't the moment to blurt it out. Bianca froze and couldn't go through with it (not, at least, until some days later). In a way, she never fully recovered from the shock of that story of Sartre's. She remained perpetually conscious that there was always someone else in the frame. According to this account, Beauvoir was jealous of her, feared losing Sartre completely, and manoeuvred – during the phoney-war period – to have Sartre dump her. (Why, indeed, Bianca never dumped him is a mystery that her book fails to elucidate.)

There was an autistic quality to Sartre's attitude towards individual women, as if they were part of some fiendish psychological experiment he had dreamed up (perhaps designed to prove that there is no such thing as love) – and was compelled to keep on repeating. Even Sartre occasionally got sick of it all, shocked by how badly he was behaving:

> I quite profoundly and sincerely feel myself to be a bastard. And a small-scale bastard at that, a sickening sort of academic sadist, a bureaucratic Don Juan.

At the same time, there was probably an element of bragging, even here (to Beauvoir), in the midst of the confessional. Bad is good. I have succeeded despite myself. But I have not been a bastard on a big enough scale. Not yet. He would redeem himself by being much, much worse.

He liked to use the word *crasseux* to describe his own life:

grubby, grimy, grungy perhaps. But *dirty* seems to strike exactly the right note. He was famously inconsiderate as regards matters of personal hygiene. Shy of using soap and water. Averse to doctors and dentists (he feared 'being turned into an object'), as if transcending merely physical concerns and requirements. There was a hint that he could transcend his demanding sexuality too, if he felt like it, but he chose to go in the opposite direction, pushing it to the limit, to see how far he could go. It was a major test of the tenets of existentialism – how many women can I seduce, despite *this mug*, these teeth, this body odour? And it was Sartre's opportunity to be more like Camus than Camus – to try to outscore Camus, on the one hand, but also to savour the delights of the real, the real that Camus was so lyrical about, the real that was typically so elusive in his virtual life. But his letters preserve the notion of the gap, the distance, the negation that was so persistent in his philosophy. Each attachment is modulated by a sense of detachment.

With several lovers at any one time, not to mention the constant presence of Beauvoir, Sartre would spend a lot of time explaining to each of them why they were apart, and why separation was really not as bad as it was made out to be. In other words, love, for Sartre, inevitably entailed love *letters*. His love – like a dodgy cheque – was always *in the post*. Sartre admitted (to his war diary) that for him love was pre-eminently a 'literary labour' (*tout un travail littéraire*). The persistent theme of the letters was *being apart* and the letters themselves served to keep a hygienic distance between Sartre and his loved one(s). Sartre's love affairs were literary and philosophical exercises, in which the *liaison* had to accommodate, from the very beginning, the notion of the *split* and circulation took priority over the one-to-one.

The affair would have scarcely begun before he had to introduce the latest *petite amie* to Camus. 'I must take you to see Camus.' So Sartre wrote in a letter to one of his lovers, Sally Swing. He almost certainly repeated the same line many times. He could never quite forget the impact that Camus had had on Beauvoir and the way he took Wanda away from him (he was still bitter about it decades later). It was the ultimate test – could he show off another of his lovers to Camus without the handsome one stealing her away from him?

I first came across the letters to Swing in a cardboard box in the reading room of the J. P. Morgan library on Madison Avenue in New York. They were not quite lost but were largely forgotten, neglected by biographers. I felt intrusive, nosey, almost salacious, poking around in these 'intimate' letters, like a pervert going through somebody else's underwear drawer. But I was compelled to keep going, since they give an answer – or a series of answers – to the question, 'Why go to so much trouble?' And I had a sneaking suspicion that Sartre expected me to read them – he welcomed gossip columnists and paparazzi into the dusty realm of philosophy. He had to be a 'public intellectual' or nothing and if that involved telling everyone about his love affairs, then so be it. He didn't really believe in privacy. He liked to keep the lights on and the door open and welcomed the peeping Tom, calling it 'transparency'.

Sartre's handwriting is small, cramped, tight, and leaves almost no margins on either side, no spaces at the top or bottom, as if he is intent on filling every square millimetre of the page, eliminating blanks. He writes a postcard that seems to contain a small novel, like a bible printed on the back of a postage stamp. All of his letters are dense and crowded, as if the whole point of writing was to fill up the available space (in a graphological analysis, he detects 'an insularity verging on dislocation' in the exaggerated gaps between *Swing*'s letters). That still doesn't fully explain why, for several days, sitting in the reading room of the Morgan library, I misread her name as 'Swinger' – and eventually had to go back correcting my own notes. I worried for a while that even Sally *Swing* was likely to be a myth – an imaginary woman, an archetype, a cartoon figure along the lines of Betty Boop. That the whole thing was a hoax. But her own letters – brimming with enthusiasm and passion and intensity – persuaded me to believe in her existence. Even so, a faint sense of the hoax lingers in all Sartre's affairs – as if there is something unreal or imaginary about them.

Swing was a go-getting young American journalist with short, boyish hair (*gamine*, the French would say), a recent graduate of Smith College in Massachusetts, based in Paris after the war. By a bizarre coincidence – if it was a coincidence – Camus had recently acquired an American girlfriend, Patricia Blake, also a student at Smith, in 1946. It was as if Sartre was

Sally Swing

trying to keep up with the Smiths, to match Camus: *Voici mon étudiante americaine!* Sent to the Cannes film festival in 1947 (only its second year) to interview the philosopher and screen-writer (*Les jeux sont faits* was having its premiere), Swing, then aged twenty-two, took the direct approach: she went up to Sartre in a restaurant and asked for an interview. Sartre gave her his telephone number in Paris and told her to call. They could have lunch some time. As she walked away he was already informing his dinner companions, an American movie producer and his wife, that his intentions were, of course, dishonourable, just in case anyone might think otherwise. Honest, as always, to the point of brutal. She, for her part, wrote to her mother that 'he is ugly as sin, but utterly charming'.

A week later they met at Cavanaugh – one of Sartre's regular haunts – on the Boulevard Saint-Germain. She asked questions and took notes, but he – impatient with the lack of progress – took the pad from her hand and wrote down his own notes for a future obituary, as usual drawing attention to his sub-optimal physical appearance. 'One lazy eye. A front tooth broken in 1915, never replaced. Never wears hat or braces. Smokes pipe.' And he sketched an unflattering caricature of his interviewer, scrawling 'Pour Sally' over the top.

Having finished interviewing himself, he started inter-viewing her. It is not surprising that the intended article never saw the light of day. (Decades later, living in New York, she tried to write a book about him too, and that similarly came to nothing.)

Over the next eight months, making the kind of heroic effort ironically noted by Camus, Sartre besieged her with flowers, chocolates, and passages from *Being and Nothingness*. The affair was consummated in May 1948 at his apartment in the Rue Bonaparte. She pronounced herself in love, even though she was resentful of the liaisons with Beauvoir and numerous other women. She gave him a full-body makeover, persuading him to improve his personal hygiene, shave every day, smarten himself up, buy a new coat, slim down, revert to his natural hair colour (a previous lover had got him to dye it red). All in all, he started to use a little more soap and water than was usual.

This was no one-night stand. She moved apartments to be closer to him. They played strange sex games in which she was 'The Little Orphan' and Sartre was her nanny, 'The Patronizing Dame' (which they both said in English). They played beautiful music together, quite literally: Schubert and Beethoven, her on the violin, him on the piano. He took her around town, introducing her not just to Camus but also to other friends, like Giacometti, Colette, Gide and the Surrealist artist Tristan Tzara (who asked her if she had a sister). They drove around the countryside in a Fiat car they nicknamed 'Rosalie' and went on picnics. They compared their favourite Parisian bars and nightclubs. When she flew back to the US, he worried about her being 'lost in the Atlantic' and went to pick her up at the airport. She would take a nap in his study, littered with books, while he worked on the next novel. All Swing's letters to her mother speak – with tremendous candour – of their amorous relations and encounters (including, for example, the revelation that Sartre suggests they make love within earshot of *his* mother, who lives in the apartment with him – so that each of the mothers gets to hear all about it, one way or another). She is lyrical and romantic in tone, but breezily pragmatic in detail, putting the emphasis on her use of the diaphragm, for example, or how she considers at one point getting pregnant or precisely how he removes her blouse and brassiere.

Sartre's letters, on the other hand, strike a radically distinct note. It's not just that he seems relatively indifferent to matters of contraception. He does not exclude the physical or talk only of art or poetry or some abstruse technical issue in philosophy. On the contrary, his writing – more like Camus than Sartre – is suffused with details of places and smells and sights and sounds. But everything is played out in a more remote key, with infinite variations on memory and anticipation, as if the carnal has to become disembodied before it can be meaningful. 'We see each other constantly,' she writes. With Sartre it is more a matter of *not* seeing constantly. More to do with visualizing, and mentally reconstructing the object of desire. It is in the nature of the letter to be always looking forward and back, to be missing out on sheer presence, it is in the nature of literature; but this literary or epistolary absence comes to permeate and define Sartre's personal relationships.

The idea of a journey to Tunis comes up again and again in his early letters to Sally Swing, '*mon cher petit animal*'. In an addendum to his self-penned obituary, he writes: '47-48: met a young American journalist in Cannes called Sally Swing – falls for her at first sight [...] becomes more and more attached to her and ends up leaving with her for Tunis.' The present tense here is misleading. Tunis lies somewhere in the future. 'Tunis will be the Thousand and One Nights for my little American' (Sartre uses the familiar *Amerloque*, which could be translated as 'Yank'). Tunis comes to stand for some Mecca of secular and sexual delight, a fantasy destination, a dream that is supposed to become real. It never quite does, not for Sartre and Swing. But this doesn't stop Sartre sketching a picture – worthy in its fantasy of Tim Burton – of a chimerical being, like some Hindu deity, with two sets of eyes (possibly looking in opposing directions), two hearts, and four arms (almost like wings), that is his idealized conception of the union between them that is expected to crystallize in Tunis. This is Sartre's archetypal relationship.

Sartre/Sally

'Each of us can point out to the other what he or she sees. You know we need two pairs of eyes and two pairs of hands in the soukhs, otherwise we allow a whole host of unperceived things to pass us by.' Or again, in another letter: wherever Swing goes, 'I have the impression that I have eyes there too.' The word *ensemble* comes up a lot: we will live together, go together, 'we will discover everything *ensemble*'. When he writes of love (to a lover), Sartre often strikes a rather Platonic note, invoking the idea of lost souls being reunited. He is anything but a materialist. Sartre argues (not in the letters alone) for some notion of transcending the merely physical, elevating the Cartesian consciousness to a heightened state – in which two are readily woven into one: entwined, entangled (like certain quantum particles), even though apart. Thus when Sally Swing complains of their separation – she is in Paris, he is in the south of France – he writes back with his theory of how to overcome the sense of absence.

> You who are so strong on Gestalt theory, you will recall how Guillaume explains how it is that one sees complicated patterns [*arabesques*] in the carpet interweaving *under* the chair leg instead of perceiving an interruption. So it is with us: we continue *underneath* this absence of several weeks and you are not truly separated from me [. . .]

Sartre denies the reality of separation – we are not really apart at all, if you think about it – and offers techniques for getting around it. Memory, in particular, becomes central to sustaining the relationship. 'I remember everything: you are always close to me, I taste you in my mouth, I smell you in my nostrils, I hear the sound of your voice in my ears, you never leave me, I carry you around with me everywhere. And you are also the sense of time that flows and leads me back towards you.'

It is a powerful statement – probably as close to poetry as Sartre ever gets. I was once sitting in Think Coffee in New York, back on 4th and Mercer, reading over some notes on these letters, when the barista, a guy named Matt, asked me what I was working on. So I told him. He said that he had a girlfriend who lived far away – Chicago as it turned out – and he was just writing to her and could I email him over a few lines. So I sent him Sartre's thoughts on separation and Matt passed them on to his girlfriend (whether he plagiarized or referenced he didn't say). She – he told me later – then decided to come back and live with him in New York. Sartre had inspired Matt's lover to move cities to be geographically closer to him, like Sally Swing moving apartments. Matt wasn't quite sure if this was in fact the outcome that he really wanted or expected (he had been planning only to soothe, not to stimulate). Nor does it appear that Sartre anticipates this effect of his writing. It is rather that he expects other people to learn to live with separation, to understand the inevitability of the split. (Matt remained philosophical about the reunion: 'Either it's going to work out – or it won't.' He didn't seem to mind much either way.)

There is a sense of circularity or eternal recurrence in Sartre's notion of time – as if nothing ever fades; no sense data can really be lost. His percepts or recollections of percepts underpin his most lyrical passages. She has 'the smell of warm, fresh-baked bread, with a light after-taste of vanilla. And then also the smell of herbs, I think: today the wind blew me a whiff of pines and *maquis* and I thought of you.' He seems to be capable of reassembling and reconstituting her, in his mind, piece by piece: arms, lips, hair, touch, thoughts, problems – almost as if he was personally sticking her together from a kit of spare parts. 'I know everything about [your body], I remember it all, I love it and I am waiting for it.'

Sally Swing writes of these letters that they are 'the most beautiful love letters imaginable'. Is she being naïve? After all, this is the same man who, in *Being and Nothingness*, is capable of arguing that there are really only two options where relationships are concerned – sadism and masochism (or some combination of the two). I must subsume your subjectivity or be subsumed by it. Love is just conflict by another name. Eat or be eaten. And it would be easy to dismiss some of Sartre's most seductive writing as cynically exploitative. Perhaps he even recycled the same lyrical vein for different lovers. But there is a genuine note of anxiety in these letters too, which seems peculiar to them – a pathos and vulnerability that are hard to find in his hard-boiled philosophy. 'I think I would have remained merely a madman if not for writing.' Writing is supposed to save him – save his sanity, save experiences that otherwise will be dispersed and lost. 'If I tell you of the moments of my life, that will save them, even for me.' He is desperate to be able to tell. 'Write to me that you definitely want me to tell you what I am doing.'

Above all Sartre seems almost pathetically concerned about being forgotten. The letters are reminders – proofs – of his existence. *Sartre was here.* He buys her a cat to stand in for him. She wants to ditch the cat and he begs her not to, as if he too is being despatched. Spare the philosopher's pet! 'If you have to sell him for snuggling up on your lap, then you would have to sell me too.' 'Don't forget me, you (I am a bit worried).' He encourages her, on her side, to cultivate her memories of him and not to turn him into 'an abstract fact'. 'Do you think you can hold on another eight days without forgetting me, without me turning into this abstraction?' He prowls around waiting for her letters and is 'worried stiff' when he does not hear from her. As with Wanda, he gets panicky when there is a possibility that he might really lose her. 'Don't add to our sadness by becoming my enemy. Let us stay together in all that befalls us, it's the best way and it's less unhappy.'

Sartre explains at one point why he needs cedar trees to back up his protestations of love: he cannot simply write 'I was some place, next to some anonymous trees, under an undefined sky, and I thought of you.' The whole thing lacks specificity – it lacks the *in-itself*. 'My love, which is the expression of my life in a particular space, will become abstract for you.' I love you, he writes – on a journey following in the footsteps of Camus – 'in every house in Algiers'. What he calls 'quotidian details', all those trees and the houses that figure in his perceptual field, are supposed to represent 'intimacy' in some way, although to Swing they seem like pure 'cruelty', because they are *not* her.

She is not a landscape, she is not a house. It seems obvious, it's a classic Sartrean point, but Sartre argues against it. For him these solid things – these memories of solid things – are like anchors that hold their love in place and stop it floating away, like a balloon.

'Didn't we always used to say everything to one another?' Sartre asks – and it is this 'everything' that he struggles to summon up, the totality of their relationship. But there is a sense that 'everything' was always elusive: 'You remember how we used to tell all about our days to one another? And yet the requisite time was always lacking to tell of them in their entirety.' It is impossible, as he writes in *Nausea*, 'to live and to tell: you have to choose'. But he has to tell, in order to 'save' the moments, to save his life in some way.

When Sally complains about him loving her only for her body, Sartre could reasonably object that his entire philosophy has been written to refute any notion of anyone being a pure sex-object or any other kind of object. But objectification is just what seems to be missing. Experience itself is lacking in intensity or what Camus refers to as 'presence'. Sartre is not joking when he recalls what took place in their meeting only the night before, Tuesday night and Wednesday morning, and says, 'By itself it was only a dream, now it is scarcely even a promise, virtually a denial.'

There is no singularity, no plenitude: everything is liable to become an empty phantasm of itself. With all the emphasis on transcending the purely physical, Sartre himself becomes subject to a phobia of the disincarnate, some sort of Invisible Man syndrome, a fear of floating away and dissolving into the ether. Like the ghosts in *Les jeux sont faits* who cannot really touch one another, Sartre suffers from a sense of unreality, his arms close on thin air. Even when he is there he is not quite all there.

Which is why he is so worried about becoming abstract and losing substance. Or, worse, reverting to the 'toadlike' aspect Sally originally perceived in him. Sartre succeeds in escaping ugliness, but he risks vaporizing into thin air, like the smoke from his pipe. He relies on his words to fix the memories of him in her mind, or quite simply to *be* her memories. When she thinks of Sartre she will think of certain words and phrases – *chat, baiser, Gestalt*, PADES ('*Petit Animal Difficile et Sauvage*', his nickname for her). Of these letters, which objectively exist. Conversely, when he writes to her it is as if he is at last holding her in his arms and they are finally united.

Sartre despises bad faith in love but especially the 'legend' that women have sex only against their will. 'French women are just as free-willed as American women, but the rules of engagement require that they have to be seduced, that they should cry out, "No, no!" and find themselves in bed giving the impression that they have been carried away by an emotion stronger than they are.' Sally Swing, on the other hand, is 'not a woman that one has despite her', she 'chooses to give herself', like a paragon of existential freedom. He often writes as if Swing is manly in her desires: she is, after all, '*mon petit animal*', she is always '*mon chéri*' not '*ma chérie*', she has hair like Chateaubriand, she has a 'man's opportunity to lead a life,' she is 'almost masculine', but an idealized masculine, frank and straightforward, knowing what s/he wants and taking it. *You* are the dominant one! Sartre appears at his most archetypally male in the conspicuous lack of commitment – the power of circulation – that so enrages Swing. And yet he will write again and again that he is 'the most faithful of lovers'. Is he simply lying? I don't think so. Swing is often furious with him as he betrays her over and over with different women. 'I would like to iron you out flat, fold you up and mail you back to Simone de Beauvoir's grave,' she wrote.

We have to understand fidelity here from Sartre's point of view: not as simply the non-multiplication of sexual partners but as the intensity of his feeling for her, which increases the further away he is. Sartre and Swing are a *love story* (he writes the word 'love' in English, to emphasize its strangeness), with the emphasis on *story*.

He fantasizes about the idea of 'making love with you all day long'. But he is too conscious of his own physical limitations and inadequacy. He cries out for the real – the objective – via sex. It is the corollary of his fear of spiritualization – of being nothing but hot air. 'There is something real and opaque and which is extended through all my senses (sight, touch, smell) and that is your body.' But the real can only be fully, safely, symbolically savoured at one remove, in the act of writing. Here he does not have to stop, he knows he can keep going, keep it up, endlessly.

> You know the Chinese say, you only speak of love, whereas we do it. I agree. It is not fair to speak of love when one cannot do it, to itemize your body when one cannot touch it. But let me assure you that it is there, your body, heavy and dense, in my arms, and I have not lost the memory of the little blue vein that throbs under your white skin and I constantly taste like a sweet fire in my mouth a continual subterranean desire for you.

Nothing is lost after all, despite the separation or because of it. 'I have not lost you, not at all. I see you. In your bed, in your pink chemise.'

There is something very Proustian about this repeated pattern of losing and then recovering paradise, mediated through language: having experiences in order to write about them later and thereby 'save' them, redeem them through art. Or perhaps it is simply magical: he is summoning her up in the ritual act of writing. In reality his sight is damaged, partial, distorted, reliant on spectacles. It's all in his 'advance obituary': 'One lazy eye [...] lost his father at 18 months, his right eye at 25 months.' On this account he is already virtually blind (we know that his eyesight failed some time in the 1970s). The physical defect, like all his other defects, didn't seem to worry him too much. That wandering eye was already seeing future visions. Rectified through his writing, his imaginary gaze – his 'mind's eye' – would become infallible: 'I see the scene, I see the bedroom, I see you enthroned on your bed.' It is through writing that he at last attained some kind of intimacy and reassurance. Unlike his mythic 'Chinese', Sartre always had to *speak* it, not just *do* it. At the same time, conversely, especially when she failed to write in turn, and the 'postwoman rose up like a wall between us', he feared that he was fading away, like the figures in the photograph in *Back to the Future*: 'I have the impression that I have become a little insubstantial.'

'That was a wild, and I admit very deep, affair,' Sartre later said of the liaison with Sally Swing (in a conversation with John Gerassi). But, according to Beauvoir and others, he was a cold, detached lover (capable of complaining about too much warmth). More – according to his own brutal self-assessment – a 'masturbator of women than a copulator'. Some said it was like having a surgical operation ('I mount and I perform,' he wrote to Beauvoir). He had to pump himself up in a frothing verbal fantasy of passion. Which is why – even apart from the mug – he had to 'go to so much trouble'. Philosophy became Viagra: the whole theory of the existential 'project' – 'rising up' and 'thrusting' out or 'exploding' into the world – is sexually supercharged. Like a blind man who compensates for his loss of sight by developing acute alternative senses, Sartre made up for his depleted or flickering sense of the real by boosting his power of imagination.

In *Richard II*, Shakespeare wonders 'who could [...] cloy the hungry edge of appetite by bare imagination of a feast? Or wallow naked in December snow by thinking on fantastic summer's heat?' And a very good thing too, says the neurocognitive scientist V. S. Ramachandran – otherwise the human race would die out, because it would be enough to imagine an orgasm, and we would all sensibly steer clear of the real thing. For Ramachandran there is a world of difference between feasts real and imagined, and in the degree of conviction between real percepts and imaginary (or remembered) ones. For Sartre, the difference was more tenuous. The image and the thing were 'two aspects of the imaging consciousness'. In *The Imaginary* (the early theoretical work he wrote in the 1930s before *Being and Nothingness*) he argued that whatever we can envisage in our own minds is necessarily real, while the real, on the other hand, is always drifting in a haze of the imaginary, populated by octopuses.

The image is not a thing, Sartre concludes, but an *act*. To imagine is to do. The imagination is like emotion, another magical way of acting on and negating and changing the real. Like an 'incantation' or a 'bewitchment'. 'The real is never beautiful; only the imaginary can be beautiful.' We know that the mysterious *Carnet* II (his journal of the phoney war) put forward a theory of 'salvation': life lived as art or text (Sartre refers to it in *Carnet* III, p. 285, citing both Gauguin and Rimbaud). The diary itself was lost – perhaps left on a train. But everything else that Sartre wrote, and especially his love letters, reiterated the same theory.

Sartre knew that he could not be making love all day long. Not really. After all there had to be time to write about it. But if Sartre developed a hyperthermic style – artificially 'hot' – Camus reacted against the temptation, leaning instead in the direction of hypothermia and the 'cool'.

Snow on Fire

WANDA DID NOT LAST LONG. She was soon displaced in Camus' affections by the actress Maria Casares. Reconstructing the trenchcoat man's erotic encounters through the Paris of the forties is like retracing the quantum collisions of a particle bouncing around in a high-energy accelerator. But there was not only a question of quantity, as in the case of Sartre, but above all of speed. And Camus knew it.

'Just play it cool, boy!' The *West Side Story* sentiment recurs throughout Camus. Keep coolly cool. He feared the rocket in the pocket. Naturally his early work was bursting with this anxiety. He had to rein himself in, to keep himself in check, lest he explode too soon. The highly personal notebooks are like a diary of his lustful urges. He could hardly walk down the street without being twisted and turned around and tormented. 'Women in the street. The hot beast of desire, which I carry around with me curled up in a hollow of my loins, stirs with a savage gentleness.' And he developed a neo-pagan ethics of love: 'If I had to write a book of ethics, it would be 100 pages long and 99 of them would be blank. On the last page I would write: "I know of only one obligation – that of loving."' But just as he had to resist his illness, actively, and take special measures to keep its progress at bay, so too he struggled against the natural impetuosity of his own body, '*cette facilité d'entraînement*' (his tendency to get carried away).

For Sartre the real issue was getting someone to fall in love with him. Everything else was irrelevant. He makes this point the core of his analysis in *Being and Nothingness*: 'to love is to want to be loved' – the problem is that I want the other to love *me*, but all this means is that I want the other to want to be loved in turn. 'Hence the lover's perpetual dissatisfaction.' For Camus there was no problem about being loved. 'The greatest misfortune is not to be unloved, but rather not knowing how to love.' The danger for Camus was at the level of demand rather than supply.

Camus' savage inclination – in accord with the desire of the hot beast – was to be crazily orgasmic. And not just in bed either. This is what he wrote in relation to reading the novels of Stendhal – as if even with a book in his hand his passion was liable to spiral wildly out of control:

> I must learn to tame my ardour, too prompt to overflow. That was my plan, to keep it cool, to conceal, a master of irony and detachment. I must do everything to overcome my capacity for bewitchment. My nature is too feverish, too prodigal, too thrusting and ill-timed. It makes me too impressionable, too easily aroused, too fast, unstoppable. As a result, I all too soon collapse into post-orgasmic lethargy.

The original French is slightly less explicit, more abstract and artistic, but the implication is unmistakable – and it is all over his early work. Camus saw himself as imperilled by premature ejaculation (of various kinds) and uncontrolled passion. He risked being a flop. He had to train himself up to become the king of cool. *I am too susceptible to the immediate*, or to translate it another way: too partial to the transient and the momentary.

He was so sensitive to changes in the weather – the patterns of light, the motions and formations of the clouds – that he seriously considered turning the *carnet* into a register of weather reports ('I ought to keep a notebook of the weather of each day), as if reluctant to miss anything. Camus once worked as a meteorologist (at the Algiers Institut de Météorologie). Meteorology became the barometer of instability, to some extent reflecting his own mercurial character. And it is just this spasmodic quality – moodiness, fickleness – that he was trying to get away from. Camus loved the *rush* but he fixated on the *lasting*. He set out early on to develop his capacity for slowness and durability, experimenting with methods of enforcing meditative tranquillity. He turned the respiratory techniques of Tibetan yogis into a methodology, scaling down his breathing, the perpetual demand for oxygen. In a rigorous programme of self-training, he aimed to shift gears – in terms of his Oriental influences – from kung fu to tai chi, 'the fusion of the Hindu wiseman and the western hero'.

Camus could be found standing in front of a clock, determined to slow himself down enough to watch the hands go around (and he is honest enough to note that he finds even five minutes of this exercise 'long and maddening'). Again and again, he positioned himself in the midst of a landscape (or seascape) and tried to become part of a still life, 'integrating himself into this rocky, aromatic world'. He would go night-swimming, but this was almost too energetic. He preferred the negation of movement and the momentary.

I also remember those small seaside villages where I would go to try and take hold of perfection by contemplating the

absolute blue of the water or absorbing through my eyelids
the dazzling polychromatic spectrum of a sky white with heat.

The imperative of stillness and calm explains why it is, at certain
times, he objects so strongly to the presence of waves. Sometimes
he cannot tolerate the slightest ripple. The Mediterranean is
required to be disciplined too, to attain perfect smoothness, the
exact opposite of a storm.

At that time not a single wrinkle cast a shadow over the
smooth face of the sea, and, in truth, the slightest appearance
of movement would have been unbearable to me.

No waves, no movement, perfect stasis, silence. No hot blasts of
emotion. No rush. The urges and impulses not so much under
control as non-existent. *What urges?* Everything is cool, everything is glassy and unruffled. Anti-torrential, anti-*pathétique*.
Camus deliberately sought out the steady-state, which he
described at different times as ecstasy, plenitude, annihilation,
renunciation, tranquillity, ataraxia. This is the philosophy of the
hard man, in which even water aspires to be non-liquid. Sartre
called this technique (in his essay on Descartes) 'the practice of
the *epoché*, in the moral domain'. The *epoché* was a 'bracketing
out' or suspension of self, of all ideas and desires and action: a
quest for the state of *wu-hsin* (no-mind).

Sometimes this would-be Zen monk was interrupted in his
training – and it was like the sound of a gun going off in the
middle of a library. One day, in March 1936, he was at a clinic
in the mountains above Algiers. There was a stiff Mediterranean
breeze blowing and stirring things up, so Camus hiked up to yet
higher ground to try to get above it all, beyond the turbulence,
au-dessus de la mêlée. Close to the summit, in the shade of a

stand of black cypress trees, he at last found a point of equilibrium, where all movement ceased.

> Above me, I admire the light falling from the sky. Below, the
> sea devoid of the slightest ripple, an imperturbable blue smile.
> Beneath the sun that is warming just one side of my face, I
> watch as this unique hour flows by without being able to
> utter a single word.

Perhaps the training had paid off. He was up to a *full hour* of stillness and silence (now he could even watch the hour hand going
around, not just the minutes). Or at least approaching (it depends
how we choose to translate *heure*). Then a patient from the clinic
happened by, accompanied by his nurse, and struck up a bizarre
conversation with him. A madman! (In Camus' book.) Perhaps
he really was mad; perhaps it was only that anyone violating the
silence – almost like a blasphemy – must have seemed like a
madman. The odd thing is that Camus already had a young
woman with him (acknowledged but unnamed) – but he had presumably been saying nothing to her, as if she too was part of the
programme of self-discipline. Camus was using her as a challenge
to his powers of contemplation, a temptation, testing himself, or
trying to dissipate or displace the feelings he had towards her in
the direction of the hills and the light and the air and the sea. 'The
ultimate sensual pleasure is attained here through ascetic self-
denial,' he would write. 'We have to understand that they are like
the two faces of the same austerity.'

Camus' attitude towards beauty in his *Notebooks* can now be
grasped not as a purely philosophical conception but rather as
a practical approach to solving a problem, a technique of self-
cultivation: 'Beauty is unbearable and drives us to despair. It
offers the flash of eternity in a moment that we would seek how-

ever to stretch out over the whole of time'. This stretching of time and spinning things out is precisely the object of his system of training. 'He can,' as Sartre wrote elsewhere, 'withdraw from time itself and take refuge in the eternity of the instant'. The idea is to sustain the peak moment in which everything appears more intense and beautiful, to string those moments together into a vast neural necklace of experience. To merge with the network.

Camus is capable of seeing the sun as a woman or a girlfriend. One particularly torrid afternoon sun is described as being like 'a mistress with whom one goes out into the street, after a whole suffocating afternoon, and who looks at you closely, shoulder to shoulder, amid the light and the crowd'. Carob trees in September emit 'an aroma of love' that spreads out over Algeria 'as if the earth were resting after giving itself to the sun, its belly all wet with almond-smelling seed'. Conversely sexual relationships appear as variations on or responses to close encounters with the environment. 'When the world is bathed in light and the sun beats down, I want to open my arms up and make love, to flow into bodies just as I merge with the light, to bathe in flesh and sun.' Sunbathing, swimming, sex: they are all part of some grand continuum of experience.

Camus worked hard on the time-extending tai chi of meditation and contemplation. Two years were not too long, he reckoned, to reflect on a single point. And he wanted his relationships with women to be more than just one-night stands, he dreamed of the long-lasting and the durable, the sustainable liaison. He aspired, in other words, to friendship. When 'the world is grey all over', he was even capable of 'loving to the point of getting married'. Which he did twice. But in the end he is unable to deny the hot beast coiled up in his loins. The calm sea gets stirred up into waves again, cyclically, before some period of tranquillity returns.

This is the process he describes in his section on Don Juan in *The Myth of Sisyphus*. Don Juan is a lucid serial lover. He is not cynical or callous, but he is disenchanted, un-bewitched, immune to myth and delusion. He knows there is no ultimate meaning beyond the multiplication of lovers. 'We use the word love for this mix of desire, tenderness, and intelligence that links me to certain other beings only by reference to a collective way of seeing derived from books and legends.' Love, like justice and truth, recedes into an elusive archetypal limit-point, half-myth, half-fantasy. 'I am only ever given the elements of a friendship, the pieces of an emotion, never the emotion, never the friendship.' Nothing but fragments. Perhaps, paradoxically, Don Juan, like Camus, is in search only of self-negation and his asceticism assumes the form of pleasure. He is the ascetic hedonist. He doesn't have to worry about impotence, but he does suffer from a very Camusian post-orgasmic 'regret for the desire that is lost in satisfaction'. He is too *prompt to overflow*. According to Camus, the original stage Don Juan, in Molina's *The Trickster of Seville*, threatened with the prospect of hell, asks only for the gift of postponement: 'May I be granted a long extension!' The idea of deferral was central to Camus' way of thinking and acting.

Given the asymmetry of demands, Camus expected all love affairs to blow up in his face, to go wrong, one way or another. To be unsustainable. 'It will collapse: I was only holding it up with my faith and my hopes – now vanished.' He is actually talking about the 'Maison Mauresque' (one of his earliest essays) here, which he half-describes and half-imagines, but so it is with all the other temporary dwellings of love. They were doomed likewise to fall apart. 'We have to fall in love – to have a great love in our lives, because that way we will have an alibi for all those irrational fits of despair we were going to succumb to anyway.' Occasionally Camus toyed with *one-love* theory – every single union is a form of communion with the whole world – but generally he preferred the plural noun, *amours*, to the singular. And the beauty of those *loves* (or *love-affairs* or *romances*) is that they were irreducible to mere *love*, which belongs to and perhaps defines the realm of the symbolic. Loves are prompt to overflow all the theories about love. 'Wretchedness and greatness of this world: it offers us not truths but only loves.'

It is hard to understand, given all his quite contrary inclinations, how it was that Camus became, like Sartre, a man of letters. Why would the savage ever really need the symbolic? Wouldn't the whole point be to stand against it, to resist the symbolic, like some anti-philosophical Canute facing down the tide? Here he is, standing on the beach again, still dripping, gradually drying in the sun:

No, there was no 'I', no 'world', only the harmony and the silence which between us gave rise to love.

Amour(s) – spontaneous feeling in general, the impulse, the urge – must override mere propositional logic. 'This singular vanity of a man – to pretend and even believe that he aspires to some kind of truth when some kind of love is all that he really asks of the world.' But the encounter with Stendhal – and any number of his lovers – clarified the issue. The idea of writing came to Camus initially as a way of holding himself back, of curbing his fiery instincts. Literature was a way of being cool, holding back the rush. It arose for Camus as a method of sexual prolongation and self-suppression. Being the hard man. 'I must coax my instinct to speak, not to gush out. It must be possible to feel it in my writing rather than in what I say or do.' When he walked around town with 'S. C.' (a potential girlfriend), he was moved to start quoting poetry 'to conceal all too natural over-excitement'. His tendency, he noted, was to love '*trop*' – too much – and he had to work to actively diminish his ardour. 'It is impossible to speak of those one loves too much.' Writing was, if not the opposite of love, then at least a coolant, a sexual inhibitor or anaesthetic. A system for stretching out and sustaining feelings in contrast to the *jet* (spurt) and the *jaillissement* (gush), short-lived spasms of emotion: 'I have taken these keen but short-term emotions aroused by the first visit to a Moorish house and tried to expand them in a system of correspondences [...]' Thus Camus could speak of writing as something like his 'secret' technique for enhancing love: 'Being able to keep on going all the way is down to the ability to keep one's secret.'

Camus switched to the pen in an experimental way but he was disappointed to discover in writing the same natural tendency to let it all out prematurely. 'I distrust my facility. It is too natural.' He feared the cliché and the commonplace, the literary equivalent of the premature climax and collapse. So the words too would have to be reined in and curbed and displaced; the great gushing orgasmic rush would have to be prohibited – it had no place in writing. Literature arises somewhere between the torrent – the wave – the impetuous *jet* and the steady-state of Zen stillness and silence, 'this white infinity of calm'. It builds, branches out from a point (a mosque, fig trees, rooftops) towards a system of correspondences and analogies. 'Art is born from constraints,' Camus suggested. 'More generally: life is born from constraints. Feeling that is constrained must be the most sustained.' Literature, then, is the art of postponement, not loving too much or too soon, not being hot: the cultivation of cool, the pursuit of degree zero. Better still: 'no literature', *pas de littérature*. 'To write, lean always towards understatement. Say too little, not too much. No chitchat in any case.' If there is one page on the obligation to love, then there are 99 others left blank.

One night Camus had been out drinking with the Beaver (Sartre was away somewhere). It was snowing. Around two in the morning they were walking down the street together. Camus suddenly sat down in the snow in the light of a street lamp – as if to cool off – and reflected on the complexities of his love life (or, in fact, life):

You have to choose: you can make it last or you can be on fire; the dilemma is that you can't prolong and burn at the same time.

SARTRE AND CAMUS
GO TO WAR

He crawled up to the parapet, then stood up and started firing. This was his big chance of revenge: every shot he fired avenged him of some ancient inhibition. One shot for Lola – I really should have robbed her; one shot for Marcelle – should have dumped; one shot for Odette – should have fucked. Another bullet for all those books I didn't dare to write, and yet another for all the guys I wanted to hate and instead tried to understand. He kept on firing and all laws were blown away, Love Thy Neighbour, pow in that fucker's face, Thou Shalt Not Kill, pow goes another two-faced bastard. Mankind, Virtue, the World – he blew them all away. Freedom is Terror. The town hall was on fire, his head was on fire. Bullets whistled around his ears, free as the air, the world is going up in smoke and me with it, he fired, he looked at his watch: he had nothing left to ask unless it was another 30 seconds, just time enough to take aim at that handsome officer – so pleased with himself – who was running towards the church. He fired: he fired at the handsome officer, he shot all the Beauty of the Earth, he shot the street, the flowers, the gardens, he shot everything he had ever loved in his life. Beauty tumbled obscenely and Sartre fired again. He fired. He was purified. He was omnipotent. He was free.

Up against the might of the German army, doomed to failure, defeat, and death. But still free. A climactic passage from *La Mort dans l'âme* (translated oddly as *Iron in the Soul*), the final volume in Sartre's war trilogy, *Roads to Freedom*. As always something is lost in translation (I have condensed it slightly), but something has also been added: I wrote 'Sartre' in place of 'Mathieu', Sartre's philosopher protagonist – a distortion that is almost justified by Sartre's repeated embrace of what he called '*my* war'. At last Sartre, like Camus, could claim to have fired a fictional gun in anger rather than just writing barbed remarks in a nausea-prone diary. Mathieu tries to top Meursault by annihilating everything, everyone, rather than just a single solitary Arab on the beach.

Philosophically, everything had prepared Sartre for war. He was already the philosopher of war even before war was declared. He was the Napoleon of philosophy, but with a defeatist spin. Or rather he was triumphalist but in the direction of negation. He was positively negative. It is classically Sartrean for his hero to zero in on the smartest, handsomest German soldier he can find – *le bel officier* – with the notion that he is finally disposing of the myth of Beauty. Fighting on behalf of all the shabbiness and ugliness of the world. On behalf of losers. This, after all, formed part of his objection to the Nazis: their obsession with *looks*. As if they were discriminating against him personally. With this one shot he has finally won his war against the Beautiful People.

Sartre and Camus would eventually stand shoulder to shoulder, in the Liberation, as they joined forces to boot the Nazis out of Paris. But they had a relatively inglorious, non-combative start to the war. Sartre originally took the view that the Nazis would never invade. He knew Germany well, spoke German fluently (and had mastered Hegel, Husserl and Heidegger), and wrote to eighteen-year old Wanda at the end of August 1939 from Marseilles, 'I don't really believe in the war'. This is his analysis of the political situation: 'Hitler can't possibly think of starting a war with the current mood in Germany.' His conclusion: 'He must be bluffing.'

The following day Sartre received his call-up papers. In September 1939 he found himself mobilized to the east of the country, on the frontier with Germany, on the front line. He was thirty-four years old, transformed from writer, philosopher and

Private Sartre

literary critic into Private Sartre (regimental number 1991), soldier meteorologist, second class. The outbreak of the Second World War marked 'the end of [his] youth'.

Sartre had visions of doing something heroic, possibly suicidal. To get in the right frame of mind he read Jules Romains' account of trench warfare in the First World War and noted that 'fear was the organ, the sense by means of which man perceived the world of the trenches'. But for Sartre fear was almost irrelevant. His main enemy was boredom. He arrived expecting a muddy apocalypse; instead he found himself on vacation in the neat, orderly countryside of Alsace Lorraine, amid cafés and bars ('something equivalent to a bar in Montmartre') and schools filled with flowers. He was even given a room in a comfortable hotel at one point, in the spa town of Morsbronn-les-bains. He fitted in a pilgrimage to Pfaffenhoffen, where his mother's family came from and he had once spent his summer holidays, and he spent several days with Simone de Beauvoir (who brought him extra notebooks, ink, and pens). The 'phoney war' (or '*drôle de guerre*') seemed to him to be summarized by Kafka – a war-without-war, more 'elusive' literary phenomenon than military:

> Since my mobilization I have often thought about Kafka; he would have liked this war; it would have been a good subject for him. He would have shown a man, Gregory K, stubbornly looking for war everywhere, feeling its threat everywhere, and yet never finding it

Sartre felt like a warrior *manqué*, a frustrated would-be hero. Here is a typical day in Sartre's war, detailing his part in Hitler's downfall, during the period when his regiment is located in a school:

7 a.m.: Hearty breakfast at Le Boeuf noir or Le Lion d'Or.

8 a.m.: Start work at school desk (either philosophy or a novel or memoirs).

Lunch: leisurely, two hours (when he 'writes less').

Then back to desk till around 9 p.m. Dinner and conversation.

One of his comrades-in-arms said to him, 'You work sixteen hours a day; you will be getting irritable.' 'No,' he replied. 'I only work thirteen hours a day maximum.' Sartre suffered from the opposite of writer's block: some form of hypergraphia, an obsessive need to record his experiences on paper. But, to be fair, he was not writing all the time: some of the time he was only reading. In just a few months after his mobilization, Sartre read (or re-read) no less than eighty-three separate works, including three novels by Kafka, the second volume of the collected works of Shakespeare (in translation), *Wind, Sand, and Stars* by Saint-Exupéry, and assorted works by Flaubert, Queneau, Gide, Koestler. And new bundles were always turning up from Paris, posted by the Beaver. For the best part of a year, he behaved, in short, more like a PhD student or Roquentin doing his research at the library than a soldier. In the midst of immediate chaos and potential danger he had an abiding sense of duty – the necessity of getting on with the job (i.e. writing), just in case the world should come to an end. At one point the Germans were only a few hundred metres away, on the far side of the Maginot Line. But they didn't drop bombs – only pamphlets, saying that this was all the fault of the English, and why should anyone suffer on that account? In the early days, in a warm autumn, it was possible for the French to disport themselves on the grass in the sun and get out their accordions and harmonicas and play cards.

Then a Moroccan recruit, who failed to understand the protocols of non-aggression, finally pulled the trigger and shot a German, and after that the French couldn't emerge from their shelters without the other side taking a pot-shot at them. 'There is always one guy who does something stupid and it's the rest of us who have to pay,' complained one *chasseur* (who had adapted to the quiet life). Sartre was shrewd enough to spot the irony. It's not the war that is 'phoney', he thought, it's the peace. This is a war of bad faith, in which everyone is deluding themselves.

Even as he left for the front, Sartre – as ever keeping the contents of his consciousness under close surveillance – found himself already yearning for (and fully expecting) 'the end of the war'. Had he not written to Wanda that 'even if there is a war there will be a time after it for all three of us'? (He still thought in terms of trios rather than couples.) But, on second thought, he realized that this idea about the future – an assumption about the end, manifestly teleological in character – made his life in the present unbearable. So he made a firm decision that the war never would come to an end, that war was just the normal, everyday state of affairs, therefore there was nothing to look forward to but war and more war. Violence is inevitable. Peace is a hoax or a delusion. There is no war to end war. War, perpetual war, is the natural, inevitable order of things. After that insight he felt a lot calmer, more relaxed, and could get on with his business, almost unconcerned about any actual outcomes.

There is a parallel here with his thoughts about love. He recalled the experience of standing at a station (before the war) looking down the tracks towards Paris. He had been visiting the Beaver at a clinic in St Cloud on the northern outskirts of the capital, where she was being treated for pneumonia. At the same time, with Beauvoir *hors de combat*, he was looking forward – as he stood on the station platform, waiting for the train, his gaze going ahead of him back along the tracks – to reigniting his passion for 'O' (Olga), who was back in Paris, in Montparnasse. But he was suffering only from a railway-induced, overly linear misconception. He realized, in retrospect, that love is not like a terminus, a station towards which one can travel and then get off at, saying, 'I have arrived, I am here, I am in love'. He gave up on the idea of love as something conclusive and earth-shattering (or, indeed, peaceful): love becomes 'this impossible love', an 'impossible rapprochement', a 'dead future' or *'avenir-passé'*. Love, if it is anything, is part of war – it resembles war itself – it isn't an end to war: there *is* no end to war. Love (as Sartre goes on to argue in *Being and Nothingness*) is just a continuation of conflict by other means.

But what if he tried looking in the other direction – in other words, back into his past, rather than into the future? But that too was an illusion, another example of railway thinking or linearity. There is little or no connection between what I was in 1929 (living and teaching in Le Havre) and what I am now, in 1939, going off to war. I am a different person now to what I was then. There is no such thing as a permanent 'self' at all – that is just a construct (a *'structure synthétique'* – of which psychoanalysis is a good example). Thus although Sartre was now under orders and forced to wear a uniform for the first time in his life, nevertheless he was at least liberated from his own past; he could not be held in check by his own earlier experiences. It's like a very speeded-up, fast-forward evolutionary theory (which Sartre derives from Pierre-Simon Ballanche rather than Darwin), in which the self is always evolving at top speed, perpetually, randomly mutating. Sartre realized that he had this great ability to 'detach myself from what I was the day before'. There is no future and no past, nothing but a hazy residual consciousness of his continued existence – which, in the circumstances, with a potential blitzkrieg on his doorstep, seemed increasingly tenuous and fragile.

Occasionally, as a certified meteorologist, Sartre would launch a balloon, follow it through his binoculars to determine the direction of the winds, then phone through the information to the battery artillery officers. 'Only pigeon fanciers,' he wrote, 'if they still exist in the army, could have as poetic and sweet a task.' In the absence of any real fighting, the war was carried on in everyday conversations with his own comrades. They argued about everything, sparring, manoeuvring for position. Every conversation was a potential battlefield, a confrontation fraught with the possibility of 'victory' or 'defeat'. '*Tu m'as cloué*,' concedes his 'friend' Pieter(kowski) – you 'nailed' me.

SARTRE: Nothing proves my sincerity, or yours, does it?
PIETER: I think I know when you're being sincere.
SARTRE: This is just a hypothesis you pay me the respect of making. But you have to admit that there is always the *possibility* of theatre, isn't there? I could be faking it.
PIETER: You nailed me.

Even without tanks firing shells or planes dropping bombs or bullets flying, there was a permanent state of drama and conflict. Can I take him or can he take me? Not world war, but *word* war.

Sartre had been dreaming of attaining some kind of 'authenticity', being a 'real man', a hero (of masculinity if nothing else). But just as he was not allowed to be a real soldier, so too the goal of authenticity receded into the distance. The trouble is, Sartre recorded in his diary, that as soon as I start thinking 'I am authentic' then I am no longer authentic, but only someone who would like to be. An authentic *what*? Authenticity becomes another 'metaphysical impossibility', a will o' the wisp, alongside sincerity, truth, love, solidarity, presence, being. Here is the joke: the more a man wants something the less he can get it. Only if you don't want something is it possible to have it. (Even then you have to not think it either – but Sartre thinks everything.)

Except when launching a balloon, or reading, he wrote all the time, including when he was supposed to be on guard. He would write standing up, if necessary. And he was determined to stick to his guns (or not). In Morsbronn he objected to being given an additional job as a telephone operator because he was too busy with his writing (he compromised in the end by eavesdropping on people's conversations and incorporating the idea of simultaneous conversations – and cutting between them – into a future novel). In nine months, aside from work on philosophy and the first volume of *Roads to Freedom*, Sartre completely filled fifteen notebooks with diary entries and reflections alone. Not to mention all the letters, mostly to women. 'Once, while he was on leave,' Corporal Pierre recalled, 'he put us in charge of sending a daily letter to one of his correspondents. He left us fifteen letters, already written, addressed, and duly numbered. Toward the middle of his leave we were also to send a telegram.' And he typed up his work on an army typewriter. In order to be able to concentrate, Sartre wore a 'Do Not Disturb' sign around his neck. Every now and then he had to explain to a superior officer that he was trying to write a novel. 'What about?' 'Hard to explain.' 'Unfaithful wives and cuckold husbands?' 'Of course.' 'Wonderful.' One biographer estimates that he must have written around 2,000 pages altogether in this short period. 'I have always considered quantity a virtue', Sartre wrote to Beauvoir.

The war was like a writer's retreat for Sartre, a sabbatical from other commitments. 'You know [...] I've never written as much in my whole life.' It was the Sartrean equivalent of the Blitz mentality: write, write, and write some more, for tomorrow we die. Every now and then he would feel a little peculiar, writing quite so frenetically while Czechoslovakia, Poland, and Norway were overrun and annexed and western civilization collapsed all around him. There was something Germanic and relentless about his writing (no wonder the Communists would later insinuate that he must have struck a deal with the Nazis). But he liked to think of it as his way of fighting back against fascism, a one-man philosophical war, digging himself into fortifications made out of pure paper, armed with pen and ink: 'I can only see my writing as a symbolic gesture *against* the fall of democracy and freedom and against the defeat of the Allies.' Every new theory that he came up with was like 'an act of conquest'.

Everything was going well. Then at last a real crisis struck. Sartre discovered that he was losing his hair (in fact, it had been coming on – or out – for a long while, but he chose this time to take note of it). And he was putting on weight, which he blamed on too many rich Alsacian desserts (combined with inaction). Oddly enough, the thick, unkempt tangle of hair came to symbolize for Sartre all the possible strands of the future that remained open to him. 'I felt that, at every step, I was losing another of my possibilities, just as one loses one's hair.' When his hair started falling out, it was 'a symbolic disaster'. Sartre was not in the least worried about dying, but he hated to go bald. Every hair in his comb was like another door shutting in his face. (In fact he managed to retain a lot of it.) Similarly, every few months he would catch sight of himself sideways in the mirror and he was desolated. He started dieting, in a desultory way, fighting his personal battle of the bulge.

In May 1940 the real war started. And almost as suddenly

stopped again, for Sartre. The Germans worked around the Maginot line defences that Sartre had been so assiduously guarding, loaded pen in hand. They headed north and west, invading Belgium, then swept south, finally coming up behind Sartre's regiment. The Luftwaffe simply flew right over the top of it. He and his entire division had been comprehensively out-manoeuvred and encircled. Sartre's commanding officers surrendered and he was captured together with most of his comrades. A few went down fighting, having taken up a position in a church tower. Which is where Sartre locates Mathieu, who intends to go out in a blaze of glory in *The Roads to Freedom*, the last man standing, one man armed only with a rifle against the might (and the beauty) of the inexorably advancing German army. It is a glorious would-be death, a classic Hollywood ending, one of Sartre's many alternate lives.

In reality, Sartre didn't get off a shot, but he had the feeling of unreality, as if he was in a film (shot by a German director) and everything was happening to somebody else. He made a last desperate stand in a girls' school in a village in north-east France, where he discovered a pile of pink notebooks – subject, French composition. The entries ceased on 10 May. Sartre can't help noticing that the last project is this: 'Your mother is ironing. Describe her.' It is just the kind of thing he would have been good at: the obsessive, minute observation of everyday life, finding drama in the mundane. But now, on a larger scale, the Germans had flattened France.

Sartre was taken prisoner on his thirty-fifth birthday, on 21 June 1940. Within a few weeks he was locked up in Stalag XII D, a wooden barracks on top of Mount Kemmel in Trier (near the German border with Luxembourg), alongside several thousand others. He picked up copies of *Around the World in Eighty Days* and *In the Country of Perfumed Tigers* by way of escape, and soon felt quite at home, getting a job as 'nurse-interpreter', and reunited with his old pipe (sent to him by the Beaver). He faked illness to get a few weeks in the infirmary, then worked his way into the 'artists' barracks' (which he calls the 'phalanstery of inverts') as a playwright. The worst punishment he suffered was to be once forcibly showered by fellow prisoners, fed up with his relaxed standards of personal hygiene. Only when another prisoner asked him if he was the author Jean-Paul Sartre was he inspired (having the reputation of authors to think of) to shave and wash of his own initiative.

This is where the real Resistance starts for Sartre: in prison, in the Stalag, locked up behind barbed wire and under machine-gun surveillance, but refusing to kowtow, sniggering behind the backs of the guards, and still writing. 'They can beat us all they want,' was his attitude, 'but in the end we'll fuck them over.' That was the business of the writer: to *fuck someone over*. He dashed off a Christmas play, *Bariona ou le fils de tonnerre*, which translated French vs Germans into Jews vs Romans in ancient Judaea ('Let's march against these mercenaries of Herod! Let's march, drunk with wine and songs and hope!'). But at last he also had the opportunity to do something other than write. Security was relatively lax – after all, an armistice had been signed between France and Germany. Non combatants (if they could prove their status) could, theoretically, be released.

Simone de Beauvoir chose this time to send Sartre an account of a dream in which two prisoners are escaping down a tunnel. Maybe it was some kind of code. In the dream they are getting away – hooray! – they have escaped, they think, freedom beckons, so far so good, and then ... the tunnel starts to narrow, to close in on them. One of the two gets stuck, wedged in, and then – as if that it is not bad enough already – a boa constrictor happens to come along, its mouth gaping, like another tunnel. Slowly but surely the struggling man is consumed, his cries finally choked off. His fellow fugitive can only watch in fascinated horror. Beauvoir, consumed – so to speak – by the dream, was terrified of going back to sleep. What is beautiful about this dream, Sartre helpfully pointed out in reply, is that the first tunnel is echoed by the second (the snake), so it is one tunnel inside another; you try to tunnel out and all the time you are just tunnelling your way further in. There is no escape. It is the deterministic image of hell again, *Les jeux sont faits*, No Exit. The jaws snap shut, the lid is closed. Everything is, in effect, contained, embryonically, in the dream of containment. This is why, perhaps, Sartre, rather than being horrified himself, seemed perversely satisfied by Beauvoir's story. 'I wonder if the Beaver's terror does not include some obscure measure of pleasurable excitement.'

But perhaps Beauvoir's letter had the desired effect. 'All in all, I was happy there,' Sartre would say later, finding in the Stalag a form of 'collective existence' and camaraderie he hadn't enjoyed since his time at the École Normale Supérieure. But after nine months of captivity, putting on plays, putting on weight, singing in the choir, giving lectures, starting a reading club (Heidegger's *Being and Time* was top of the list), and finishing the first draft of *The Age of Reason*, Sartre finally devised a plan of escape. Together with Father Perrin (Sartre must have been attracted to him in part by the name – his own childhood fictional hero who defeats the Kaiser), he forged a medical certificate stating that the prisoner Sartre was 'affected by a partial blindness of the right eye, entailing difficulties of orientation', thus enabling him to pass himself off as a civilian. No tunnels, no clambering over barbed wire, no motorbikes to freedom. Then an even better scheme fell into his lap when he came into possession of a genuine safe-conduct, signed by the camp commander, 'Please allow the bearer and two accompanying prisoners to pass'. In the end he was able to stroll out of the camp, dressed as a farmer (Farmer Sartre – and yet so deeply anti-agricultural, it must have appealed to some notion of far-fetched existential personae) and make his way back to Paris, partly on foot but mostly on trains.

The drama of his own captivity and escape was a gift to Sartre (like a broken love affair to a poet). It provided him with the overarching narrative and allegory of *Being and Nothingness*. Philosophy became his safe-conduct – a *laissez-passer*. Nationality, birth, family, the body, destiny: these are all so many variations on a form of intellectual captivity from which it is possible to just walk away in the direction of freedom and an undefined horizon. Sartre's theory is part philosophy, part reportage: the working-out of his story of Occupation and Resistance. Freedom resides in struggle *against* something, hence the idea that we are never freer than under the Occupation.

So too with the struggle of writing. Writing is just like skiing, Sartre suggests. In skiing you have the snow, the mountain, the Arlberg technique (for turning). Without them you couldn't even ski. So, similarly, all the rules of the language game cannot be conceived of as constraints – a 'prison-house' of language. Rather it is a 'terrain' on which to exercise liberty, like skiing downhill. Gravity is dragging you down, but – with the right technique – you can carve your own lines across the face. 'Man is a being who flees from himself into the future.'

Had he been a coward? No, it was only that the opportunity for heroism passed him by. But the anxiety was still there. Garcin in the hell of *No Exit* is tormented by the suspicion of cowardice for all eternity. 'Where are the dead and the wounded?' Sartre asks in *Iron in the Soul*. 'If you've seen them you're lucky. All I've seen is a bunch of pussies like you running along the roads, scared shitless.' Sartre lived through a 'phantom war, a phantom defeat, a phantom guilt'. The sense of unreality, of living through a film, continued to haunt him. It was not until Camus recruited him to the cause that Sartre was able to feel a real sense of participation in the wider war.

Still in Algiers, Camus (quoting T. E. Lawrence) saw 'a great wave of death' approaching. But at first he refused to have anything to do with the war, almost as if it was none of his business. In 1939 he was a reporter working for the *Alger Républicain*, an ex-communist, a literary critic, and an avowed pacifist. He was more concerned with putting on plays at the Maison de culture (they were planning a production of *Hamlet* and an adaptation of Malraux's *La Condition humaine*). His first books – meditations, lyrical essays, travel stories, non-travel stories that still involve feeling like an outsider – *L'Envers et l'endroit* (*Betwixt and Between*) and *Noces* (*Nuptials*) had come out, rather quietly. Now he was taken up with work on *L'Etranger*, based on real clashes between French and Arabs that had taken place on the beaches around Algiers. Meanwhile he attended court proceedings as a reporter and took sides in murder trials. Perhaps, rather like Hitchcock in his films, Camus makes a fleeting courtroom appearance in his own novel: 'One of the journalists, much younger than the others, dressed in grey flannel with a blue tie, put his pen down and looked at me. In his slightly asymmetric face, I only saw his pale grey-green eyes which examined me attentively, without expressing anything you could put your finger on. And I had the weird impression of being looked at by myself.'

He attacked the mayor of Algiers for being pro-fascist. But when war finally broke out it found him writing articles mainly about crime, elections, finance, welfare. And road accidents, like this one involving an old lady who had been out shopping: 'In this very place, some minutes later, only a few scattered vegetables, and a bunch of grapes on the bonnet of the car, remain as derisory witnesses to this distressing accident.' He wrote a series about poverty among Arabs and the first stirrings of anti-colonial revolt. And he went to a brothel with some bored high-school teachers in Tiaret, where it snowed. 'Still the same desolate wasteland,' he noted on leaving, 'but white this time.' War remained marginal in his mind.

While Sartre was putting on his uniform and setting out for the phoney war, Camus, like Sartre, was reading Kafka (*The Castle* and *The Trial*) and writing an essay, 'Hope and the Absurd in Kafka'. In September 1939, he was barely able to credit that war was real. This is the 'phantom war' in Algiers.

War has broken out. But where is the war? Beyond the news reports that we have to believe and the posters we have to read, where can we find any signs of this absurd event? It is not in this blue sky or the blue sea, or in the singing of the cicadas, or in the cypress trees which line the hillsides.

But he knew that the absurd was real – he embraced the absurd ('we embarked on this war with the idea that it was absurd, but that we could not do otherwise') – so, despite remaining, in theory, a pacifist, he duly presented himself at the recruiting office to join up, only to be rejected on account of his tuberculosis. Altogether Camus tried to join up at least three times, and was turned down every time. Perhaps this explains, in part, why there is no mention of war in *The Outsider*. There is a war on, but it is not – as Sartre would say – 'his' war. Camus remains an outsider all over again, even from the war. His divorce from his first wife, Simone – an unreformed morphine addict – was coming through, but he had a feeling too of being 'divorced' from war.

He went back to journalism. His newspaper was anti-Nazi – just as it was anti-Franco – anti-fascist, and sympathetic to Muslims and the working classes. Camus came out as anti-Hitler, but also anti-French warmongers too. He was, in short, anti-war and denounced 'this hatred and violence that can already be felt welling up in people'. He quoted the German philosopher Fichte: 'In order to show courage there is no need to take up arms. Often in our lives, we must show more courage to remain true to our convictions by rising above the world's opinions.' Some of his friends rejected him as an appeaser – this was not the time to be wandering lonely as a cloud over hill and dale or listening to the cicadas and going for a swim! Soon his newspaper was being censored for its manifest lack of a warlike spirit and blank pages appeared. As more and more of his colleagues went off to war, Camus found himself writing most of the paper himself, adopting a variety of pen names (Vincent Capable, Nero, Petronius, Cesare Borgia, Irene). Later his articles would be denounced in a lawsuit as 'insane' and 'detrimental to the national interest'. The editor, Pascal Pia, and Camus tried publishing quotes from the classics, but even extracts from Montaigne were liable to be censored. Camus still refused to back away from his pacifist (but would-be soldier) position. Finally, in January 1940, *Alger Républicain* was banned altogether and the newspaper offices shut down.

Camus was now officially unemployed, as well as an army reject. He had no notion of changing the world, only of changing himself. Just as Sartre had to hold back from desserts, so too Camus imposed a punishing new regime of abstinence: 'Hence the absolute necessity of proving oneself [. . .] Through rigorous chastity'. He suspected himself of being a sex addict, just as his wife was a drug addict ('Sex [. . .] is his opium', he noted of himself), and was trying to wean himself off. 'It is so difficult,' he wrote to Jean Grenier, 'not to yield to beings and to beauty'. He spent a blissful week of celibacy camping in the dunes outside Algiers ('Long dunes savage and pure!'). In February 1942, the idea of attaining 'inner peace' was still uppermost in his mind. He appointed himself fixed hours of work and came up with a new method of concentrating his thoughts (and keeping them chaste): 'A single constant subject for meditation, and refuse anything else.' And his method worked – he finished both *The Outsider* and *The Myth of Sisyphus* in this period, and a play, *Caligula*. But it might also explain why, when his old editor, Pascal Pia offered him a job (on the *Paris-Soir*) in 1940, Francine – his new fiancée – refused to go with him. From Paris he wrote home to both Francine and unofficial girlfriend Yvonne. He was torn as usual between more than one woman. 'I want so much to embrace you, and also to turn away.' It was his equivalent to not being able to fight: he wasn't allowed to have sex either. It was almost a 'Make Love Not War' philosophy, but with a double negative. Perhaps, like Sartre, he feared that love was war by another name. In any case he continued to obsess about sublimation.

It was during the war years that Algeria mutated into paradise lost for Camus, while Paris became the locus of exile – a land of outsiders. The woman who lived above him threw herself off her balcony into the courtyard below. 'Everything is still splattered with her blood. She died after saying "At last!"' Camus was hardly even surprised (after all, suicide was the only serious philosophical question). 'All French people,' he noted, 'look like *emigrés*', carrying old suitcases held together by string. At this stage of the war, it was enough for Camus, like Sartre, just to keep on writing. 'The people who create – I mean great artists, not literary journalists – are almost always men of action, contrary to popular belief, who have chosen this form of action to exercise their will.' The real heroes of *The Plague* are all variations on the theme of the writer, journalists and journal-keepers, and perhaps Camus' most affectionate creation, the figure of Grand, who is writing a novel but never gets beyond the first sentence, which he is forever polishing and enhancing ('One fine morning in the month of May an elegant young horsewoman was riding a handsome sorrel mare along the flowery avenues of the Bois de Boulogne'), agonizing over every stray conjunction and preposition (he can't even make his mind up about 'and' or 'but'). We never find out what happens next to that elegant young horsewoman.

Grand is Camus' protest against what Flaubert called the 'stupidity of concluding' and a measure of his sense that language cannot say everything he would like to say. 'I don't know how to define it very well, but I can feel it [. . .] No, I will never be able to define it.' In this sense *The Plague* is another of his anti-literary works of literature. No wonder he struggled so much to finish it. 'Literature,' he noted in August 1942. 'Distrust this word.' The plague must be resisted at all costs, but it is clear that for Camus the virus was more than just a metaphor for the war: it seems to stand for everything in his life – specifically his own addictions and compulsions – that he felt driven towards and therefore actively resisted. Anti-book and anti-sex. Like Hemingway's collection of stories, *The Plague* could be subtitled, *Men Without Women*: his characters live out Camus' rule of asceticism, perhaps involuntarily, but with the intensity of a monastic brotherhood.

Some of his anxieties are manifested in his thoughts on meteorology. Camus was an obsessive weather-watcher. That both he and Sartre had been meteorologists was a kind of bond: the coincidence must have led to some well-informed conversations about cloud-formations, or at least theorizing about the point of it all. Sartre saw his balloon experiments as a waste of time that simply distracted him from his more serious undertakings. Camus, on the other hand, saw connections between meteorology and his own writing. He thought that he might as well turn his *carnet* into a pure collection of meteorological observations, since that was what it mostly consisted of anyway. But, at the same time – the old nagging absurdity – he felt he was never going to get it quite right. 'The temperature varies from one minute to the next. The experience is too chaotic to be stabilized in mathematical terms. And yet any observation I can make is only an arbitrary slice out of reality.' Meteorological observation, clearly, is not the same as the weather. But Camus was also thinking about his work generally.

> As in all the sciences of description (like statistics, which collects facts), the great problem of meteorology is a practical problem: how to replace all the missing observations. Our methods for compensating for the lack always resort to the concept of a 'mean average' and therefore presuppose the generalization and rationalization of an experience that is far from being obviously rational.

The virus of *The Plague* is, in part, an allusion to this fear of over-generalization and abstraction that is built into all language and thought. In this respect, *The Plague* is an anti-philosophical novel.

Camus retreated south to Clermont-Ferrand with the staff of *Paris-Soir* while the Germans marched down the Champs-Élysées. The city made him think of Sartre's Bouville: 'precisely the stage set for *Nausea*.' Stray dogs (he named them Proto and Kirk) were attracted to him and in Lyon he adopted a dog that he called Blaise in honour of Pascal (whose *Pensées* he was reading at the time), and he was still thinking in terms of living a reclusive, contemplative life, ignoring all *divertissements*, and scorning the pleasures of Paris. 'There are times when the only companions I feel good with are animals, especially dogs', he wrote. Even walking the dog could conceivably be too exciting. 'To be able to remain in a bare room for a year,' he noted in his *Carnet*, 'teaches a man more than a hundred literary salons and 40 years of *la vie parisienne*.' Camus probably had in mind Pascal's notion that all our troubles stem from being unable to remain at rest in a room. At the same time he was also reading the Bible (Prophets), Chang Tzu (or Zhuangzi, 'the third of the great Taoists'), the Qur'an, Hindu literature, and Nietzsche.

While he was back in Algeria for a few months he started to play football again, this time as striker (and he scored), relinquishing his customary position of goalkeeper. Until – typically fragile – he dislocated his wrist. Around the same time he went to watch the European champion Marcel Cerdan fight at the Galia stadium. Later, in Lyon, more enthusiastic than before, he went along to other boxing matches with René Leynaud (a poet, fan of *The Outsider*, and regional chief of the Resistance). It marked a significant shift in his attitude towards boxing and this alternative art – the Sartrean sport par excellence – started to seep into his consciousness and his metaphors. 'Until now,' he wrote in a letter to Yvonne (dating from 1941), 'I have always known what I wanted to do with my life, and I always did what was needed. Now I have the impression that I am losing the match. I feel myself nibbled away, put under a glass cover, annexed bit by bit. It's as if I were dispossessed of my own life, simply by lassitude, as if I had given up in a boxing match.' Perhaps this helps to explain the distinctly non-Pascalian note in his diary, regretting his inertia: 'The Frenchman has kept the habits and traditions of great thinking, he only lacks the guts

[. . .] He remade the world without moving his backside out of his armchair.' Although still spitting blood, and occasionally having his lungs deflated and reflated, and forced to live up in the mountains of the Massif Central ('Illness is a monastery with its own rules, asceticism, silence, and inspiration'), Camus finally made the decision to get out of his armchair: in his vocabulary, the 'absurd' was giving way to 'revolt'. He had been used to resisting his own impulses and desires for so long; it was simply a question of turning that resistance outwards towards others. Back in Paris, he adopted another dog, Pauline, took her for long walks through the streets, and evolved at the same time from Resistance sympathizer to militant activist.

Camus was a natural anti-hero. He was sceptical about heroes and heroism and epic adventures. But some time in 1942 or '43, he overcame his scepticism, or was persuaded to. 'We had to vanquish one more time this suspicion in which we held heroism' (*Letters to a German Friend*). He completely renounced pacifism, swinging around to Sartre's more adversarial, agonistic point of view. Unlike Sartre, he could not say that he 'chose' war – but rather that war had chosen him. If he could not join up with the conventional army, he would take up with the Resistance instead. By the time he fell in with Sartre in Paris in 1943, at the opening of *The Flies*, he was already involved with the MUR (Mouvement Uni de Résistance).

It was one of the things that impressed Sartre about the younger man (even though Camus thought of his own efforts as 'derisory'). Sartre's own valiant attempts to organize a Resistance unit – Socialism and Liberty, also known as 'the Sartre group' – had by this time collapsed in disarray (Malraux, for one, declined to join up when Sartre and Beauvoir, cycling through the Free Zone to his villa in Cap-Ferrat, called on him) and he had had to go back to writing plays. In Paris Camus became, in effect, head of the Resistance, writers' section: he was given the job of editing *Combat*, the clandestine Resistance newspaper (a fusion of two earlier publications, *Liberty* and *Truth*), published more or less monthly under threat of execution. It was the perfect title for Sartre the boxer, but Camus had become more pugilistic, more Sartrean and combative. Camus naturally invited Sartre – who all along had plotted and dreamed of 'terrorist actions' – and the Beaver along to secret meetings and was able to initiate them into the fringes of the Resistance (Sartre acquired the nom de guerre Miro). Camus' mission was to collect information and writers and to write editorials or 'leaders'. His writing was uplifting and inspirational and explicitly heroic, setting up a choice between freedom or death. Setting aside the Militia as 'traitors', he asserted the 'solidarity' and 'unity' of France: in his vision the whole of France had risen up as one against the invaders – 'total war' echoed by 'total Resistance' by the 'totality' of France. It was in this period that Camus became the poet of 'fraternity'.

Many of his co-Resisters were captured, killed, tortured, or sent off to the camps. *Combat*'s printer, André Bollier, had to blow his own brains out when he was surrounded by Gestapo and the Militia. Camus said that writing *The Outsider* was like walking on a 'tightrope, in passionate and solitary tension'. Editing *Combat* was even more risky and precarious, with the prospect of a terminal drop in every direction. He would go to sleep with air-raid sirens going off, as if indifferent to his own mortality. When one of his immediate colleagues, Robert Antelme, was arrested, Camus had to go and pick up a load of incriminating documents from his apartment. Another time he was nearly captured with the evidence on him. He was with Maria Casares (the Spanish actress girlfriend he nicknamed 'War and Peace'), outside the Réaumur-Sebastopol Metro station, one day in early 1944. And he was carrying false papers under the name Albert Mathé, his Resistance pseudonym. Unfortunately he was also carrying the mock-up of the next *Combat* issue in his briefcase. It had the word 'COMBAT' right at the top, together with the cross of Lorraine (the symbol of the Free French) on the masthead, just so there was no ambiguity. However, on this particular day the French police and the Germans had blocked off the street in a security swoop. Camus, passing himself off as an innocent civilian – like Sartre – shoved *Combat* into his coat pocket. But up ahead in the queue men were being made to empty their pockets. Then he noticed that they were only searching men: the women had to show their papers, nothing more. So he slipped this text that was also a death-sentence to War and Peace and she put it in her coat pocket instead. The Germans duly searched him, but not her, and Camus and Casares and *Combat* made it through.

The literary image Camus so often had in mind – and almost certainly here, while standing, waiting to be searched, arrested, tortured, executed – was the episode in Malraux's *La Condition humaine* in which prisoners are queuing up next to a locomotive (which is not going anywhere, but is nevertheless fired up), waiting to be thrown in the boiler. This was probably the closest he came to feeling the flames licking at his flesh. Soon Camus had to clear out of town completely – on a bicycle – when other members of his group were picked up, and took refuge in Verdelot, ninety kilometres east of Paris, at the house of Brice Parain (whose philosophy of language Camus had enthusiastically reviewed). As the network fell apart Sartre, likewise, got out and headed south with Beauvoir, concerned that if he was tortured he would not be able to hold out and would reveal the name of Camus. Their terror was a shared terror.

Camus and Sartre finally joined forces in an active way in the Liberation of Paris. The 'insurrection of Paris' – more symbolic and political than military – began on 18 August 1944. With the Allies closing in, and the Germans poised to retreat, for the first time members of the Resistance started to appear openly on the streets, carrying weapons. There was a hazy armistice, an internal struggle between Communists and Gaullists, and German snipers on the rooftops. Camus recruited Sartre to write a series of eye-witness accounts of the liberation for *Combat* under the title '*Un promeneur dans Paris insurgé*' (which he wrote in collaboration with the Beaver). The *Combat* team seized 100 Rue Réaumur, which had become the seat of the collaborationist press. Sartre, a member of the National Theatre Committee, was assigned a mission of his own: to re-occupy the Comédie française, on the Place Colette, between the Louvre and the Bibliothèque nationale.

This was the nation's premier theatrical institution, but it had cultural significance only; its military value was zero. Moreover, it was already empty. Nobody was expecting Sartre to start firing a gun from the top of a church tower. Sartre asked Michel Leiris to accompany him, but he was too busy occupying a museum. So he duly marched into the building and occupied it on his own, entirely unopposed. Mission accomplished. Camus, on his way to the Rue Réaumur, dropped by the theatre to check how his protégé was doing, and found him fast asleep in a plush seat in the orchestra section, exhausted after trooping through Paris. Camus gently jogged him awake, laughing. And he cracked a joke that, although not hilarious in itself, neither of them would forget: 'You aimed your armchair in the direction of history!' Sartre, Camus appeared to be implying, was still an armchair fighter at heart, more theorist than man of action. He never really got out of his armchair, not even for the liberation of Paris. He was never going to walk through a door with a gun in his hand.

But, still, they probably laughed together. They would never be closer than they were right then: comrades, standing shoulder to shoulder as the bullets flew, sharing in the euphoric carnival atmosphere of Paris, intellectually and emotionally united, with the Nazis put to flight and General de Gaulle marching down the Champs-Élysées. For one brief but epic summer, for one ecstatic, heroic moment – almost as if they had scripted it in a play, in a movie – they were partners, kindred, comrades, a team: the grand synthesis. Paris seemed to them like the centre of the world and together they had liberated it from oppression. They had won back the future. They signed up together to write the 'Ethics' essay for an encyclopaedia. They got drunk together, they partied together, they picked up women in bars together. They even shared (for a brief while) one girlfriend. Not only did they collaborate on *No Exit*, but they also acted together in Picasso's surrealist play, *Desire Caught by the Tail*. They both sat on the jury at Gallimard for a literary prize. Sartre was reading Camus and Camus was reading Sartre.

And then Camus made Sartre an offer he couldn't refuse.

New York/New York

I N SOME ODD WAY, existentialism was going home. Some said that, in part, it had come out of the metaphysical turmoil of the United States at the end of the nineteenth century, and retained elements of the pragmatism of C. S. Peirce and the psychologism of William James. Camus and Sartre had both learned from writers like Faulkner, Hemingway, John dos Passos (not to mention the films of Humphrey Bogart). And it was certain that both would have an enormous impact, in return, on writers like Richard Wright and Ralph Ellison and Norman Mailer, and, later, on the Black Power movement, and anyone else who felt like an outsider (practically everyone, at one time or another). Perhaps if they had travelled together, exchanging views, comparing notes, gradually working towards some kind of common ground, everything could have turned out differently. But, after Liberation, Camus offered Sartre the job of American correspondent for *Combat* and Sartre jumped at the chance to get out of Paris. They would, in the end, have radically divergent impressions of America. In a way America came between them, just as Wanda had.

Theoretically, Sartre should have been in his element. He was, after all, an existential cowboy, an intellectual gunslinger who could annihilate all-comers. A fundamentalist libertarian, philosophically. His very imperfect English notwithstanding, he was made for the USA. And yet, in January 1945, Sartre was complaining that, after getting off the boat, he started to suffer from '*le mal de New York*', New York-sickness, just as one has sea-sickness. It took him a while to get his bearings in a city that didn't seem to him like a city at all. But perhaps he never really recovered. He was staying at the Plaza Hotel, and walked up 5th Avenue beneath a frozen sky. He was looking for New York and he couldn't find it. There was nothing on which to focus his gaze; it was a city for 'the long-sighted', since the natural focal point was somewhere around infinity, over the horizon, lost in space. He missed the quartiers of Paris, finding in their place only 'atmospheres, gaseous masses longitudinally elongated, with nothing to mark either a beginning or end'. Oddly enough, just the kind of place where an existentialist in exile ought to feel right at home. And yet he was anything but. 'In the numerical anonymity of roads and avenues, I am just anybody anywhere.' It reminded him of the steppes or the pampas.

But soon enough he started to realize what his fundamental objection to New York really was. The whole point of the city was, he thought, to fortify itself *against nature*. But New York signally failed to do that: an 'open' city with a limitless sky above, it let nature in on every side. It was too exposed to the elements: to storm, hurricane, snow, heat, wind, floods. It had no real protection against anything. 'I have the impression that I am out camping in a jungle swarming with insects.' Therefore he learned to appreciate it only while crossing it in a car, as if he were 'driving across the Andalusian plains'.

In his report on New York, Sartre went so far as to offer a prophecy. All those skyscrapers? Obviously they were doomed; they had had their day. 'Already they are somewhat neglected:

tomorrow, perhaps, they will be torn down. In any case, to construct them we needed a faith that we no longer have.' The Chrysler and the Empire State already appeared to him like ancient 'ruins'. None of which prevented him from embarking on an affair with Dolores Vanetti, who was his interpreter and minder in New York, an ex-actress, brought up in France, who had been working for the French-broadcasting section of the Office of War Information – and had even had some poems published in a surrealist magazine. She would become a fixture for some years among his girlfriends, and she thought seriously of marrying him and taking up with him in France. But like his other American lover, Sally Swing, she could never quite reconcile herself to his complex distribution of sexual labour. 'Her passion literally scares me,' Sartre wrote back home, 'particularly since this is not my strong suit'. Beauvoir would eventually retaliate by going off to the US herself and having a long drawn-out love affair with the writer Nelson Algren.

'I am killed by passion and lectures,' he wrote home to the Beaver, as usual sparing her nothing. But Sartre went on giving lectures on existentialism (at Harvard, Yale, Princeton) and kept on filing articles (thirty-two in all), phoning them in to Camus back in Paris, just as he used to make his meteorology reports to HQ.

Camus himself sailed west a year or so later, in 1946. Now the father of twins (Catherine and Jean), he was a cultural emissary of the French government, and likewise met up with the effervescent Dolores. This time, however, he refrained from availing himself of Sartre's girlfriend (perhaps in part because she had the habit of reminding him of this point: 'Do you know I've slept with Napoleon!'). Following in Sartre's wake, he provided a kind of ironic commentary on his predecessor. Where Sartre was obsessed with architecture, Camus was indifferent, oblivious. 'I notice that I have not noticed the skyscrapers, they seemed to me perfectly natural. It is merely a question of general proportions. And then it is impossible to live with your head tilted upwards all the time.' He admired colours, foodstuffs, smells ('iron and cement'), taxis, women. Especially women. And tie shops ('You have to see them to believe them'). He enjoyed the 'orgy of violent lights' that was Broadway – and this:

The Camel sign: 'an American soldier, his mouth open, puffing out clouds of real smoke'. He was conscious of 'a society of signs', but perhaps he could still feel himself dissolving again into the smoke, floating up into the light. There was so much to enchant Camus. Ice cream, for example: 'I savoured yet another of these ice creams that make me feel so happy. A good moment.

Another good moment.' Camus noted that one New Yorker had the habit of taking his giraffe out for a ride in the back of his truck, and that a woman took her gazelle for a walk in Central Park. He had dinner in Chinatown, listened to jazz in Harlem, went up the Empire State (he didn't notice that it was an ancient ruin), and even tried out roller-skating. On the subway he saw 'an unforgettable face'.

At Vassar, where he was giving a lecture on 'The Crisis of Mankind', he was dazzled by the spectacle of 'an army of long-legged young starlets, lazing on the lawn' (Sartre had turned down their invitation and predicted that Camus would surely accept). Back in Manhattan, he fell in love several times over, most notably with Patricia Blake, a nineteen-year old student and *Vogue* apprentice, who saw him as a young Humphrey Bogart and guided him around town. He read her pages from *The Plague* and she took him to the Bowery Follies, where he

Patricia Blake

concluded that 'it is necessary to be either very ugly or very beautiful'. Since Camus was fascinated by the American way of death, and admired the funeral-parlour ad 'You die. We do the rest', Blake found him issues of undertakers' trade magazines, such as *Sunnyside*, *Casket*, and *Embalmer's Monthly*.

Unlike Sartre, Camus was reminded of home. 'When you look down from the heights of Riverside along the Hudson, the uninterrupted stream of cars, smooth and well-oiled, sends up a song, at once grave and distant, that is exactly the sound of the waves.' And yet, all the same, there was something missing. There was an 'American tragedy' that Camus struggled to put his finger on, amid all the girls on lawns and ice cream and jazz bars and clouds of cigarette smoke.

Afternoon with students. They don't feel the real problem; however, their nostalgia is evident. In this country where *everything* is done to prove that life isn't tragic, they feel something is missing. This great effort is poignant, but one must reject the tragic *after* having looked at it, not before.

What was the tragic for Camus? Perhaps it had something to do with all the clouds of smoke and the waves. It should be said, there was an obvious difference of context between Camus and the young students he was talking to. He was coming from Europe, which had just spent several years tearing itself apart, whereas they remained more or less physically untouched by the war. Camus was welcomed both as literary luminary (the translation of *The Outsider* came out during his stay) and Resistance hero. But he found himself already trying to get away from the subject of recent history. One student at Columbia asked how many people were in the Resistance. '360,728,' Camus snapped back, slightly acerbically. Of course, how could they fully comprehend the notion of a historical tragedy on a vast scale such as Camus himself had just lived through and worked – very hazardously – to diminish? But his tragic perception of life was not reducible to the question of the Second World War.

Sailing back from New York to France, at night in the middle of the Atlantic, staring down from the deck into the ocean, Camus pulled out his notebook again:

> Marvellous night on the Atlantic. This hour when the sun has disappeared and the moon has just barely been born, when the west is still luminous and the east is already dark. Yes, I've loved the sea very much – this calm immensity – these wakes folded under wakes – these liquid routes [...] I've always been torn between my appetite for people, the vanity and the agitation, and the desire to make myself the equal of these seas of forgetfulness, these unlimited silences that are like the enchantment of death. I have a taste for worldly vanities, other people, faces, but, out of step with this century, I have an example in myself which is the sea and anything in this world that resembles it. O sweet-ness of nights where all the stars sway and wheel above the masts, and this silence in me, this silence which finally frees me from everything.

It was fully ten years after that sunny day, lying in bed, in 1936. We have followed the tubercular postgrad out of his house in Algeria, to France and the war years, and then beyond, to America and 1946. No sun this time, only a lingering luminosity in the west. No smoke, no foliage, no flash of enlightenment. But the two episodes, lying in bed in Algiers and leaning over the rail of a ship at night, somewhere in the Atlantic ocean, ten years and one world war later, were connected. On this occasion, looking down, Camus could feel himself vanishing into the abstract patterns left by the wake of the ship ('wakes folded under wakes'), almost as if he were throwing himself overboard, losing himself in the great 'seas of forgetfulness'.

Camus identified two kinds of relationship between himself and the rest of the world. On the one hand, there was the smoky metempsychosis effect, in which the psyche faded away into the Brownian motion of liquid and photons, becoming a kind of disincarnate gas or vapour, dispersed out into vacant interstellar spaces, merging with the immaterial and oblivion. On the other, there was the more incarnate experience – talking to the Vassar students lying on the grass – mingling with the masses in New York, looking into people's 'faces', and finally conversing with them, giving lectures, answering questions and so on. And the one did not translate well into the other. The 'silence in me' urged him to seek consolation and a kind of ecstatic self-erasure in the non-human, in things, in the sky and the sea, in light and in darkness: in other kinds of silence. He could experience a form of empathy with things that do not in fact feel any emotions and are devoid of language. Whereas, when it came to other beings, to this extent like him, who do feel emotions and form intentions, the horizontal dream of being like smoke faded away and made any notion of a meeting of minds curiously and frustratingly elusive. Yes, I can have a meeting of minds with you, providing you don't actually have one; but if you do then, no, I can't. As soon as it becomes possible it also becomes impossible. Pure X-theory. It is this realization – marginally autistic perhaps – that informed not just his sense of the tragic but also his theory of 'absurdity', which relied on a teasing, bewitching but elusive counter-opposed expectation of 'unity' and belonging, exemplified by the Vassar students and the United States generally. And here Camus must for once have found himself agreeing with Sartre, who discerned a 'myth of happiness' at work in America and concluded that 'nowhere else is there a greater disparity between people and their myths'.

Despite which, even while all alone, in the night, between continents, far away from everything, Camus had to stress, for the benefit of his own diary, that he would never be an existentialist, that he was explicitly 'against modern existentialism', which increasingly seemed to him to be another form of messianism. He had already had to repeat, for the benefit of the students, that, no, he was not nor ever had been an existentialist. Camus was not Sartre. As to what he was precisely, he replied (at a press conference), 'I am too young to have a system'. There could never be a full understanding between Camus and Sartre and that too was part of the 'tragic'. Perhaps Camus, in thinking about getting away from other people, all those faces, was also thinking of one face in particular, a face with one lazy eye and nicotine-stained teeth.

Asked on his return to publish his take on America, he replied: 'Everywhere I went I received a warm welcome, and everywhere I expressed myself with total freedom. I'm not going to spit in the plate after having eaten the soup, the way Sartre did.' But the essential difference between them may have been touched on in Canada, when Camus saw Quebec for the first time. While Sartre after the war was increasingly drawn towards a form of philosophical journalism in which he was trying to provide an exhaustive description of the world, as it was, had been, and would be, more than ever a 'writing machine', Camus in contrast – increasingly *hypo*graphic, almost graphophobic, shying away from writing, haunted by a 'disgust for all forms of public expression' – was falling out of love with journalism, to the point of pulling out of *Combat*.

Now Camus was struck – for the first time on this continent –

'by the real impression of beauty and grandeur'. He could (he wrote) probably write something quite decent about Quebec and its history, perhaps feeling drawn towards it by virtue of its being a French-speaking community outside France. But anything along these lines would be pointless, even if technically proficient.

> The one thing that I would like to say – I have been incapable of saying it hitherto. And I will doubtless never say it.

There was 'one thing' that did not translate well into language. He didn't of course say what that one thing was, since he was after all incapable of saying it. We can infer that it was something akin to the 'secret' to which he referred that must be held back in writing. Perhaps the 'one thing' was the sense of oneness, an elusive underlying unity that he occasionally experienced but that could never be fully expressed. Or, to put it at a minimum, the thing that both he and Sartre were always really interested in saying, what it felt like to be alive, was the one thing that resisted being written. Books always ended up being *against* the author. This may help to explain why on another ocean voyage, this time to South America two years later, when we find him again standing on the deck and looking down into the Atlantic flowing by beneath, Camus is seriously considering heaving himself over the side and diving in and becoming one with the waves.

14

PHILOSOPHERS STONED

W HEN IT CAME TO substance abuse, Sartre and
Camus really had a lot in common. Always assuming we can count alcohol and tobacco. Sartre, with
his robust constitution, liked to get drunk on a regular basis;
Camus more rarely. They were all 'hard drinkers'. 'No one in our
circle was reluctant to get drunk,' Beauvoir recalled, 'and some of
us saw it as a duty.' 'I get drunk,' wrote Sartre, 'but only every other
night' (this was during a transatlantic voyage). Both smoked
cigarettes, making this 'little crematory sacrifice' as Sartre put
it (in *Being and Nothingness*), symbolically turning the world to
ashes ('the world [...] going up in smoke'). Camus favoured the
corn-paper Gitanes, famously toxic, while Sartre was more attached
to the pipe. But they differed significantly on the subject of more
powerful intoxicants and hallucinogenics.

Sartre was never openly evangelical about drugs. He didn't
issue any commandments: turn on, tune in, drop out (although
it is plausible to infer an attitude like this). But when it came to
his own habits, he had an anything-goes attitude. The mescaline
was purely an experiment. Aldous Huxley would later argue that
the drug, derived from the Mexican peyote plant (a form of
cactus), opened 'the doors of perception'. But for Sartre it

A Gitanes smoker

induced psychotic episodes and waking visions of his worst nightmares. His psychiatrist friend Daniel Lagache first introduced him to the drug, in laboratory conditions, at St Anne's hospital in Paris. He started taking it in 1935 and carried on, on and off, for a year. It probably impacted on the writing of *Nausea* (the episodes with the pebble, the seat in the train, the chestnut tree could virtually be explained away by reference to mescaline). But it certainly led to the lobsters.

First of all it was devil-fish. Beauvoir found him fighting them off. And of course the inevitable octopus (when she telephoned he told her that she had just saved him from a struggle that he was about to lose), squid, and crabs. Later, on the train, he noticed she had giant beetles on her shoes where the tassels ought to be. And there was an orang-utan swinging from the luggage rack. Eventually the lobsters turned up, chasing him down the Champs-Élysées, following him around town, into class, keeping him company in Les Deux Magots. 'I would wake up in the morning and say, "Good morning, my little ones, how did you sleep?" I would say, "Okay guys, we're going into class now . . ." and they would be there, around my desk, absolutely still, until the bell rang.' They didn't leave him completely until the war years. In 1959, in his play *The Condemned of Altona* (also known as *Loser Wins*) they reappeared as a race of morally superior crustaceans, sitting in judgment on humanity. Jacques Lacan attributed the lobsters to Sartre's anxiety about being condemned to a career as a schoolteacher. They became a kind of conscience for him. He was almost sorry when they finally left him alone. 'I would have liked my crabs to come back. Sometimes I miss them [. . .] I remember how they used to sit on my leg.'

But even then he was on a diet of uppers and downers. He always relied on Belladénal to get him off to sleep. Later on he became addicted to amphetamines. They were produced in large quantities during the war to get soldiers and pilots through the stress of battle. Sartre took to them as a way of getting him through books. At a certain point in the fifties he was munching them like popcorn or jelly babies, handfuls at a time. Corydrane – a mix of aspirin and amphetamines – was his drug of choice and legally available at the time (it wasn't prohibited until 1971). At the same time, a bottle of Orthodrine a day, a prescription drug that he obtained from a variety of doctors, was supposed to keep the blues away. He knocked it back like Balzac and coffee. The Beaver, anxious for his health, suggested he might want to ease up on the dosage. Sartre would argue in classic existential terms that he could always *choose* to stop – he just didn't want to, that was all: he liked to 'see the sun that switched on in [his] head'. Some claim that they can detect a vein of Corydrane – like letters in a stick of rock – running right through the middle of *Critique of*

Dialectical Reason as he upped the intake from ten to twenty. But the fact is that his writing was naturally hyper-writing with a hallucinatory tendency. In the way that some drunks like to get drunk to justify the fact that they are always loud and uninhibited, so Sartre found that the drugs were a convenient way of making sense of – perhaps covering up – his real addiction. 'Sartre's true drug,' writes Bernard-Henri Lévy, 'was neither mescaline nor Corydrane, but writing.'

Camus came at the usage question from the angle of a sceptical spectator. He had first been seduced by drugs, or a drug-addict anyway, at the age of nineteen, back in 1932. Simone Hié was sexy, mysterious (known to everyone as S), funny, quoted surrealist poets, sang obscene songs, and painted her eyelids. She

S

already had a boyfriend, but she was even more hooked on morphine (which her mother, an ophthalmologist, had first given her for menstrual cramps). Camus tried to wean her off the habit just as he unhooked her from the boyfriend. He knew a friendly pharmacist who would supply her with boxes of progressively diluted ampoules. And he would wait around and watch, fascinated, while she shot up.

'I want to get married, kill myself [...] do something desperate, you know what I mean?' He opted for marriage, when he was only twenty, convinced that he was doomed to die young, and she was nineteen. His friend Louis Benisti reckoned it was a mistake and that Camus was trying to be an angel or a St Bernard and save her from herself. Whether or not he was right, the fact is that Camus did not succeed. He tried to distract her with his writing and came up with a fantasy about the water fairy Mélusine: 'it is time to create new worlds, to escape from the intense melancholy one expects'. And he left sentimental notes on her pillow when he left their apartment to go to classes. 'You are sleeping. I daren't wake you. You are beautiful. That is enough for me.' Or this, more fantastic, perhaps sympathetic to hallucinatory experiences:

> We would like to break through the all too narrow frames of thought and the human, and live above time, beyond space. And since we wish it, so it must be. I will take my little girl by the hand and I will sit her down next to me. We will gaze into one another's eyes and there we will follow Sinbad's ship on its slow navigation, carving out a path towards unknown seas. Look and you will see us on board.

When this approach didn't work, he persuaded the doctor who was treating him for tuberculosis to put her on a diet of glycerine water. He resolved to break up with her only when he discovered that she had a lover. They were in Salzburg in the summer of 1936 and Camus picked up their mail from the post office. One of the letters was for S from the doctor who was not only supplying her with drugs but getting sexual favours in return. *He* was being her angel or St Bernard instead. Camus gave up his career as saviour. Perhaps he felt that, in a way, he too had been drugged and he needed to break free of the habit.

Over the years, Camus would see a lot of doctors and even made one of them into his narrator-hero in *The Plague*. But he remained sceptical about drugs and drug addiction. He was not against happiness, but he didn't think it could be artificially induced by a pharmacological supplement. He believed rather in the power of the opposite, in taking away, not adding, in composure: in falling out of love. But more than that he developed a resistance to the ecstatic mentality, to any form of hype, or 'hyperthermic' discourse (as I have called it) whether it was journalism or – increasingly – political ideology. Around ten years after falling out with his wife, he started to think he detected a similar vein of addictive thought in the other 'S' in his life.

15

SQUARING UP

BORIS VIAN – WHO ALSO went by the name Bison Ravi (an anagram), 'Delighted Bison' – was a one-man artistic band. He was not just a writer (*L'Écume des jours*, most famously, and a handful of parodic *romans noirs*, published under the name Vernon Sullivan), but a jazz trumpeter at Le Tabou, jazz critic, poet, composer, engineer, and translator (of Raymond Chandler's *Farewell My Lovely* and *The Big Sleep*). He would die in rare and distinguished circumstances, when attending a preview at the Cinéma Marbeuf of a film version of one his own novels, *J'irai cracher sur vos tombes* (*I Will Spit on Your Graves*), so appalled at the distortions wrought upon his work ('You call them Americans? My arse!') that he fell back in his seat and promptly died of a cardiac arrest at the age of thirty-nine. But prior to this spectacularly aesthetic death he was also a great party animal and thrower of parties. And, acquainted with Camus and Sartre, he invited both of them to one he and his wife Michelle were organizing at their apartment in Paris, in December 1946, in the tradition of the great all-night 'fiestas' of the Occupation. Which was risky, because Sartre would go on to have an affair with his wife and destroy their marriage. But this was also the beginning of another long-drawn-out and definitely-not-amicable divorce. Vian had written a popular anti-war song, 'Le Déserteur', but in this case he was lighting a particularly short fuse.

One war had come to an end. But another was just beginning. Colder, but more personal. The very idea of peace began to seem like an illusion. 'I am a battleship. I can't be sunk.' So said Sartre in 1944. But Camus set out to torpedo him. The two old comrades were drifting further apart. But perhaps all would yet have been well between them that night if not for Merleau.

Maurice Merleau-Ponty, following Husserl, identified himself (as did Sartre) as a 'phenomenologist'. He wrote a classic work of the genre, *The Phenomenology of Perception*, trying to rescue subjectivity from science. Perhaps he could even have found common ground with Camus in his emphasis on the 'communing' between consciousness and the 'flesh' of the world. But in fact he now worked with Sartre on *Modern Times*, the journal Sartre and Beauvoir had founded, taking the title from Chaplin's comic film about capitalism. Merleau-Ponty, like the entire staff of *Les Temps modernes*, had swung around towards Marxism in the post-war climate, and he had recently published an article attacking Arthur Koestler, 'The Yogi and the Proletarian'. Koestler was an avowed anti-communist, who had denounced Stalinism, the purges and the pre-scripted Moscow show 'trials', notably in his great novel *Darkness at Noon* and more recently in his essay 'The Yogi and the Commissar'. From the point of view of *Les Temps modernes*, the end of the war did not mean an end to hostilities. Now the fight against fascism had been won, the point was to keep on going and overthrow capitalism too. For anybody who hadn't had a particularly good war, it was an appealing concept.

Koestler was at the party too. Camus, in contrast to Merleau, was a supporter of Koestler. They had become fast friends – doomed, therefore, to have the occasional punch-up – since he arrived in Paris. They found they shared a liking for Orwell's anti-Soviet satire *Animal Farm*, and used the informal '*tu*' in speaking to one another while out drinking in Paris brasseries. Which did not, however, stop Camus falling madly for Koestler's wife. The two of them wound up in a hotel in Avignon together. 'I cannot leave you', he said to her in the Metro (but of course he did – the lasting, the durable remained elusive). Koestler, meanwhile, was distracted by his parallel affair with Beauvoir. Not exactly one big happy family, but it was a tight network, held together by ties of love and suspicion and antagonistic reciprocity. In 1946 they could all be found knocking about Paris together, in various permutations, in bars and restaurants and nightclubs, gossiping, drinking, dancing. Another time, between bars, Sartre and Camus and Koestler competed to see which of them could cross the Place Saint-Michel fastest on all fours.

At a certain point in the Vian party, Camus and Merleau-Ponty were thrown together. Everyone had already consumed a fair amount of alcohol. According to Beauvoir, Camus didn't turn up till eleven and was already in a bad mood on account of some long journey from the south (and possibly, adds Beauvoir, at her bitchiest, because he felt his 'golden age' was coming to an end). But he was not too tired to lay into Merleau over his article, championing Koestler, and accusing Merleau of tacitly supporting the Soviet show trials and mass purges. He would have said something like, 'As writers we are traitors to ourselves if we do not denounce what must be denounced.'

It was a clear sideways swipe at Sartre, so he got in the ring too, taking sides with Merleau, and similarly denouncing Koestler. These two already had history. Koestler had riled Sartre less by flirting with Beauvoir than with his blunt assertion that 'You are a better novelist than I am, but not such a good philosopher', and Sartre had given him such a tongue-lashing in return that he actually wrote an apologetic letter to Koestler afterwards. But now all Sartre's fighting instincts were aroused and he tore into Koestler once more, condemning him as a capitalist collaborator and rabid anti-communist. His catchphrase of the moment was: 'An anti-communist is a dog!'

Camus, according to some, had Merleau in a headlock and had a mind to thump him except that his adversary 'refused the delights of violence' (as Sartre would write). Sartre, devoid of any such reserve, took over the fight from Merleau, like some experienced gunslinger standing in for an amateur, cranking up the level and the ferocity of the attack a few notches. The other partygoers turned their attention in the direction of the showdown and clustered around, like kids in the playground. Naturally the entire editorial team of *Modern Times* and Simone de Beauvoir were rooting for Sartre. Fight Night. Sartre vs Camus: amid so many minor disputes, this was the Big Fight everybody had been half-fearing, half-longing for. It had been simmering away in secret for so long, and now it had finally erupted, bubbling up into the public domain, spilling out on to the boulevard.

Camus wasn't one to shy away from the fray. He had turned down the offer of working on *Modern Times* and sometimes Sartre made him think more of another of Chaplin's films, *The Great Dictator*. Sartre was a little dictator who could punch above his weight. Maybe all dictators tended to be short and tyranny was a way of overcompensating for the lack of height. But he couldn't quite bring himself to get personal and dirty, so he fumbled for words. This, it must be emphasized, was only an indirect confrontation after all. For the time being the argument was, technically, about Koestler and Merleau rather than Camus and Sartre. Camus of course knew that Sartre's defence of Merleau was, covertly, a direct attack on him just as Sartre knew that Camus' support for Koestler was a coded assault on him. But at this point Camus found it hard to believe that Sartre could be so hardline, so unyielding, in his anti-Camusian harangue. Could he really be that dogmatic? Surrounded by Sartrean lieutenants, Camus felt outnumbered, out-generaled and demoralized: disappointed by his friendship with Sartre (whom, let us not forget, not so long before he was commissioning to write for *Combat*). He grabbed his trenchcoat, slammed the door and rushed out into the night.

Everybody realized that this was a bust-up not – as it began – between Merleau-Ponty and Camus, but between Camus and Sartre. This was certainly the way Sartre saw it. And almost immediately he began to have regrets he wanted to apologize, as he had to Koestler, but in person. Maybe this was overkill and – Sartre was self-conscious enough to realize it – clearly imbued with all his personal resentment of Camus, the way he swiped Wanda from right under his nose, the movie-star looks, his affectation of the trenchcoat. But they were still comrades, after all, survivors. Which is why he and Jacques-Laurent Bost – not only another close collaborator at *Les Temps modernes* but also the husband of Olga and, intermittently, Beauvoir's stand-in lover – went running after Camus. They caught up with him already sulkily striding down the street and tried to humour him into coming back to the party. It was all a *malentendu*: Sartre was only *joking*, after all (as he would say to Sally Swing); nothing personal, don't take it so seriously. They were not Nazis, this was not *Combat*, Camus didn't have to be the great Outsider. Why couldn't they just continue the conversation inside? It was cold out in Paris in December. Sartre would probably have denounced himself: I feel myself to be nothing but a bastard, and a small-scale bastard at that. And I am a bourgeois after all, and so are you (as he would say later, at the time of their definitive rift).

But Camus was sensitive, prickly, quick to flare up. Sartre would probably have said he *chose* to be sensitive. But either way he was still hurt, wounded by the skirmish, and could not be readily persuaded, jollied, into turning around. No laughter. He had to be somewhere else, do something else – a rendezvous? – and stalked away into the night. Despite the apologies and the jokes and the patching-up, he felt frozen out. Sartre and Bost (and subsequently Beauvoir too) reckoned he liked to feel excluded, just as he refused to sign up to socialism.

Camus walked out on the party – just as he'd pulled out of the Communist Party, aged thirty, back in the thirties, disappointed with their Algerian policies. Oddly it seems like the kind of thing that, in theory, Sartre – the radical individualist, the cowboy philosopher – should be doing. And yet it was Sartre who was yearning for the embrace of the collective, the 'group-in-fusion'.

Only two months before, Camus and Sartre had been out drinking together with Koestler and Beauvoir and Koestler was ranting and Camus had been inspired to say what he thought they all (at least he and Sartre and the Beaver) had in common: 'Individuals are paramount for us: we prefer the concrete to the abstract, people to doctrines, and we put friendship above politics'. His *Carnets*, likewise, speak of a collective *nous* in a conversation between Sartre, Camus, Koestler and Malraux and the idea of setting out some moral common denominators between them. But now there was no more 'we' – nothing but individuals and a series of collisions, force and counter-force. The Sartre-Camus axis had morphed into Sartre vs Camus. And ironically the split was over the right to speak on behalf of a collective *nous*, a band of brothers, beaten down by and yet rising up against the bourgeoisie. The two old comrades found themselves on opposite sides of an abyss, and the intellectual landmasses they occupied were shifting steadily further apart. This was only the first and perhaps the most trivial of their public showdowns. The *froideur* – the coolness – lasted only a few months, until March 1947, but it provided a snapshot of the tension between them. Barely an overture, an introductory chapter, but their *agon* was now out there, in the open; they had become official antagonists, even if they tried to postpone the moment of reckoning as long as possible.

As Camus stormed into the night, he likewise began to be afflicted by *l'esprit de l'escalier* (staircase wit – one more reason why writing was so important to both of them): the familiar situation where you leave the party and go down the stairs and then you realize exactly what you *should have said*. The devastating one-liner, the killer comeback that is guaranteed to overwhelm all opposition. Only you didn't say it. But it comes to you now, when you've already left. Do you go back and try to find a pretext for delivering the knockout punch? Or, better still, keep on going and write it down, and make it even stronger? Camus, reluctant though he was, really had no option. Perhaps it is not so surprising that, around this time, we find him jotting in his diary 'Unbearable solitude' and 'What makes a man feel alone is the cowardice of others'. Nor that he was soon writing a satirical play, *L'Impromptu des philosophes*, in which an existentialist philosopher, named Monsieur Néant (Mr Nothingness), who carries around with him an enormous book that nobody wants to read, is finally locked up in an asylum. (Camus himself tried valiantly with *Being and Nothingness* but, as he admitted, never got much beyond page 179.)

One way or another, they were always arguing. Sartre and Camus were adversarial right from the beginning, and even before. And they shared the kind of geographical and intellectual intimacy that was always liable to end in a fight, to de-cohere, with one or the other storming out and slamming the door behind them. It was Camus – the savage – who was the more likely to issue an ultimatum and then make a dramatic exit. Sartre, with his higher regard for the symbolic, and his history of boxing, was always up for another round of verbal pounding. In the end, Camus would run out of words, or would lose faith in the power of argument, and would feel that the truth ought to be manifest; Sartre could always give the dialectic another twist, perhaps turning it around 180 degrees.

Like boxers dancing around the ring, Sartre and Camus readily traded positions, even though they kept to their underlying agonistic stance. Even so there was more than a hint of cross-fertilization. If Camus was gradually shifting and shuffling in the direction of a more existential perspective – adopting and adapting some of the vocabulary even if he gives it a lyrical twist – Sartre was similarly replicating some of Camus' old moves, but translating them into his own distinctive way of thinking. If their dual intellectual trajectory had to be written down in a single letter, it would look like this:

X

Jacques Derrida used to refer to this crossover effect (which is also deferral and aporia) as a 'chiasmus' (thinking of the original Greek letter). I am going to stick with the X because I like to think of Sartre and Camus as, if not 'existentialists' (a label even Sartre initially refused), then 'X-men' – or even 'ex-men' – subject to random mutation. Sartre and Camus contain an anti-Camus, an anti-Sartre, and in their opposition to one another they also oppose themselves. The X is an X-ray, illuminating not so much two adversarial individuals as a larger, composite, conflicted consciousness, the 'universal singular' (in Sartre's phrase). X-theory is the meeting, the clash, between existentialism and the absurd.

Even though he was a symbolic writer and thinker par excellence, a man better at visualizing than perceiving, someone for whom codes and formulae and novels and philosophies made infinitely more sense than, say, a love affair, nevertheless Sartre remained jealous of the savage way of being. A thinker and a writer who yearned to be a doer: sitting in his 'armchair', he dreamed of a life of action. Words were acts, he insisted. But in the post-war years he could never forget that, in the period of the Occupation and Resistance, it was Camus who was always more the man of action, the X-man, than he was. A meteorologist who got locked up as a prisoner of war, talked his way out, then spent the rest of the war in cafés writing or going to fiestas (a way of 'magically' conjuring up victory, Beauvoir said): it was not a manifestly glorious record and always liable to be queried or trashed.

When he spoke, on the very last page of *Being and Nothingness*, of finding some kind of new morality or at least a 'moral terrain' (and promising to devote 'a forthcoming work' to the question) – this was Sartre looking for some cause to adopt, another war to fight, this time more heroically. In the early philosophy, there is no reason to do any one thing more than any other. Existential phenomenology is completely open and egalitarian and non-prescriptive as regards any course of action. All actions appear equally absurd and futile, perhaps rather laughable; there are no values; everything is a long way beyond good and evil. The waiter and the skier are the classic exemplars of existential activity – both trying to be something they can never really be, and comically never far from falling flat on their faces. Perhaps it is because the waiter is clearly doing something for someone else that he is seen as such as faker, a con artist. It is clear that every individual is a Resistor at heart, that he is in search of (to borrow Isaiah Berlin's terminology) 'freedom from' (the Nazis, for example), but there is no logic to determine what freedom is 'for'. You might as well be a waiter or a skier as a footballer or a writer, a collaborator as a Resistance hero. *Trans-ascendance* and *trans-descendance* were equivalent.

The end of the war changed all that, if it wasn't already changing. In *Nausea* Sartre jeered at any idea of 'ending' anything. After the war, he accommodated then espoused ends – not just purposes, objectives ('praxis' was his new word) but the very shape of the future – and started to work out means. So the revised theory gradually took shape: existentialism, inflected with Marxism, evolved into acting as lifeguard on behalf of a new supercharged individual, the magic figure of the worker – and by extension the working class – whose freedom was perpetually circumscribed or cancelled out by the ruling class. One against all: now it was *the* One, the 'unanimity', the collective of the for-itself pitched in battle against the in-itself, the self-satisfied ruling classes. *They* (at various times, the government, anti-semites, empires, General de Gaulle and his ministers, the entirety of the bourgeoisie, America, the West) were the octopus that Sartre had to grapple with and overcome. His whole philosophy of extreme selfishness segued readily into extreme altruism, mediated by the boxer's overarching binary, antagonistic instincts. It was no longer individuals like the waiter (or, in another war-time essay, Baudelaire) suffering from bad faith, giving away or abdicating their options: rather they were victims of higher powers, conspiring to rob them. The worker was thus the incarnation of the ideal existential soul, set at an angle to the rest of the universe, threatened by a sadistic conspiracy to turn him into a tool. 'He is condemned to fragmented and semi-automatic tasks whose meaning and purpose escape him [...] forced to repeat the same gesture a thousand times a day.' Increasingly the figure of the worker appeared as a stand-in for the embattled figure of Sartre himself. Thus the writer was, above all, a worker, writing was – or *ought* to be – productive work, and what it produced was truth, converging on the elusive 'totalisation' – an updated form of secular transcendence.

Finally Sartre found he had something to *do*, a cause to fight, beyond analysing and writing. In the revised theory, the requirements of freedom had been significantly upgraded. What you had taken for freedom – just being alive, being unpredictable, indeterminate, quantum, an infinite bundle of possibilities – shook out as purely theoretical, and had to be toughened up, made practical. Freedom had to become real. '*Une liberté qui se veut liberté*', a freedom that seeks (or intends) to be freedom (or perhaps 'a self-conscious freedom') is a phrase that had already appeared on p. 692 of *Being and Nothingness* (coming close to undermining the whole of the previous 691 pages). It could only metamorphose from theory into practice (or praxis), from the minimum into the maximum, via the catharsis of revolutionary violence. Without violence, in this new understanding, there was no freedom. 'Since nothing can be got unless an order that is sacred is smashed by force, the worker sees the affirmation of his own reality as a man in a manifestation of violence.'

Sartre liked to end his plays with a good murder. Orestes kills his mother and her lover in *The Flies*. After a lot of Hamlet-like hesitation, Hugo – hero of *Les Mains sales* – finally assassinates Hoederer, the Communist Party boss. At the end of *The Devil and the Good Lord*, Sartre has his hero, Goetz, stab to death an officer who is objecting to his leadership of a rebel army. Increasingly this dramatic climax came to seem more than just a theatrical gesture. Under the heading of militant *engagement* (or commitment) and 'original violence', Sartre was trying to merge the symbolic with the savage life of true action and find the 'solidarity' with others and sense of sheer presence that Camus seemed to have automatically. He seemed to need *the affirmation of his own reality*. In this new way of thinking, it was no longer enough to be a waiter or skier; you had to be a revolutionary or nothing. In his emphasis on 'reality *as a man*' there was too more than a hint that Sartre – completely unreformed by Beauvoir's *Second Sex* manifesto – was hankering after a display of machismo. He lived in fear of losing his manhood, or at least in a state of equivocation and anxiety.

Camus joined the Communist Party in a spirit of youthful idealism as a student (and almost immediately dropped out again when he realized how atrocious those ideals could become in practice); now Sartre, without ever signing up as a member, espoused the cause. He was an avowed anti-anti-Communist, even if not officially a Communist either. After years of fumbling for a third way, somewhere in between the competing superpowers, and at the same time distinct from the Euro-centric nationalism of General de Gaulle, Sartre could speak of a semi-religious 'conversion'. 'After ten years of ruminating, I had come to the breaking point [...] I had to write or suffocate. Day and night, I wrote the first part of "The Communists and Peace".' In the spring of 1952, he 'rushed' back to Paris from Italy to knock out a full-blooded defence of the leader of the French Communist Party, who had been arrested by the police on trumped-up charges (they claimed bizarrely that some pigeons that he was taking home for dinner were being used to transmit messages to coordinate rioting against a visiting American general). It was a point-by-point deconstruction of the arguments put up by anti-Communists and probably the first time he had used, in any favourable way, the word *unanimité*. I am not my story; but *we* are our 'history'.

Sartre reckoned he had been evolving in this general direction for a decade, perhaps ever since the camaraderie of the Stalag. But the fact that he had recently read *The Rebel* – not to mention heard Camus on many occasions articulate the same arguments – was certainly a factor in the shift. Only when Camus came out as an anti-Communist did Sartre begin to set out his pro-Marxist stall, 'rushing' back dramatically from Italy, feeling under pressure, in a hurry, to define himself by opposition. It was just like the party at the Vians': as soon as Camus took up an argument, Sartre had to get involved; he couldn't stay on the side-lines. Camus, in turn, from the very beginning, sought to define himself in opposition. Hence his whole political theory was erected to hold back the tide of Sartre's growing revolutionary sympathies. Camus remained the goalkeeper, intent on defending the absurd from the encroachment of tyranny, while Sartre, more than ever the boxer, dreamed of landing the knockout punch on the chin of the oppressors. Thesis and antithesis were locked in combat.

While Sartre was convinced that his task was to lay out the truth for the future (which he started to call 'history'), Camus increasingly came to doubt not only his own but anyone else's right or ability to get anything – much less everything – quite right. During this period, he and Beauvoir – especially in the absence of Sartre – became particularly close and Camus opened up to her in a way that he never did with other men, confiding his intimate anxieties. One night they were out in Paris together, drinking champagne, at the Lipp and Pont Royal. 'If only,' Camus lamented as they headed back to her hotel, 'we could write the truth!'

16

THE REBEL

OVER THE 382 PAGES (in the paperback edition) of *The Rebel* (*L'homme révolté*, literally 'Man in Revolt'), Camus mentions approximately 166 separate thinkers or writers or poets or artists in total (I know: I counted them, rather laboriously, one by one – and I probably missed a few). He does not mention Jean-Paul Sartre once. Which is odd, considering that by this time – 1951 – Sartre was probably about the best-known living philosopher in the western world. He was virtually synonymous with the word *philosopher*, certainly of the adventurous, continental variety. Tourist buses stopped outside his place of work to gawk. Existentialism had acquired celebrity status in Europe and America. As early as 1946, according to one of Sartre's letters to the Beaver, 'Here [New York] is just like Paris: everyone is speaking about me'. Not just on land but at sea too. 'I must be *really* famous, poor little Beaver, because although I only stuck a few shabby labels on my suitcases, still the whole boat knew who I was and demanded a lecture on existentialism.' His public lectures were packed, pop-star sensations, with fainting fans and more media than philosophers.

And yet, in a work that refers to so many *philosophes*, that alludes, among other contemporaries, to André Malraux and

René Char and André Breton, there is not one single explicit reference. Everyone gets in *except* Sartre. It is almost as if Camus' whole point is to remind us that there are thinkers other than Jean-Paul Sartre in the world, and also that he can get along without him very well. Maybe, in other words, and this is the subtext of the whole book: we ought to try to forget 'Monsieur Néant' for a while and think about something else entirely. Or perhaps – in some Zen-like way – not think too much at all and try to *be* more spontaneously. But, like Freud's repressed, Sartre is certainly latent if not manifest. The more Camus tries to forget the more the figure of Sartre keeps on forcing himself on his attention. Sartre, in other words, rather like God – or possibly Satan – is everywhere in the book, even if nowhere visible. The book reads like a considered reply to Sartre's classic jibe, 'I'm more intelligent than you are.' It is possible, Camus argues, to be *too* intelligent and at the same time completely stupid.

We find the idea already sketched out as early as the first *Carnet*, the resistance to ideas: 'What has done me the most harm is abstract ideas.' At first sight, it seems that Camus is holding philosophers and their bad ideas to blame for all our ills. The philosopher is his *bête noire,* the *éminence grise* behind all conspiracies. Camus was haunted by the spectacle of organized mass slaughter in which, by its mid-point, the twentieth century had become so proficient: Nazism in western Europe on the one hand, and Stalinism in the East on the other. And, hanging over the future, the atom bomb that had already been tested out on Japan. Camus saw them as broadly equivalent, variations on the 'apocalyptic' mentality, capable of wiping out all or at least large portions of humanity with a view to improving it. The problem was to explain how this 'Apocalypse Now' attitude – the Final Solution mentality – came to be so pervasive in the world at this point in our history. *The Rebel's* explanation, on the face of it, is: *philosophy and philosophers.*

Nietzsche, the philosopher Camus links most closely to the rise of Nazism, is the archetypal case. The doctrine of the 'will to power' leads in the direction of a real will to total power: from theory to practice. But all of Camus' vocabulary, almost like the page of a thesaurus, hammers away relentlessly at this same theme: irrespective of any particular set of propositions, it is always too much *discourse, reason* (or *rationality*) *metaphysics, intelligence, doctrine, logic, theory, syllogism, argument* (even *mathematics*) that is to blame for the rise of tyranny. It is as if Plato's vision of a society ruled by philosopher kings has come into being – and it is a disaster. The trouble with 'metaphysical revolt' is that it is a protest against everything which therefore values nothing and produces 'absolute negation'. In *The Plague*, evil is decoded as arbitrary, random – pervasive but inexorable and ultimately inexplicable. Here killing on an industrial scale is linked with certain widespread intellectual errors, in fact with intellect generally. The symbolic mind, injecting aesthetics into politics, tends towards a ritual purification of the world.

In this approach, Camus has something in common with George Orwell and Karl Popper, writing in the same post-Second World War period, who attributed the horrors of totalitarianism to the contagious spread of some very lethal ideas (Popper focuses on Plato, Hegel and Marx; Orwell on Lenin, Trotsky, and especially Stalin). Philosophy in the cause of mass murder. But Camus gave his argument a distinctive twist that reflected some of his own personal experiences and leanings. And here he goes off in an altogether different direction. Camus blames totalitarian societies and the concentration camp and our genocidal tendencies on too much sex. So he seems at first to have two rather competing and conflicting arguments going at once, attributing political vices, in the first instance, to too big a brain and then, in contrast, to our super-sized sexuality. Both are maladjusted.

The section in *The Rebel* on the Marquis de Sade helps to clarify the issue. Sade, says Camus, is 'our contemporary' in his 'dream of universal destruction'. The holocaust takes the remote Sadeian castle that is also a torture chamber and turns it into Auschwitz. Sade is a variant of the Don Juan figure of *The Myth of Sisyphus*. But more than a decade has passed since Camus argued that Don Juan was a natural expression of absurdity: the absurd world-view applied to the realm of sexuality. Don Juan kept on repeating himself, but he had no plan, no theory as such, there was no programme. Now the Sadist has a plan, a whole philosophy. Then it appeared that there were no victims, unless it was Don Juan himself. Now, after the Second World War, liaisons have come to seem much more dangerous to Camus, so that the gluttonous satisfaction of sexual appetite – the realm of the hypersexual – is more sinister, more manifestly sadistic, entailing the coercion or repression of others. Absolute war is an extension of rape, but rape on a mass scale. Sade embodies for Camus 'the immoderate energy of desire', 'the inexhaustible law of desire'. Sadism implies not just pain and murder but, more fundamentally, the conviction that one's own personal pleasure takes priority over everything. *If you want it, take it*. Or, as Camus puts it rather more elegantly, in a phrase that seems like a snapshot of so many other episodes, 'the unlimited liberty of desire entails the negation of the other and the suppression of pity'. And 'the maximum of pleasure coincides with the maximum of destruction'. Although Sade is clearly understood as a particular perversion of the sexual instinct, nevertheless the smallest impulse of desire is seen to lead, somewhere down the road, sooner or later, in the direction of 'universal annihilation'. Love and death are intimately entwined. With this perception in mind, it is easy to understand why Camus himself became so troubled, tormented by his own sexuality, because every relationship appeared to him like a potential rehearsal for murder. Somebody was going to get hurt.

But the Sadeian libertine is not just an inexhaustible and immoral sexual athlete. Unlike Don Juan – more of an instinctive pleasure-seeker – he is a thinker too, and a writer. Sade is more of a theoretician of pleasure, and is only a practitioner to prove a point. Herein lies the nexus of the two lines of argument, the one anti-symbolic, the other anti-sexual, that Camus pursues in *The Rebel*. Sade is a sexual philosopher. He had to be, as Camus points out, since he spent most of his life behind bars of one kind or another, notably in the Bastille before the Revolution. Thus Sade articulates the theory of the orgy. He is the 'perfect *homme de lettres*'. Camus traces the roots of the apocalyptic mentality in other writers, notably Dostoyevsky (revolutionary nihilism) and Baudelaire (a 'dandy' and fan of Sade who formulates an 'aesthetics of crime'), Lautréamont and possibly the whole of Romanticism and the poet Milton (a preference for Satan), and certainly André Breton (who said 'the simplest surrealist act consists of dashing down into the street, pistol in hand, and firing blindly, as fast as you can pull the trigger, into the crowd') and the surrealists. But to Camus' mind, they all smack of the Marquis. They are all *ecstatic* writers, conjuring up or invoking an 'antiworld' (in Sartre's phrase), a parallel universe more total and more intense than the real (consider Dalí, for instance, who claims, in the 'Surrealist Seminars on Sex', to be able to induce orgasm at twenty paces). Sade thinks about sex too much, writes, dreams, fantasizes about it; he plans and calculates and develops strategies, rather like Napoleon. For Camus, he is the application of brain to body, the symbolization of the sensual. And this is where the destructive, ultimately apocalyptic logic of sex kicks in, at the point where the savage is transmuted into the symbolic, and the virtual becomes real.

Not that Camus is necessarily against strong emotions. He doesn't expect others (not even himself, most of the time) to sign up to the stipulations of degree zero. Camus is even sympathetic towards the thwarted figure of Heathcliff in *Wuthering Heights* in his furious lust for revenge. He entertains the idea of murder, as he did in *The Outsider*, so long as it is a 'crime of passion' – committed spontaneously, in the heat of the moment – and not a highly premeditated, coolly executed 'crime of logic'. The savage life is sacred for Camus, so long as it remains 'hot', spontaneous and 'passionate', not twisted and perverted by 'cold' reasoning. This may explain why Camus talks about Sade's purely 'mathematical notion' of equality, for example. *The Philosophy of the Boudoir* exemplifies all his work, 'these dozens of volumes stuffed full of atrocities and philosophy'. Sade brings a philosophical mind to bear on the instinctive. He takes the physical and makes it 'metaphysical'. In this sense Sade represents the exact opposite of sex. The philosopher of negation. At the same time he is writing a theory of passion, a literature of orgasm. The philosophy of overstatement not understatement – the advocate of the *hyper*, the ecstatic.

Camus, from his earliest writing on, even in his commentary on Stendhal, thought of writing as a way of curtailing and cooling the rush, the *jaillissement* and the *jet*. He was the *anti-ecstatic* writer and thinker par excellence. For Sartre, in contrast, writing existed in order to stiffen and enhance. The erotic was essentially a literary labour. The ecstatic had to be affirmed in writing if it was to exist at all. The divergence in their attitudes was already clear on that night in a bar in Paris. 'Why are you going to so much trouble?' Sartre was overexerting himself, verbally, to Camus' way of thinking: all he had to do was let it happen. Don't push so hard. It ought to be possible, Camus implied, to have sex spontaneously, without plotting and planning and turning it into semiotics and charade – without thinking about it too hard, without all the emphasis on seduction ('I don't seduce,' he wrote, 'I surrender'). Sade, in other words, sounds a lot like Sartre. Sade was a version of Sartre and Sartre was always potentially Sade. They became a double-act in Camus' mind. It is hard not to hear something of Sartre's voice (denouncing a tree, for example) in the lines Camus quotes from Sade:

> I abhor nature [...] I would like to subvert its plans, thwart its progress, halt the wheeling of the stars, overthrow the spheres that spin through space, destroy everything that serves it, protect whatever harms it, insult it in every one of its works – and yet I cannot succeed.

At the same time, Camus offers a distinctively Sartrean-style critique of Sade. His apocalyptic sexuality bubbles up out of the practice of objectification: he is apt to think of people as things. They don't have feelings or intentions of their own, or at least none that matters; they are not 'for-itself' at all – they are only accessories subordinate to Sade's own feelings. The sadist's capacity for pleasure is maximized at the expense of everyone else's. It is as if he is sucking up all the pleasure in the world and siphoning it off into his own being. But he can never quite get enough, so he must repeat himself endlessly like a darker Don Juan and become a serial murderer, or one of the 'executioners' in Camus' vocabulary.

> At the same instant that sexual crime suppresses the object of pleasure, it also suppresses the pleasure that only exists at the moment of suppression. Then it must procure itself another object in order to kill it afresh, and then another, and ultimately an infinity of all possible objects.

And human beings can become objects only once they have already become symbols or signs in the symbolic mind. To use Camus' mathematical perspective on Sade: individuals become notations in a cold-hearted calculus of pleasure. Camus, then, sounds more like the early Sartre than ever here: defending the freedom of the individual from the oppression of a heartless collectivity. This is the right of the 'deviant' (which might be a better or at least less melodramatic translation than the 'rebel') to deviate. And this is where the writer comes in, for writing is or should be an act of deviation from the existing paradigm of thought, the *epistémè* (to use the term Foucault will later appropriate) – which is exactly what he is doing.

The Rebel used Sartre to critique Sartre. But the logic of the absurd was still at the core of the book. The problem with all mass political movements of the twentieth century, whether utopian or dystopian, was that they promised to fix the absurd, to heal the split between demand and supply. This is one form of ecstatic discourse, 'infinitely demanding' (as the contemporary philosopher Simon Critchley would say). Whereas for Camus we would have to learn to live with the absurd, to love the absurd, not strive to eliminate it, particularly not at the expense of wiping out humanity at large. In *The Myth of Sisyphus*, suicide offered a quick fix. But suicide had evolved into genocide, 'apocalyptic' murder, 'dragging the whole world down too' in a more inclusive annihilation ('suicide and murder are two faces of the same order'). The idea of revolt tweaked the absurd. What 'revolt' revolts against is not so much revolution as *resolution*. The sense of the absurd detects a discrepancy between what is and what could be. There is a temptation to try to make the real rational. The more Camusian idea of revolt is to revolt against, or deviate from, the total fix – 'deliverance' or 'salvation' (with all its religious resonance) in Camus' terms –

and preserve the contradictions and paradoxes rather than trying to iron them all out. The absurdist rebel remains in two minds. And Camus was still tempted by some kind of anti-literary degree zero: 'perfect absurdity aspires to the condition of silence'.

Camus had shifted away from some of his earlier positions, and relinquished the dream of 'unity', for example. Unity, he now believed (as in, say, Rousseau's Social Contract with its theory of the 'general will' and people being 'forced to be free') was always coercive, a fiction laid over the top of disunity. He was still broadly attached to some notion of 'solidarity', but in this more sceptical perspective, there is a risk of over-identification with others, a hyper-empathy that is tantamount to dictatorship. 'One loves humanity in general in order not to have to love any individuals in particular'. Fascistic empathy. It sounds like a typically autistic Sartrean perspective to adopt – it comes close to saying that 'hell is other people', without the bitterness – but Camus and Sartre had never been more divided than now. And, ironically, Camus was at his most Sartrean when he was attacking Sartre.

One of the classic existential themes that Camus wove into *The Rebel* was the insistence on the openness of history, the chaotic unpredictability of outcomes. In *Nausea* Sartre argued that the teleological attitude – the anticipation of an end – is the definition of fiction. Every novelist has an ending in mind when she is telling a story. The beginning makes sense only in terms of an ending. But life isn't like this. We don't – as Heidegger would have it – 'live towards death'. The destiny of the individual is not predestined, the *telos* is just a fiction. In his spirited reply to the ferocious critique of his work published in Sartre's journal, *Les Temps modernes,* Camus complained about existentialism that it was no longer existentialist enough, that it had been inflected by Marxist historicism, whereas it ought in theory to be opposing 'the idea of a foreseeable end to history'. So he would have to do the job instead. *The Rebel* is emphatically anti-historicist: the future is not closed; it cannot simply be inferred from the past. Camus is fond of the *clinamen* – in Lucretius the unpredictable 'swerve' of atoms – as the flag and anthem of the open (but also chaotic or aleatory) society. All those theories – Camus thinks of Hegel and Marx – which derive a 'law' of history, comparable to the laws of physics, that would enable us to predict and order what is to come are fictions, but fictions that when taken seriously lead us down the road to apocalypse now. To the realm of the Final Solution and the Terminator (which might be a better translation of Camus' *le bourreau* than 'Executioner'). 'Revolt, for human beings, is the refusal to be a thing or to be reduced to mere history or narrative.' Revolt (or deviancy), the refined, reaffirmed absurdism, is a form of self-negation, it is the right to contradict oneself: 'Man is the only creature who refuses to be what she is' ('*L'homme est la seule créature qui refuse d'être ce qu'elle est*' – the '*elle*', grammatically correct, introduces a definite twist).

It was a classically disjunctive Sartrean perspective, which could almost have been lifted straight from the pages of *Being and Nothingness* (I am not what I am and am what I am not), but one that Sartre himself no longer so readily subscribed to. Sartre had had enough of sitting in the 'armchair of history'.

17

THE LAST SUPPER

INTERMITTENTLY, IT WAS almost like old times. In 1951 Camus attended some of the rehearsals and the opening night of Sartre's new play, *The Devil and the Good Lord* (the fact that his lover, Maria Casares, was starring in it, was not irrelevant, but still he was there). Sartre offered to publish Camus' chapter on Nietzsche in *Les Temps modernes*, sight unseen (later he said he didn't like it but the offer stood and they published it anyway). Even though they were diverging all the time, there were still flashes of the old comradeship and mutual respect.

There were convergences too, like the reunions of an old band. On 22 February 1952, Camus and Sartre stood together on stage for the last time, at a rally in Paris, united by their common hatred of fascism, supporting Spanish trade unionists who had been sentenced to death by Franco's government. At the end, with night falling, they found a bar and went for a drink together, just as they used to. There was some banter about women, as usual. Then Sartre finally addressed the thorny question of *The Rebel*. After months of post-publication silence, Sartre told Camus that there would be a review appearing in the May issue of *Les Temps modernes*. He anticipated, however, that it would not be a positive review. Camus, who had been feeling ignored (had the book not been published in October?) was more relieved than concerned. It couldn't be that bad, could it? Mixed, perhaps. At least it was an acknowledgement from the intellectual engine room of the Left Bank.

A couple of months later, April 1952, a small bar in the Place Saint-Sulpice, just off the Boulevard Saint-Germain: Sartre, Camus, and Beauvoir were meeting for the very last time as a trio. It could have been like the good old days, almost ten years back, in the middle of the war, when they were all bound together by the threat of a common enemy. Camus was his old self, joking about some of the bad press *The Rebel* had received. Panned by the Right and the Left – it can't be too bad! (In fact it received a whole range of reviews, mostly complimentary, but Camus was apt to fire off angry letters to negative journals.) Sartre and Beauvoir were sympathetic to the classic street fighter's attitude. But it became like a soliloquy from Camus. His old comrades looked away, not quite knowing what to say. Camus had, from their point of view, gone off the rails. According to Beauvoir, Camus 'just took it for granted that we liked [*The Rebel*]'. At the very least he must have supposed that they would give him the benefit of the doubt, some respect, some loyalty – out of friendship.

In reality, they didn't like it. In fact they hated it: the book was so anti-Communist, so anti-existentialist, virtually anti-philo-sophical, it was like he'd gone over to the opposition. He was starting to look like the enemy. But they didn't like to say so, flat-out, to his face. They had, after all, a history of common causes that still bound them together, in principle. So they said nothing. Sartre struggled to work out how to tell Camus the truth about what he really thought without insulting him. Normally he wouldn't think twice about insulting anybody, but, for all the tough-guy talk, he knew that Camus was easily wounded and Sartre (for the time being) was pulling his punches. His solution to the problem was (for once) to climb out of the ring and bring in a surrogate – one of his *Modern Times* team – to take up the fight for him (at least to begin with). The cold war between the two men was about to warm up considerably. Soon there would be no more indirection and displacement and diplomacy. They were moving towards the confrontation that Sartre would later call 'the final break'. Sartre had become enthusiastic about finality in a way he never was before – and about the *break* or *break-up* (or '*rupture*').

In *L'Homme révolté*, Camus is still theoretically in favour of 'revolt'. He makes himself out as a rebel. But he is not so much a fan of the convulsive, blood-spilling, final break as Sartre. He is a toned-down sort of rebel – not planning to take up arms against a sea of troubles, but only to challenge specific injustices. He sees the idea of revolution as a way of trying to rectify the absurd, which cannot be rectified, and which therefore ushers in tyranny and repression, replacing one kind of injustice with another. By trying to make things perfect, revolution makes them considerably worse. If the rebel becomes a revolutionary he can no longer be a true rebel; he has to conform to some political orthodoxy. Clearly he is speaking about – among others – Sartre, but Sartre has become He Who Cannot Be Named. The closest Camus comes to identifying Sartre and possibly Beauvoir too is when he uses the umbrella term of 'our existentialists'. On his analysis of the post-war period, Sartre and Beauvoir are being drawn into the camp of the dogmatic revolutionaries or 'metaphysical rebels'.

Revolt is not clearly defined when it is said, as it is by our existentialists for example (who are also subject, for the time being, to historicism and its contradictions), that there is a progression from revolt to revolution and that the rebel is nothing if he is not also a revolutionary. But the contradiction is, in reality, more complex. The revolutionary must be at the same time a rebel or otherwise he is not even a revolutionary any more, but rather a policeman and bureaucrat who turns against revolt. But if he is a true rebel, then he will end up turning against the revolution itself. Thus there is no progression from revolt to revolution, but only co-existence and ever increasing contradiction.

This could be read as a coded critique of *The Devil and the Good Lord* and the transition of the figure of Goetz from revolt to full-blown revolution. But it was clearly an attack on the position of Sartre himself. If 'our existentialists' were coming out as pro-revolution, then Camus was redefining himself as anti-revolution. The dialogue between them had crystallized into a showdown: the revolutionary vs the rebel. There was scope for *co-existence* but also *ever-increasing contradiction*. Sartre thought in terms of a radical *final break* with the past, Camus more in terms of a continuum – in which old adversaries can keep on squaring up to one another and still share a drink at the bar. If Sartre was Marxist, then Camus had swung around to the school of Groucho Marx: 'I don't want to belong to any club that would have me as a member.' For each man there was still an evil empire at work that had to be stopped and overthrown, but they identified it in opposing ways. Each man thought of himself as fighting injustice but at one level they were fighting one another, in Sartre's binary praxis of antagonistic reciprocity. Each provoked the other, just by being alive. Whenever they delivered some further clarification of what they were about, they sparked one another into going off in divergent, almost opposite directions, forever sharpening the divide between them.

The Boxer and the Goalkeeper, in their mutual caricatures, had evolved into the Great Dictator and the Preacher: Saint Camus vs General Secretary Sartre. If Camus was still counting on some underlying friendship – that initial quizzical, tenuous bond – to overcome and outweigh the increasing friction between them at the level of ideas, he was about to be disillusioned.

18

EASTER 1952

EASTER 1952 FOUND Camus back in the heights of Le
Panelier, far from Paris, breathing cleaner air, fishing and
night-swimming. He had attained some measure of
peace and composure; he was floating, not even writing. Which
was when he received his advance copy of Jeanson's review of
The Rebel. It was like having the mad man interrupt his meditation.

Francis Jeanson was a staffer at *Modern Times*, at twenty-nine
one of the youngest. He had written an exegesis of Sartre's philosophy and, like Sartre, like Merleau-Ponty, had become
increasingly Marxist (he engagingly described himself as 'more
Marxist than the Marxists'). Sartre gave him the job of writing
the review. He didn't want to do the job himself, but he must
have known Jeanson was going to be negative. Perhaps he didn't
realize quite how negative. More hatchet job than review: a
J'accuse-style denunciation. 'I tried to find someone who would
be willing to review it in *Les temps modernes* without being too
harsh,' Sartre recalled later, 'and that was difficult [...] Everybody
loathed the book.'

Jeanson, writing as if – like Sartre – he knew Camus personally (which in fact he didn't), but didn't like him at all, laid into

Camus with almost unabated ferocity for all of twenty pages. Camus (as per Sartre's original jibe) was reviled as 'the Great Priest of Absolute Morality' and an anti-Communist dog. He had not read Marx and Engels and Hegel properly, according to Jeanson, and he was not enough of a materialist to take note of the 'substructures' of economic reality and was only really interested in the intellectual and artistic (the precarious 'super-structure' of society in Marxian terminology). On the one hand, Camus was denounced as an anti-philosopher; on the other hand he also gave too much credit to mere ideas. Jeanson especially objected to the link Camus set up between Marx and Stalin (even though Stalin himself claimed to be the inheritor and exponent of Marx). Camus was a has-been, an old fighter whose glory days were over (Beauvoir's theme) and really ought to retire. His fire had gone out. The whole tone was mocking and derisive – so 'harsh' (to use Sartre's word) that Merleau-Ponty, editing the journal in Sartre's absence, begged Jeanson to reconsider. They compromised on letting Camus have sight of it first, giving him advance warning.

Camus, reading it at his retreat in Le Panelier, felt as if he had been mugged, almost assassinated. Not to mention – reviewed by one of the underlings! An office junior! An *apparatchik*! – treated with contempt. The notebooks capture his state of mind: '*Modern Times*. They allow sin and refuse grace. Thirst for a martyr.' On the same page the word 'hell' comes up more than once, like an echo of Sartre. 'Hell is here, we are living in it. Only those who extract themselves from life can escape.' Clearly, even if he was not actually suicidal, he did not take this review well. 'Paris is a jungle, filled with flea-bitten wild beasts'. He spoke of 'intolerable solitude', but also came close to speak-ing of the binary praxis of antagonistic reciprocity: 'The tragedy is not being alone, but rather *not* being alone.' Aside from being nearly arrested by the Gestapo, this was probably his most paranoid period (on the other hand, other people really were after him). 'Everyone is on my case, they all want to destroy me.' Camus had taken over the mantle of Sartre's older alter ego, Pardaillan: one against all and (especially) all against one. 'This explosion of long-suppressed hatred is striking,' (he wrote to his wife) 'and it proves that these people were *never* my friends and that I always offended them by what I believe, hence this nasty spewing and incapacity to be generous.' Camus felt under attack from all sides, doomed to be misunderstood by even his closest friends. Especially the friends. 'Who will bear witness for us? Our works. Alas, who will defend them? No-one.' In an adjacent entry (September 1952), he named Sartre explicitly, attaching just one bitter epithet (italicized) to the name: *déloyal*, disloyal or unfaithful. Like a lover who had jilted him. 'We only really betray the ones we love.'

It was obvious to Camus that Sartre must have been pulling Jeanson's strings. The assumption was not unreasonable. Even if Sartre was not directly scripting Jeanson's review, Jeanson was anxious to mimic the master – to be more Sartrean than Sartre. In any case, in this context of the increasing polarization between them, Jeanson had taken sides squarely with Sartre and against Camus. In France in the middle of the twentieth century, at this precise moment in history, it was almost impossible not to take sides, politically and philosophically. West or East? Sartre or Camus?

While Sartre was dashing back from Italy and dashing off *The Communists and Peace*, Camus was writing his dignified reply to Jeanson, to be printed in the following issue. Perhaps, all in all, just a little too dignified (certainly for Sartre's taste). At the same time he allowed too much of the wounded pride to show through. Jeanson had drawn blood. Camus might have been better off slugging it out with Sartre; Sartre would have appreciated that. As it was, he didn't even mention the name of Jeanson nor of Sartre, confining himself to addressing 'Monsieur le directeur'. This was verging on ridiculous, even by the standards of formality of the period. He was trying to be too cool, going for the degree-zero attitude even here. And he must have realized that his strategy could not fail to rile Sartre, who feared invisibility and expected to be cited explicitly.

'You call me *Monsieur le directeur* when everybody knows that you and I have been friends for ten years?' Sartre objected to being subsumed into a collective '*vous*', as if 'Jeanson was one of my pseudonyms'. Again, just as in *The Myth of Sisyphus* ('a writer of today') and *The Rebel* ('our existentialists') Camus seemed to be trying to suppress the very name of Sartre, as if he didn't exist. Or as if, by not mentioning him, he could make him cease to exist. A vain hope. Camus spent half the article complaining of distortion and clarifying and defending his original argument. He was not anti-historicist, but he refused to make history into an 'absolute'. If I say the sky is blue and you say that I describe it as black, either I am mad or you are deaf; my work is evolving in the direction of solidarity – if you say the opposite you are dreaming or lying.

But he could not resist taking a poke at Sartre towards the end. As one of the old militants 'who never refused any part of the struggles of their time', he was getting 'a little tired' of receiving lessons on political action from 'schoolteachers who only ever aimed their armchairs in the direction of history'. Referring back to his joke at the expense of Sartre when he found him snoozing at the opera, Camus was reminding Sartre as explicitly as possible (without of course mentioning him by name) that you never really did enough for the Resistance, did you? (Unless you count *teaching* during the war.) Yet now *you* lecture *me* on the virtue of engagement? You cannot be serious. And, by the way, I notice that *Modern Times* has remained silent about the gulag – the Communist concentration camps – as if it prefers to take no notice of the practical consequences of its own theories. Maybe the old existentialist would at least have mentioned Stalinism, *n'est-ce pas*? It was a retort aimed at Sartre in particular, not at Jeanson (who was of a younger generation). Camus was effectively admitting that everything he wrote in *The Rebel* was a direct assault on Sartre's position. The fight was right out in the open now; the seconds were out. The old boxer was honour-bound to hit back.

19

GLOVES OFF

ND HIT BACK HE DID (in the following issue of *Modern Times*) – with another twenty pages and even more aggression than Jeanson and Camus combined. He was like a poker player upping the ante, trying to burn out the opposition, leaving just one player still in the game. Just as he had taken over the argument from Merleau-Ponty, now he took over from Jeanson. 'Unfortunately you have so deliberately put me on trial, and in such an ugly tone of voice, that I can no longer remain silent without losing face. Thus, I shall answer you, without anger, but unsparingly (for the first time since I have known you).' The gloves were finally off.

Sartre begins flat-out with the end of their relationship. It is a farewell, a valediction, almost an obituary. He assumes that the knockout blow has already been landed. 'My dear Camus, our friendship was never easy, but I will miss it.' He fuses the personal, the political, and the philosophical, and finds Camus wanting in all these categories (conceited, timid, shallow). 'A mix of gloomy arrogance and vulnerability always discouraged people from telling you the whole truth.' Well, it isn't going to stop Sartre, not this time. But if Camus was wounded by the review, Sartre – for all his fighting talk – has clearly been hurt over the long-term by Camus' neglect of his work, which may explain why he has to reassert, in his haughty professorial way, that he is simply *more intelligent* than Camus: my stuff is just too hard for a country bumpkin like you. His greatest crime is 'philosophical incompetence'. 'I don't dare advise you to consult *Being and Nothingness*. Reading it would seem needlessly arduous to you: you detest the difficulties of thought.' Perhaps he knew that Camus couldn't get through it. At least he and Hegel had this in common, Sartre argued: that Camus had read neither of them. There are flashes of the classic Sartre – he takes Camus to task for treating Jeanson as if he were 'an object, a dead man'. 'You speak *of him* as though he were a soup tureen or a mandolin, never *to him*.' By the same token, there is the old resentment, masquerading as a kind of respect. 'What is disconcerting about your letter is that it is too *written*.' Camus' attitude is 'pure literature', he is 'Chief Prosecutor' for the 'Republic of Beautiful Souls', but he is therefore guilty of a 'racism of moral beauty'. Sartre has to heap scorn on any concern with style – to 'shoot down Beauty' just as his hero Mathieu did. It explains why he now scorns not just poetry (Baudelaire) but fiction (Camus) too.

He has to concede that Camus *used* to be a role model. 'How we loved you then,' Sartre writes, harking back to 1944. 'You had been for us – you could again be tomorrow – the admirable conjunction of a person, an action, and a work [. . .] then you were not far from being exemplary.' Sartre is so generous, so effusive, in his admiration that it threatens to throw the argument off kilter. 'If I say "your first contact with History", it is not to imply that I had another kind and that it was better. All of us intellectuals had the same one then, and if I call it *yours*, it is because you *lived* it more deeply and fully than many of us (myself included).' Only Camus attained some kind of elusive 'synthesis', a perfect 'equilibrium [...] that could be realized once only, for one moment, in one man.'

But, Sartre hurries to add, this is all past tense. Camus belongs to the past because he lacks a sense of the present. He doesn't live in the real world any more – like a ghost. Just as Camus took up some of the tenets of existentialism to attack the arch-existentialist, so too Sartre starts to echo the old Camus, even as he is attacking him. Now *I* am committed, and *you* are running away from conflict like a coward. It is as if Sartre is trying to be more like Camus than Camus. He has taken over the baton from his old rival and proceeds to beat him with it. Now I am the man of action, the man of the people. Whereas Camus is a lonely existential soul, refusing to belong to any clubs or to take sides, retreating (or 'retiring') into 'solitude', determined to deviate. Sartre mercilessly maps out the X in their crossed intellectual paths. Sartre himself is now more anti-literature than Camus ever was, and therefore, by the same token, anti-Camus. From his point of view, Camus has gone from being the outsider to the insider. On the one hand, he describes Camus as a 'dictator' and even a 'terrorist', and represents him as the bourgeois establishment that he, Sartre, must overthrow at all costs. On the other, the boxer is accusing the goalkeeper of being a pussy, of chickening out of the big moments (of 'History', always now with a capital H). 'The problem [of History] is not to know its end, but only to give it one.' To Sartre's way of thinking, Camus can never bring himself to be quite violent enough. The rhetoric is an example of the tough-guy attitude that he is recommending, an exercise in verbal GBH, an attempt to annihilate Camus once and for all, to deliver the KO.

Sartre admits that most people (and especially all their enemies) are going to laugh at this classic '*querelle des auteurs*'. But perhaps the funniest line of all he saves for the very end of this letter/essay/indictment: 'I have said what you meant to me, and what you are to me now. But whatever you may say or do in return, *I refuse to fight you*' [my emphasis]. Yet for the previous twenty pages he has done nothing but that: he has had Camus on the ropes, pounding him to a pulp. It is the end of a friendship, but still not quite a knockout. 'So much brought us together; so little separated us. But this little was still too much: even friendship tends to be totalitarian; it demands agreement in everything – or else the bust-up.' But Camus – 'a wounded bull' according to Maria Casares – is still standing. Nothing has ended. The relationship may be broken, but one way or another the fight will continue until one or both are dead.

This is something that Camus, for one, accepted, looking back fondly to the tradition of the duel – as if the fight was only just beginning:

> In other times, now regarded as backward, one at least had the right to challenge [to a duel] and to kill without being ridiculed. Idiotic to be sure, but this made it less easy to be insulting.

Given the options, he would have preferred pistols at dawn, the clash of steel, or fists. As it was, words dominated. 'Art is a revenge,' he wrote. Beauvoir, piling in behind Sartre, was quick to stick the boot in. She wrote *The Mandarins*, her autobiographical novel of the post-war period, partly to pay homage to Sartre (Robert Dubreuilh) but largely to analyse and deride Camus – under the name of Henri Perron, a self-tormented writer and newspaper editor. His novels are derided as 'mortally classical', his left-wing slogans are a cover for right-wing sympathies, and the only 'action' he seems to be capable of is having affairs that depress his wife.

Camus was probably right to take it all personally. The personal was philosophical and philosophy was personal. And he was justified in assuming that there was an element of sexual friction or frisson amid the rhetoric. He recalled how they would meet up every week, the three of them, Camus, Beauvoir and Sartre, and then one day the Beaver walked through the door and said a 'friend' of hers would like to sleep with Camus. He brushed it off saying that he was 'accustomed to making [his] own choices' – and realized that she bore a grudge on this account. Whether or not the 'friend' was real or imaginary, it was clear that Beauvoir, having enjoyed the intimacy of Camus, and his confessional relationship with her, was bound to start hyping up all his inadequacies as a human being, just as Sartre did.

In *Being and Nothingness*, Sartre spoke of the law of perpetual conflict with the other. In his response to Camus, he used the terms 'split' or 'break' (*rupture*), uncoupling (*décrochage*), and also, more dramatically, 'torn by civil war' (it was no longer clear if this was supposed to be France or the two of them or philosophy at large). Camus adopted the same stance when he said, in 1957, in his address to the University of Uppsala, 'perhaps there is no other peace for the artist than what he finds in the heat of combat'. The word *combat* recalled not just the era of the Resistance but also the journal Camus edited, which carried a slogan on its masthead: 'In war as in peace, the last word belongs to those who never surrender.' The binary praxis of antagonistic reciprocity had reached its peak. Friend had morphed into foe.

'There are always good reasons for murdering another man,' Camus wrote in *The Fall*. 'It is, on the other hand, impossible to justify why he should live.'

20

WAR OF WORDS

AFTER THE WAR, the French army did to Algeria what the Nazis had been doing to France. Massacres and torture were commonplace. The 'Algerian War' (in effect between the government and the FLN, the National Liberation Front) lasted from 1954 (when the French finally pulled out of Indochina) to 1962, when the colonial regime was brought to an end and around a million European (mostly French) *pieds noirs* were forced out. Perhaps it went back to the nineteenth century, when French settlers (and Camus' ancestors), backed up by force of arms, first began to arrive in Algeria. And perhaps, at some level, it has never really finished. But it was clear that Sartre and Camus were always going to be on opposite sides in any war of words.

In the thirties and forties Camus was already reporting on the 'crisis in Algeria' and studying famine and unemployment in Kabylie. Sartre espoused the logic of decolonization and by the mid-fifties was underwriting and supporting guerrilla warfare, while Camus protested against 'the logic of violence' and conjured up elusive forms of rapprochement (for example, could Algeria become like Switzerland?). In 1946 Sartre wrote of the 'nationalization of literature', thinking of how he and

Camus and other individual writers were being called upon to embody or express the whole of France. He might just as reasonably have used the word 'globalization'. But at the same time it is possible to speak of the *personification* of vast and enduring conflicts. Sartre identified fully with the colonized; Camus found himself not exactly on either side, 'neither a victim nor an executioner' as he maintained, but whether he liked it or not identified with the colonial power – the *colon* that Sartre detested. It was a stand-off between the 'Communist' (Sartre from Camus' point of view) and the 'fascist' (Camus seen by Sartre).

Like shadow boxers, Sartre and Camus conducted their dialogue indirectly or vicariously over many years, through essays and interviews and polemic (which I quote from here), but it still seems as if they are addressing one another. As Tony Judt observed, 'the various books and articles of [. . .] Camus, Sartre and others constitute one long conversation, in which close attention was paid to the arguments of one's colleagues and opponents – more attention, in fact, than was ever paid to the events they were purportedly discussing.'

SARTRE: No one today can be unaware that we have ruined, starved, and massacred an already impoverished population in order to make them fall to their knees.

CAMUS: I have defended all my life (and you know that this has cost me exile from my country) the idea that we must have wide-ranging and profound reforms.

SARTRE: These reforms will be a matter for the Algerian people themselves, when they have achieved freedom.

CAMUS: Some kind of progress is always achieved whenever a political problem is replaced by a human problem. It is up to us to bring down the walls that separate us.

SARTRE: Colonization is neither a collection of chance events nor the statistical aggregate of thousands of individual undertakings. It is a system that was put in place around the middle of the nineteenth century. Algeria is simply the clearest and most readable example of the colonial system.

CAMUS: From what you say, it would really seem that Algeria is populated by a million colonists wearing cravats, smoking a cigar, and riding around in Cadillacs. Whereas 80% of French Algerians are not colonists but wage-earners or shopkeepers.

SARTRE: It is not true that there are good colonists and bad colonists: there are only colonists, end of story. Exploitation and oppression require the application of violence and the presence of the army.

CAMUS: Speaking for my own family, they have always been poor and without hatred, and have never exploited nor oppressed anyone.

SARTRE: The colonist has even created new additions to culture that reflect the needs of the metropolis far more than those of the natives. He is therefore double and contradictory: he has his 'homeland', France, and his 'country', Algeria. A republican in France, he becomes in Algeria a fascist who hates the Republic and who loves the army. Could it be otherwise? No, not so long as he remains a colonist. The colonist's only real interest is to sacrifice Algeria to the profit of France.

CAMUS: The time of imperialism is over. And the West which, in a space of ten years, has given autonomy to a dozen colonies deserves more credit, respect and patience in this regard than Russia which, in the same period, has colonized or placed under an implacable protectorate a dozen countries each with a great and ancient civilization.

SARTRE: Any intention no matter how pure, if it arises inside this circle of hell, is automatically corrupted from the very outset.

CAMUS: Presuppositions and a bundle of ideas taken off the shelf become odious when they are applied to a world in which people are dying of cold and children are reduced to eating the food of beasts without having the instinct that would prevent them from perishing.

SARTRE: The system is pitiless.

CAMUS: We need a confederation of peoples, based on principles of justice and reason [...] Either we have a marriage of convenience or a fight to the death between two xenophobias.

SARTRE: A lot of fine words: liberty, equality, fraternity, love, honour, homeland, etc. None of which ever prevented us in the slightest from using at the very same time a lot of racist pejoratives: filthy nigger, filthy Jew, filthy Arab.

CAMUS: It is absurd to describe a whole country as racist on account of the exploits of a minority.

SARTRE: Our beautiful souls are racist.

CAMUS: Everything we do for truth, whether in French or any human language, is against hatred. At any price we must bring peace to those peoples who have been torn apart and tormented by suffering that has gone on for too long.

SARTRE: Colonialism is in the process of destroying itself. It is infecting us with its racism. It forces our young people to go and die for Nazi principles that we were fighting against together ten years ago. Colonialism over there, fascism here: one and the same thing.

CAMUS: The world today is immersed in hatred. Everywhere violence and force, massacres and shouting, darken the atmosphere even after we believed we had inoculated it against this most toxic poison.

SARTRE: We have to confront this unexpected spectacle: the striptease of our humanism. Here it is, at last, stripped naked and not beautiful: it was only ever an ideology of lies, the decorative justification of pillage; all its sweetness and light and its concern for language underwrote our aggression. They look so fine, the pacifists: neither victims nor executioners! Come off it! If you are not a victim then you are undoubtedly an executioner.

CAMUS: When violence responds to violence in an escalating delirium that makes the language of reason impossible, it cannot be the role of an intellectual to excuse from afar the violence of one side and condemn that on the other.

SARTRE: There is no 'Third Way' [...] We, the colonized, have a choice: remain terrified or become terrible. We must kill: to take out a European is like killing two birds with one stone, wiping out simultaneously both the oppressor and the oppressed. The result is: one man dead and another man free.

CAMUS: Some of our pundits seem to have the obscure idea that the Arabs have acquired the right to slay and mutilate.

SARTRE: It is not their violence in the first place: it is ours, turned back against us, which only grows as it tears them apart. Murderous madness is the unconscious of the colonized. Hatred is their only precious possession. This is the time of the boomerang.

CAMUS: We must condemn with the same force, and without mincing our words, the terrorism applied by the FLN to French and, even more so, Arab civilians. This terrorism is a crime that cannot be excused or allowed to continue.

SARTRE: They don't give a fuck. For all the difference it makes to them, you can shove it up your arse.

CAMUS: Whatever the origins of the Algerian tragedy, no matter how ancient and profound, one fact remains: no cause justifies the death of the innocent.

SARTRE: The signs of violence will not be wiped away by any gentle touch: only more violence can destroy them. And the colonized will be cured of his colonial neurosis only by hunting down the colonist.

CAMUS: Someone will always reply: the time for reconciliation is past and now all that is left is to fight a war and win it [. . .] The role of the intellectual is to clarify definitions in order to disintoxicate minds and pacify fanaticism, even against the tide.

SARTRE: Too many of our pseudo-intellectuals have said, 'Our colonial methods are not what they ought to be, there are too many inequalities in our overseas territories. But I am against violence from wherever it comes: I don't wish to be either executioner or victim and that is why I am opposed to the revolt of the colonized against the colonial powers.'

CAMUS: Gandhi demonstrates that one can struggle for one's own people and overcome, without for a single day ceasing to remain honourable. Whatever the cause you are defending, it will always be besmirched by the indiscriminate massacre of an innocent crowd where the killer knows in advance that he will be killing women and children.

SARTRE: Understand this if you can: if violence had begun this very evening, if exploitation and oppression had never existed on earth, then perhaps the display of non-violence could conceivably calm the storm. But if the whole regime and even your own non-violent thoughts are conditioned by an age-old oppression, then your passivity only serves to place you on the side of the oppressors.

CAMUS: Then we are returning to the jungle in which the only principle is violence.

SARTRE: On the solution to the Algerian problem, friends can differ without ceasing to have regard for one another. But what about summary executions? What about torture? Is it possible to retain friendship for someone who would approve of them?

CAMUS: Reprisals against civilians and the practice of torture are crimes. Personally speaking, I am now only interested in actions that, here and now, are capable of sparing further pointless bloodshed.

SARTRE: Can we cure ourselves? Yes. Violence, like the spear of Achilles, can heal the wounds that it has made.

CAMUS: Then we are locked into an agon, doomed to commit the maximum harm against one another, implacably [. . .] These two personalities, linked to one another by the force of circumstances, can choose to associate together – or destroy one another.

SARTRE: You, so liberal, so humane, pushing your love of culture to the point of precocity, you pretend to forget that you have colonies and that massacres are carried out in your name.

CAMUS: And yet you and I, we resemble one another so much, sharing the same culture, the same hope, a sense of fraternity for so long [. . .] We are condemned to live together.

21

THE CALL

IT IS THE ULTIMATE writer's fantasy. Posterity calling: 'You have been awarded this year's Nobel Prize for literature. Congratulations.' All those years of struggle and abuse and doubt and the terrible feeling of futility – finally, you are justified, this is the accolade, the vindication you have been waiting for, a message from the (Nordic) gods. And, in purely material terms, it translates out as: 'Who Wants to Be a Millionaire?' The best pay cheque of your writing career. It happened to both Camus and Sartre, but neither of them could just lie back and enjoy it.

First floor, Chez Marius, Paris, 16 October 1957. Camus (a month short of turning forty-four) was having lunch with Patricia Blake, the attractive young Smith College graduate he first met and had an affair with in New York. A courier from Gallimard, his publishers, came up to them and informed Camus that he had won the Nobel. What did he do? Crack open a bottle of champagne and celebrate? No. More like: have an asthma attack. He could hardly breathe. He muttered that Malraux, the older French writer who influenced the young writer, 'should have had it'. He had taken to rating Malraux above Sartre. Malraux, he would assert from time to time, was his master.

When Sartre heard the news from his secretary, he said, with a degree of grudging admiration, 'He didn't steal it.'

In old francs, the prize was worth 18,777,583 (now around a million euros or 1.4 million dollars). Camus' first thought was to turn it down. He felt as if he didn't really deserve it. His second thought was that the decision made about as much sense as anything else so he decided to go ahead and accept, but in a mood – as usual – of uncertainty. As if it was really a mistake and eventually he would be exposed as a fraud. 'Nobel,' he recorded in his *Carnets*. 'Strange feeling of despondency and melancholy. At 20, poor, naked, I knew true glory.'

His twelve-year-old daughter was not too impressed either. 'Is there a Nobel for acrobats?' she asked. Her twin, his son Jean, denounced him as an insignificant 'writer about nothing at all' [*un petit écrivain de rien du tout*]. Overwhelmed by parties and official dinners and well-wishers and journalists and photographers, Camus turned to yoga to calm down and de-stress – to bracket it all out in a self-editing *epoché*. At the same time he was enjoying free champagne at La Coupole and a telegram of congratulation from William Faulkner, who won the prize in 1949. When his head cleared he took the trouble to write a letter of thanks to his old school teacher, Louis Germain. 'Without your teaching and your example, none of this could have happened.'

Camus' last novel, *The Fall*, had been published the previous year, with its 'judge-penitent' hero, Clamence, reminiscing (as Ronald Aronson demonstrates) in ways that subtly recall episodes of the Sartre/Camus drama. But we now know – it was suspected at the time – that one of the factors in his election was the essay he had written in 1957 denouncing the death penalty. This work, among so much else he had written, in the view of the Swedish Academy, fitted the explicit Nobel criterion of 'the most outstanding work in an ideal direction'. At this time the guillotine was still the standard form of execution in France (and therefore its colonies likewise). Hence the title of the essay, 'Reflections on the Guillotine'. Camus recalls his father getting up early one day and taking a long bus-ride to go and witness a public execution (the story came from his mother since he had no personal memory of his father). The condemned man was guilty of robbing and slaughtering an entire family and Camus *père* felt that justice was 'being done' and he ought to be there to bear witness. But even he had been revolted by the spectacle of organized state-sponsored brutality and when he came home he threw up and flung himself on the bed and kept silent afterwards (the family story comes up in *The Outsider* too, when Meursault, contemplating his own execution, harks back to his father's experience).

It was clear that the goalkeeper would always try to save the condemned man. Camus put forward many arguments against the guillotine and the death penalty more generally – statistics, logic, sympathy for the convicted, the fallibility of the judicial system, the fallibility of the system of execution – but the main reason he objected so strongly to the guillotine is that it symbolized calculation and premeditation. It was a point he had already made in *The Rebel:* he could accept the crime of passion but not the crime of logic, the emotional Heathcliff and the *crime passionnel* but not the guillotine. Since most murders are not premeditated, Camus argued, the threat of execution could not serve as a deterrent. But more than this, the guillotine, coming out of the French Revolution (introduced by Joseph-Ignace Guillotin in 1789), reminded Camus too much of the metaphysical demand for purification that was characteristic of the Revolution and the post-revolutionary state. Even the

Marquis de Sade, so enthusiastic about inflicting pain, was against it. Locked up in the Bastille, forced to witness many executions, Sade could not accept that murder was compatible with the law. With the guillotine, the law was committing the very crime that it claimed to be punishing.

But there is one more *reflection* that, in all the arguments ever brought against the death penalty, remains (so far as I know) unique to Camus. The much-touted advantages of the guillotine were its speed and efficiency. Compared with hanging or the axe, there was never any need to repeat the procedure. Once the blade started to drop, the guillotine was not only infallible, but – so it was widely believed – clinical. And supposedly painless (inducing at worst, according to Guillotin, 'a slight sensation of coolness in the neck'). Virtually altruistic, as if we were actually doing the condemned a favour by guillotining.

But hold on, said Camus, things were not quite so transparent as they were made out. How did we really know how the condemned felt about it? Specifically at the very moment when his or her head was being so efficiently removed. Camus, as he did with Meursault, put himself squarely on the side of the victim. And found himself in a twilight zone between life and death. Lavoisier, the great French chemist (and co-discoverer with Priestley of oxygen) was condemned to die on the guillotine by the Safety Committee of the French Revolution ('The Revolution has no need of scientists,' declared the prosecutor). He devised (it is said) a final experiment to be carried out at the time of his execution: he would keep blinking even after he was decapitated and his assistant would keep a tally of how many times he managed to blink. He was supposed to have blinked more than twenty times. Similarly, Camus theorized that consciousness must persist even after the removal of the head. It was of course impossible to say for how long – Camus thought minutes or even hours – but since it was possible to think of 'stretching out a moment across the whole of time', it was as likely to apply to horror as to beauty. Therefore the guillotine became, contrary to received wisdom, an instrument of torture. Camus cited one case where the head, although separated from the body, was supposed to have responded to his (its?) name. The victim was still alive and yet on the very threshold of death, or perhaps somewhere ambiguously between the two states. It was not hard for Camus to imagine since this was exactly how he lived his own life. 'You are zombies!' Sartre once suggested (to French people at large, especially of a colonial mentality). Perhaps Camus felt that it applied to him in particular – and to anyone else with their head on (or off) the block. This was just what it feels like to be alive. To be one of the condemned, awaiting execution.

Handing down a sentence, passing judgement: Camus was sceptical about it even in *The Outsider,* where Meursault is found guilty and sentenced to death (and therefore the guillotine). He was always painfully sensitive to other people's opinions, especially published reviews, no matter how established he became. He revolted against Sartre's judgement and Jeanson's verbal assassination ('the fifty pages are deliberately insulting' he wrote to his wife). Whereas Sartre was self-confident and insouciant, Camus was always plagued by doubts and regrets. Ironically, he felt similarly tormented by the judgement, even though positive, by the Swedish Academy. He found that it reminded him too much of a life-sentence. The Swedish ambassador said that, as a great Resistance fighter, Camus was like a hero from Corneille. But Camus couldn't help but feel that the Nobel judges were entombing him with their verdict. Perhaps this explains why, according to Patricia Blake, he appeared 'suffocated'. To his friend Roger Quilliot, Camus seemed 'as anguished as if he had been buried alive'. Camus wrote to his cousin Nicole that the award of the Nobel aroused 'more doubts than certainties [...] the malaise of the artist remains incurable: he dies without ever really knowing anything.'

Having drinks with some of his old *Combat* comrades, he came out with a mock-Stockholm speech: 'Remember that shit thou art and unto shit thou shalt return.' And having lunch with his old mentor, Jean Grenier, on the Boulevard Montparnasse, he shook his head again, regretfully: 'I am going to have more enemies than ever.' He turned down the offer of an interview in *L'Express*. He wanted it all to go away. The Nobel would not do him any favours, he knew, would not reconcile him with anyone. The war would go on, one way or another: one against all and all against one. Inevitably, in his acceptance speech on 10 December 1957 in the Concert Hall in Stockholm, he returned to the theme of war, recalling that he was like many others 'who were twenty at the time of Hitler's rise to power and the Moscow show trials, who received their further education via the Spanish civil war, the Second World War, the realm of concentration camps and the Europe of torture and imprisonment.'

Camus was particularly irked – it was virtually his worst nightmare – when he was twice praised as 'an existentialist' by members of the Swedish Academy, almost as if they had mixed him up with someone else, inflaming the old anxiety of influence. Whatever he did he couldn't seem to get out of Sartre's shadow. Returning to France he said that the Nobel 'aged me overnight'. He refused to have a portrait medal cast by the National Library. He didn't want to be turned into an icon. Despite which he was a celebrity in Paris, pursued by admirers in restaurants, and an American radio broadcast rhymed 'famous' with 'Ka-mus'. He was probably the most notorious writer of his time.

This perhaps explains why he went back to Algiers at this point – to escape his own notoriety. When he got in a taxi, the driver said he thought he looked familiar. I'm Albert Camus, said Camus. 'Of course,' exclaimed the cabbie, 'the goalkeeper!' Then he ran into an old schoolmate, who had become a plumber. 'Well, Albert,' said the plumber, 'what's new? What are you up to these days?' He was just one of the boys again, back on the beach, sun-tanned and salty. It was a brief moment of friendship and harmony: soon they would all be either dead or exiled from Algeria.

Sartre, when his call finally came through, in October 1964, when he was fifty-nine years old, was entirely different. He was sure he deserved the Nobel but he didn't want it any more. There was no question of Malraux here, nobody more deserving; it was long overdue, in fact. The headline in *Aurore* magazine summed it up neatly: 'SARTRE DOES THE DOUBLE'. That is:

1. He is awarded the Nobel.
2. He rejects the Nobel.

François Mauriac, the Catholic novelist who received the award in 1952, paid homage: a Nobel rejected was worth more than one accepted. 'This great writer is also a true man, and therein lies his glory [. . .] It is because he is a true man that Sartre can touch even those most alien to his thought and most hostile to the side he has taken.' Sartre had managed to top the writer's fantasy by telling the Swedish Academy to get lost. But while ardent supporters praised and congratulated him for the grand gesture, anti-Sartreans came out with a string of derogatory hypotheses to explain the rejection.

1. He is so shabby he can't face smartening up to receive it.
2. He doesn't want to upset the Beaver.
3. He is after yet more publicity by slapping the Nobel judges in the face.
4. He is annoyed that his old rival Camus (even though now dead) got it before him.

Sartre, in his clear-sighted way, had long been expecting the call. Perhaps ever since Camus got his. When he got wind that he was likely to be awarded the prize he tried to head them off at the pass and warn them that he had already taken the decision not to accept if offered. In his letter of 14 October 1964 he was polite, expressing his 'profound esteem' for the Swedish academy, but firm. He regretted the presumption implicit in assuming he could be a candidate. But the letter failed to reach them in time and the decision was formally announced anyway. 'The Nobel Prize has been awarded this year to the French writer Jean-Paul Sartre for his work, which, in the spirit of freedom and in the name of truth, has had a great impact on our era.' Which was then followed by a subsequent message from Stockholm: 'The nominated laureate has just informed us that he does not wish to accept this prize. The fact that he is declining this distinction does not alter in the least the validity of the nomination. The Academy announces that the awarding of the prize cannot take place.'

Sartre was not the first writer to assert that the Nobel had a strong political element. But the complaint generally came – however legitimately – from those who had been passed over. Even though it was clear that the Nobel judges tended to disapprove of right-wing writers (Malraux's association with General de Gaulle probably sank him, for example), and that Sartre was therefore the beneficiary of a leftish swerve, nevertheless the whole thing was too anti-East, insufficiently socialist, for his taste. He was supposed to be giving an interview at the Café L'Oriental to the very same Swedish journalist who had once interviewed Camus when he got the Nobel. But it quickly turned into a lecture or a sermon. 'Today, the Nobel prize appears to be a distinction reserved for writers of the Western bloc and rebels of the Eastern bloc [. . .] I do not mean to say that the Nobel Prize is a "bourgeois" prize [. . .] I know that, in itself, the Nobel is not a prize limited to the Western bloc, but it is what one makes of it [. . .] The only possible combat on the cultural front should aim at the peaceful coexistence of the two cultures, that of the East and that of the West [. . .]'

The rejection was more than a just political gesture, however. Sartre had consistently shied away from objectification by others, any kind of official label or status, which he feared would turn him into a thing (like a mandolin or a soup tureen, as he would say), instead of no-thing. He pointed out that he had likewise refused the Legion d'honneur after the war and the offer of a chair at the Collège de France in the fifties. 'It is not the same thing if I sign Jean-Paul Sartre as if I sign Jean-Paul Sartre, Nobel Prize winner. A writer must refuse to allow himself to be transformed into an institution, even if it takes place in the most hon-ourable form.' In other words, he feared the same fate as Camus: being buried alive and suffocated under the weight of success.

Many years later Sartre would explain that he rejected the Nobel because he couldn't tolerate the notion of a 'hierarchy' in literature. Did it mean that he was a 'better' writer than any non-Nobel laureate? The idea made no sense. Sartre was too egalitarian to accept the Nobel, refusing the kind of pre-eminence it implied.

But there was an even more compelling reason for the rejection. The prize, after all, was for 'literature'. And Sartre had ceased to believe in literature. He thought of it all as some kind of hoax. It was implicit in his critique of Camus – he was too 'beautiful', too much of a stylist (even though Camus thought of himself as a degree-zero writer). Of course Sartre couldn't give up writing as such, he was addicted for life, he would continue to 'rush' it out, working 'day and night' – write or suffocate! – but he was determined to make his writ-ing as unliterary and as purely pragmatic and workmanlike as possible. A description of the world, nothing more. No more style, no more literature (but no degree zero either). Just as Roquentin gave up on biography, so too Sartre had long ago given up on *The Roads to Freedom* novel sequence, halfway through the fourth volume, disillusioned with the whole fic-tional game. His writing had a job to do, 'to call a cat a cat' as he puts it in *What Is Literature?* No more poetry for me. In the forties, at the end of the war, Sartre had published a long essay denouncing Charles Baudelaire, France's best-known poet, as an exemplar of 'bad faith', denying his own freedom and attributing his malaise to society and his step-father. Perhaps all poetry, he thought, was like Baudelaire: too many flowery metaphors and similes, something was always 'like' something else, there was no firm principle of un-relatedness. Now he extended his scepticism to include any literature of a poetic persuasion, or perhaps all of it. Why go around making stuff up? We had the Nazis, who needed ... rats, for example?

Whereas for Camus in *The Rebel* the whole point of literature is that it is deviation (or 'revolt'), an admission of our failure to be perfect realists (God alone could be one), Sartre tried increasingly to exclude the detotalized in favour of a hypothetical 'totalization' of pure information. It was something that Jules Verne once said scathingly of the work of his rival, H. G. Wells: '*Mais il invente!*' (But he is making it up!). Sartre, the great reader of Verne, might have said something similar. In his autobiography, *Words* (for which, ironically, he was in part awarded the prize), Sartre dedicates himself to demystifying 'the literature myth'. Flaubert would become the great *bête noire* and icon of literariness in his massive *The Family Idiot* project. In his grand gesture of rejection, he was rejecting his own overly literary childhood, but also rejecting other winners of the Nobel Prize for literature.

Unlike Camus, Sartre appeared not in the least torn or tormented or angst-ridden about his decision. He was perfectly cheerful and unequivocal. What eventually came to haunt him was the 250,000 Swedish kronor that he so blithely passed up. 'With the sum the laureate receives, one could support a number of important organizations and movements. Personally, I would begin with the Apartheid committee in London.' There was talk he would have given the cash to the Tupamaros Marxist guerrillas in Uruguay. Perhaps this was the closest Sartre had come to a personal act of literary guerrilla warfare – as if he was planting a small bomb, however politely, under the hated bourgeoisie, by rejecting their supreme accolade. But, again, as so often, he was at the same time defining himself in opposition to his old adversary, Camus. Sartre refused to belong to any club that would have Camus as a member.

22

WHAT IT FEELS LIKE
TO BE DEAD

CAMUS' FRIEND AND PUBLISHER Michel Gallimard (along with Ringo Starr, Ava Gardner, and the King of Morocco) owned an unusual, expensive, and elegant car. This is (roughly) what it looked like:

One advert described it as 'the fastest 4-seater sports coupé in the world'. It had a 360 horsepower engine and was capable of up to 240 kph.

The car was a Facel Vega. Facel (an acronym standing for Forge et Ateliers de Construction d'Eure et Loire, i.e., Steelworks and Construction Workshops of the *département* of Eure et Loire) switched from metal stamping to car manufacturing in the early 1950s. The Vega was introduced in 1954. It began as a two-door but in 1956 Facel developed a four-door model, with a bigger engine and rear-hinged doors – known as 'suicide doors', because it would be relatively easy to open them at speed and fling yourself out. They virtually open themselves and invite you to jump (and were popular with gangsters of the thirties because they enabled you to dispose of people with style). But the main problem with the four-door was that – although it was known as the 'Excellence' – a central pillar had been taken out, which made the car less rigid and its handling much less secure. In the early sixties, Facel attempted to penetrate the sports car market with the Facellia. It was a disaster. The Vega had used a Chrysler engine, but the Facellia's was all French, which sounded like a good idea – demonstrating the independence of France from American influence – except that it had a bad habit of not working. The Facellia sank and the company folded in 1964.

The sporty, speedy two-door Vega had its own problems. Michel Gallimard, for example, had some anxieties about the rear left wheel, which had a tendency to seize up. And there was known to be a lot of freeplay in the Facel Vega's steering. The mechanic who repaired Gallimard's said: 'This car is a coffin on wheels.' This is what Gallimard's car eventually looked like:

Michel Gallimard was a friend to both Camus and Sartre and one of the family behind the company that published all their works. He tried to remain on good terms with both men despite the clashes between them (his brother, Robert, called their split 'the end of a love story'). He was a kind of go-between, but he was more sympathetic towards Camus and remained one of his keenest admirers. He was also well-off. Once Camus had said to him, 'Michel, you have no experience of poverty.' In the first week of January 1960, he offered Camus a lift from the south of France back to Paris. Clearly, it wouldn't make any sense. Camus was due to take the train with Francine and the twins. And he already had a ticket.

Over the winter, Camus had been living and working in the village of Lourmarin, between Aix and Avignon in Provence. He and Francine had bought an old house there in 1958 with his Nobel Prize money. Here he was as contented with life as he had ever been. Aged forty-four, he quoted Nietzsche at the age of forty-three: 'My life is at this instant at its meridian: one door closes, another opens.' He could have written a lyrical pitch for a real-estate agent or the Lourmarin tourist office. 'The intense light, the infinite space transport me.' He rhapsodized about lizards and wisteria. Here he felt at home, mingling with poets (René Char, an old friend from Resistance days) and footballers (members of Lourmarin United).

He would not, on the other hand, have written quite so positively about an apartment in Paris. 'Sordid' was one of his habitual words for Paris – one of many words, nearly all derogatory. Even after being awarded the Nobel, in October 1957, he was writing 'I need to get out of this place', adding 'But where do I go?' In 1958 he found the answer. Lourmarin was in France but out of it. It belonged to the vague and vast 'South', the Mediterranean civilization that Algeria too was part of. The 'Nordic' (especially Paris) was for Camus the land of the cold philosopher kings, of Descartes and Sartre and the symbolic, while the savage 'South' was the realm of instinct and passion and wellbeing. Camus was always desperate to leave Paris in the rear-view mirror, almost like a fugitive, a man on the run. In September 1958, for example, he was in Paris to finalize arrangements for the performance of *The Possessed*, his adaptation of Dostoevsky. He woke at five a.m., ate a hearty breakfast, then hit the road (he was driving an old, beaten-up Citroën 7). 'I am at the steering wheel for 11 hours straight, nibbling on a biscuit from time to time, and the rain keeps on falling all the way down to the Drôme. Finally it starts to thin out until at last around Nyons the powerful smell of lavender comes to meet me, wakes me up and lifts my heart. The landscape that I recognize nourishes me anew and I arrive happy.'

For most of 1959, far from Paris, Camus was working away on his semi-autobiographical novel, *The First Man*, in the loft room on the second floor, which he had converted into a study. He didn't work feverishly like Sartre, 'rushing' night and day, but he was assiduous: he could sit for hours at a time, recalling key experiences, struggling to reformulate them, just as he used to stare at a clock or practise doing nothing, trying to imagine all the time that writing was just like swimming in the Mediterranean. Despite feeling torn, he turned down an offer to appear in a film by Peter Brook in order to concentrate on the book. The house itself seemed to him about as close as he could get to Algeria without crossing the Mediterranean. 'I feel as if I only have to stretch out my hand and I can touch Algeria,' he said. Everything reminded him of his homeland, the vineyards and the mountains, and in his writing Camus returned full-time to his Algerian childhood. That one thing could be like another, that one being could resemble another – a metaphorical principle – underlay all his thinking. For Camus in this last phase of his life, Algeria represented the degree-zero state: it was pre-literary; it was truth. Everything that came afterwards was already removed from the truth. Truth was something that one had to return to, to recover. Perhaps it was also the 'one thing' that could never be fully expressed.

It would be too narrow to say that – like some intellectual foreign legionnaire – he was trying to forget. Or that he was specifically trying to forget Sartre. But it is clear that he was trying to go back to before Paris, to before 1943 and the Boulevard Saint-Germain. To recover everything that had been lost along the way. Sartre, Paris, the 'Nordic': they belonged to the realm of the symbolic and now he was aiming to recover his own aboriginal life far from the metropolis and the 'society of signs'. Arriving in Lourmarin on 28 April 1958, Camus lingered outside, soaking it all in, embracing the countryside and the sky and the evening:

Grey sky. In the garden marvellous roses weighed down with water, as delicious as fruit. The rosemary is blooming. Go for a walk. In the evening the violet of the irises even deeper.

He added a final word: *Rompu*. Broken. That he was talking about himself here is suggested in his next entry. Even if he *believes* in the communion of all beings, he doesn't *feel* it:

For years I have tried to live according to a collective code. I forced myself to live like everyone else, to resemble everyone else. I said what had to be said to bring people together, even when I felt apart. And what I ended up with was a catastrophe. Now I wander amid the debris, I am lawless, torn apart, alone and willing to remain so, resigned to my singularity and my infirmities. And I have to reconstruct a truth – having lived all my life in a sort of lie.

In times past he had argued – intermittently – that it should be possible to utter the truth or write it down. By this point, amid the marvellous roses of Lourmarin, he seemed to have given up the idea altogether. There was no question of writing anything. The point was to live the truth, to *be* it, and embody it, just by being alive. In this perspective, literature couldn't really get near it (whatever *it* was). The *mensonge* – the lie – was Paris and the Left Bank and literature and philosophy and Sartre (the 'catastrophe'). And bound up with them was his notion that it would be possible to 'bring people together', no matter how different. This is Camus' farewell to all that.

It marked a return to the Tao. Camus once described himself as 'a mix of Fernandel [the comedian], Humphrey Bogart, and a samurai'. His Oriental leaning in the south of France took the form of what Peimin Ni has called 'a kung fu of philosophy', with its privileging of being and living and doing and, say, swimming, and devaluing of propositional truth and getting the logical 'system' (as Sartre would say) fully articulated (or 'totalized'). Camus' notebooks offer a collection of aphoristic fragments, and still more observations of meteorological vagaries. A collection of his haiku-style minimalist responses to the environment, *The Posterity of the Sun*, written in conjunction with René Char, was published posthumously ('Tomorrow, yes, in this fortunate valley, we will find the nerve to die happy'). Perhaps, like an antithesis of Sartre, Camus was always a poet of nature at heart. So we find him, for example, enjoying – so simple – the 'rustle of the grass' beneath his feet. Or hymning the wisteria. These are the same plants in Lourmarin that he knew in Algeria, perhaps the same (or similar) foliage that he saw through his bedroom window, when – for an instant – he became a ray of light. Wisteria was to Camus what the *petite madeleine* was to Proust, opening up a lost world of truth ('involuntary memory' in Proust's phrase), and overcoming the *mensonge*:

Bad night. It is raining on the golf course and the hills. Wisteria flowers: they filled my youth with their perfume, with their deep, mysterious ardour [...] They have been more alive, more present in my life than many beings [...] except for the one who suffers beside me and whose silence has not stopped speaking to me for half a lifetime.

Who was '*celui-là*', this other 'one'? Which 'being'? It is unlikely to have been Beauvoir, tempting though that hypothesis is, given that she was the exact opposite of 'silence'. Was he talking about his long-suffering and uncomplaining wife? (Plausible.) His mother? (Also feasible – he speaks about her in adjacent entries.) Or (we cannot know for sure) could it be that he was thinking about some alter ego, another part of his being or consciousness that was therefore 'beside' him, speaking to him although silent? The savage, degree-zero part of him. It is hard to find any other candidates in his life who really were silent. One piece of evidence in favour of this theory: he also spoke of being at war with himself: 'I make war against myself and I will either destroy myself or be reborn, that is all.'

'I love the little lizards,' he wrote, 'as dry as the stones they run along. They are like me, all skin and bone.' The key word in this sentence, to my way of thinking, is the word 'like': Camus – perhaps it is the silent *alter*-Camus, the Camus that is not Camus-the-writer – found it easy to identify with lizards, with wisteria, with abstract patterns in the foliage or the ocean. To see the 'family resemblances' (as Wittgenstein would say) – a coefficient of relatedness – between himself and other beings; to understand one creature as a simile of another. It is only when it came to other human beings that there was more of an issue.

> It is myself that, for the last five years, I have put on trial, everything I believed, the way I lived. This explains why all those who shared the same ideas as me believe they have been targeted, and hold such a bitter grudge against me.

Camus felt himself to be more of an outsider than ever. He lived perpetually in a state of exile anyway, but he chose to exile himself from Paris. When Camus asked himself what he shared in common with other humans (after all he uses the words 'man', 'men', and – more rarely – 'men and women' freely enough), he came up with different answers at different times: a feeling of being alive, the night, the sun, stars, oxygen, grass beneath our feet, desert, sea. But it seemed as if he only half believed his own argument. The one common denominator, the universal, that Camus really seriously believed in is death. Still afflicted with tuberculosis (he had to learn to breathe through only one nostril) he was often preoccupied with thoughts of death, but rarely just his own.

In Lourmarin, in September 1959, he calculated how many people were dying at any time, around the planet: '140,000 people dying per day; 97 per minute; 57 million in a year.' (I am quoting from his notebooks. By my calculations if we start with the figure of 140,000 in a day we end up with a figure more like 51 – rather than 57 – million for the year. Camus – like anyone else, we could say – is capable of making mistakes: I think that he would probably count that as another universal.) Perhaps he had in mind that scene from Malraux in which prisoners are queuing up to be flung into the boiler of a train engine. Then there was the retirement of M. Mathieu, his old literature teacher at high school, which Camus inevitably saw as a rehearsal for dying.

'He died instantly.' It is a phrase often used, about Camus for one. But it is an idea that Camus himself derided and rejected, notably in *Reflections on the Guillotine*: nobody died instantly; death was always a long drawn-out affair. And if consciousness appeared to Camus to persist, so too, backing up, extinction beckoned him and provided him with hints and clues about non-being. He was always guessing at it, imagining, living it. He thought (as Sartre once had) of the condemned man in a novel of Faulkner's who recognizes his guilt and is resigned to death. The prisoner on death row, again, was a dead man walking, which is how Camus tended to see himself and why he identified so readily with the condemned. He – like Stendhal's hero, Julien Sorel; like his own, Meursault – found himself at home on the scaffold, waiting for the blade to fall. He had so many premonitions of his own death. He told his wife he wanted to be buried in Lourmarin. He even got his daughter to hop into a big chest they kept in the loft to see what it looked like being in a coffin.

And yet, for all his dark, doom-laden thoughts, now – at the end of the 1950s – he felt more intensely alive than ever before. On the brink of attaining immortality, or at least a sense of eternity in the everyday. If only it were possible to attain absolute truth in one's very being. To be, without ambiguity or equivocation, and enjoy the kind of intensity Sartre too once dreamed of:

> The lie is a form of sleep or dream, like illusion. Truth is the only power, effervescent, inexhaustible. If we were capable of living only on and for truth: youthful, immortal energy that is in us. The man of truth does not age. One more small effort of will and he will never die.

As he struggled to relive his early life in Algeria, to be the young goalkeeper once more, he had to cut out everything that stood between him and what he once was, anything that did not correspond to the truth. This was his personal 'war' against himself, a built-in, unceasing conflict. No more films or television broadcasts or talking about his own work. No Paris. 'Destroy everything in my life that is not this poverty. Ruin myself.' He wrote himself a to-do list, which reads like 'the stages of a cure':

1. Eliminate all vain polemic.
2. Exalt what must be.
3. Silence the rest.

The trick lay in exalting – in this case writing about Algeria – and at the same time preserving the 'complete silence that I have found here'. This was the 'degree zero' state that he had sought when he was a student: the impossible, savage state of 'being truth' that implies making war against oneself. Camus' answer was to split off the writing and attribute it all to his magic pen (just as a surfer speaks of his board doing the work for him, or a golfer of a club letting him down): 'I am a writer. But it is not I but my pen that thinks, remembers or discovers for me.' Camus strained to juggle the savage and the symbolic. It was like a high-wire balancing act or one of his unfeasible yoga positions that could be sustained for only so long: 'this precious vibration' alongside which 'nothing else exists'. And if he fell off? 'If I can't stick to this discipline, given the way things are, then I accept I have to pay the price and be punished.' This constant striving to attain truth or to be truth – perhaps that was all that truth could really be.

Nietzsche was the philosopher he kept closest to him. Even if Camus had condemned his *Will to Power* in *The Rebel*, a copy of Nietzsche's *Le Gai Savoir* would be found in his mud-spattered briefcase. On his way south from Paris to Lourmarin, in the winter of 1959, he was reading a biography of Nietzsche. 'N. man of the North, finds himself suddenly confronted by the sky over Naples, one evening: "And to think you could have died without seeing that!"' The North vs the South, Sartre vs Camus. Perhaps it was this link that inspired Camus to zero in on Nietzsche's break with Wagner and his nostalgia for a lost friendship, to which Camus added the following thought: 'Unless he has access to God, a man with real heart needs friends.' But if Nietzsche's theory of eternal recurrence is true, then nothing is ever really lost – Algeria, Paris, everything is somehow preserved, ageless.

In the house in Lourmarin, Francine had her own room, on the same floor as Camus but on the opposite side of the corridor. So she came to stay in December 1959, along with their children, the twins. You are like a sister to me, he told her, adding: 'But one should not marry one's sister.' Camus had arranged things so that 'Mi', his twenty-something Danish artist girlfriend (he had picked her up in the Café Flore in February 1957) was at the same time living in a neighbouring village. Camus liked to riff on her name – part-code, part-nickname – so that he referred to himself as being 'mi-*riant*, mi-*serieux*' – half-laughing, half-serious, as if torn or divided in two. Intermittently, Camus would become a family man and father, but episodically would take off and pick up Mi, and they drove around the countryside together in his old Citroën, going as far as Marseilles. They would go swimming together and Camus intuited a connection with waves, as if they too were wave forms, doomed to rise up and then, finally, unfurl and collapse on the beach. During this period he developed a long-distance view, whether though space or time, feeling in tune with – on the same wavelength as – the vastness of terrestrial history.

It is in the sea that life is born. During the whole immemorial time that led life from the first cell to the advanced marine being, the continent, devoid of animal and vegetable life, was only a land of stone, filled only with the sound of rain in the midst of an enormous silence, alive only with the flickering of the shadows of great clouds and the racing of tides over ocean basins.

For Camus the sea, this 'divinity', was pre-eminent. But doesn't the sea sit on top of a buried landmass? No. Camus inverts the relationship of land and sea. 'Terra firma, in conclusion, is only a very thin layer on top of the sea. One day the ocean will reign over it.' In this vision the land and sea exist in the same relationship as North and South, the symbolic and the savage. One day the land and everything that goes along with it will be swept away and we will be returned to our primordial state of flow. And everything that has been lost will be restored. And then it will be possible to love everyone – and everything – all at once.

At other times, moodily wandering the countryside, Camus wondered if it was possible to love anyone. He had been reading Boris Pasternak's *Dr Zhivago* and he read it as not just, obviously, a love story – the relationship, torn by Revolution, of Zhivago and Lara – but a meditation on love: 'this is the kind of love that expands to encompass all beings at once. The doctor loves his wife, and Lara, and others, and Russia. If he dies, it is from being separated from his wife, from Lara, from Russia and everyone else.' The implication was that if only it were possible to love enough, then you would never die. It was a new theory of his: love as a form of immortality. 'For the mature man, only happy love affairs can prolong youth.' While Sartre was wrestling with Marxism, Camus was translating Groucho Marx's theory, 'You're only as old as the woman you feel', into a more lyrical vein.

On one of their excursions, Mi sobbed, 'I am so in love with love.' The fact that he troubled to write the thought down suggests that something similar was true of Camus. He developed a concept of 'a love without object', intransitive love, and made it the overarching thematic of the 'cycle' of books he was working on (including *The First Man*). Camus recorded his flashes of jealousy, his frustration when she was away, but also his 'violent gratitude' to Mi, and noted that 'my heart is finally alive'. For Camus there was no potential tragedy in sex any more, no absurdity. 'Carnal love has always been tied for me to an irresistible feeling of innocence and joy. I cannot love with tears in my eyes but only in a state of bliss.' In December 1959 there was no more contradiction between carnal love and love. No more Don Juan. 'There is no more Don Juan since love is free. There are men who are more pleasing than others. But there is neither sin nor heroism.'

Distracted from his novel ('a fiasco of the pen' in his self-critical phrase), he fired off a volley of love letters to addresses around the world.

To Patricia Blake in New York. 'New York, for me, is you, has been you for the last thirteen years.'

To his mother in Algiers. '*Chère Maman*, may you be forever young and beautiful. And may your heart remain the same as always, the best in the world.'

To Mi in Denmark. 'This awful separation will at least have made us feel more than ever the constant need that we have for one another. I knew it already, now I know it even more, I bless my need and I am waiting for you, full of strength and passion, my beloved, my ardent one, my little girl, my dear lover.'

To Catherine Sellers in Paris. 'This is my last letter, sweetheart. See you Tuesday, my dearest, I am kissing you already and I bless you from the bottom of my heart.'

To Maria Casares, also in Paris, making arrangements to see her too, always allowing for 'the hazards of the road'. 'This is a last letter to say I am arriving Tuesday by car.'

Camus didn't give too many interviews around this period (he would pretend to be the gardener if he picked up the phone and an unknown voice asked for him). In the one that he did give (a written questionnaire from an Argentine magazine), he was asked: 'How can we bring about a world less oppressed by need and more free?' His answer was a toned-down version of the thoughts he confides to his notebook: 'By giving, when you can. And by not hating, if you can.'

The exact opposite of the gospel according to Jean-Paul.

In 1960 Sartre and Beauvoir were living in the apartment on the Rue Bonaparte. They considered this a good joke because (a) Sartre was small, like Napoleon but (b) unlike Napoleon, all their work was directed against the Empire – the French Empire in particular, but just about any and every empire in the history of the world would do. Sartre had translated the struggle of the proletariat to overthrow the bourgeoisie into the nationalist movements of colonized people around the world, in the post-Second World War period, to be done once and for all with their old colonial masters. He applied the same ruthless revolutionary logic with the same fervour to each and every uprising. But especially when it was against the French. And especially when it was Algeria. Camus, with his even-handed, Third Way, perhaps utopian approach, remained right in his firing line.

Sartre had been arguing against Camus and his hazy, optimistic thinking, one way or another, for the best part of a decade. Just as, in the Second World War, there had been a simple choice to be made (you were either with the Nazis or against them) so now – to Sartre's way of thinking – you were either with the anti-imperialists or you automatically became one of the colonizers. Camus, from this point of view, was still hopelessly wedded to the old colonial system. Contrary to Camus' 'neither executioner nor victim' attitude, Sartre thought that everyone was *either* an executioner *or* a victim. There was no third way. Nothing in between, no happy compromise (other than myths and delusions). When you were in a historical jam, violence was the only way out. Violence was the solution (for Camus, of course, it was the problem). There was no scope here for Gandhi-style civil disobedience. Sartre identified himself with the position of the colonized, and identified Camus as his colonial master, fated to be overthrown and destroyed. What was left after all the fine words ('humanism') had been stripped away? A clash between two human beings, one of which sought the death of the other. In this respect Sartre had never forgotten the lesson of Hegel that Beauvoir signposted in her epigraph to *L'invitée*. So he remained, at heart, a dualist (hence conflict-driven); while Camus, still intellectually lying on his bed and gazing out of the window at the light beyond, remained firmly monistic in his sympathies, always expecting to overcome those temporary misunderstandings and work through to some state of harmony.

Sartre fully identified with Che Guevara ('the most complete human being of our age') in the jungles of South America. He went to Cuba to support Castro, seeing himself as a more intellectual Che.

Beauvoir, Sartre, Che. Sartre has a cigar in one hand and a pen in the other.

But Che himself (who read Sartre in his youth) was rumoured to be unsympathetic or impatient: 'Let Jean-Paul Sartre philosophize about revolution; we who carry it out have no time for theories.' The revolution had no need of philosophers: but Sartre was sure that it did, that there was scope for a marriage of ideology and praxis, theory and violence. Wherever he went (which was almost anywhere *except* the USA) the annoying thing for Sartre was that everyone still wanted to know (and this was the kind of question he tended to get), 'What is the meaning of existentialism?' There was relative indifference towards his take on Marxism. Sartre remained undiscouraged. He forged links with the FLN in Algeria and provided material assistance. Intellectually, he formed an alliance with Frantz Fanon, author of *The Wretched of the Earth*. Fanon, a contemporary of Guevara's, was a French-speaking psychiatrist from Martinique who gave a potent psychosocial analysis of what might be called 'the colonial syndrome'. The therapy he recommended to colonized people was killing the colonizers. Sartre agreed to write a preface to Fanon in which the 'negation' of the other recommended in *Being and Nothingness* evolved explicitly into annihilation. While Camus was pondering, privately, the theme of love, Sartre was writing openly about the 'treasure' of hatred. 'Violence is a cleansing force,' wrote Fanon, with the Sartrean seal of approval. 'It frees the native from his inferiority complex and inaction; it makes him fearless and restores his self-respect.'

The *pied noir* had to be sacrificed for the good of all. It was the message he had been sending out to Camus for several years: that he was a dead man walking ('Somebody had to tell you. It might just as well be me'). It was an almost religious-sounding doctrine of purification and rebirth, with the rhetoric of a 'new dawn'. Camus the colonist represented a Christ-like figure doomed to suffer and die for our sins ('the only Christ we deserve' as Camus said of Meursault). Perhaps even Camus himself, in *The First Man*, admitted some part of Sartre's analysis: 'We are made to get on,' says a *pied noir* farmer of the Arabs and the French Algerians.

> They are as stupid and brutish as we are, and they have the same blood we do. Still, we are going to go on killing one another for a while, cutting each other's balls off and torturing each other. And then we'll start to learn to live together again. It is the country that wants that.

Sartre would scoff only at the happy ending.

When a gendarme, in Lourmarin, learned that Monsieur Camus, Albert, was writing a novel, he asked: 'Is it romance or detective fiction?' Camus replied, in his *mi-mi* way, 'Half and half.' And perhaps this summary of *The First Man* and the story of Algeria was fair. The book is about a long love affair that ends in killing. All liaisons turn out to be dangerous. Sartre would have agreed with the last part (it was only the romance that was deluded).

On Saturday 2 January 1960, Camus saw off Francine and the twins at Avignon railway station. Then he got back in the car and put his train ticket in his pocket (where it would later be found intact). Michel Gallimard, the great go-between, had persuaded him to drive to Paris in the Facel Vega. René Char, who was also going to Paris, decided to take the train, seeing that the car was going to be fairly crowded.

'I'll only be gone for a week,' Camus told his housekeeper when they finally drove away on the Sunday. Gallimard was driving, together with Janine, his wife, Anne, his daughter, just turned eighteen, and their dog, Floc. When they stopped to fill up at the garage, Camus had to sign a copy of *The Outsider* for the *garagiste*. They gradually wended their way north, having lunch in Orange then stopping overnight near Mâcon, 100 kilometres north of Lyon, in a hotel called the Chapon Fin. They set off again the next morning, Monday 4 January 1960. After lunch in Sens – for the last leg to Paris – Camus, who was forty-six years old, switched to the front passenger seat. Janine said to him, 'You're bigger than I am, you have longer legs.' No one bothered with seatbelts.

Perhaps every significant road journey includes anticipations of one's own death. This one certainly did. Camus and Michel amiably discussed life insurance. It was impossible for either of them to get any, on account of their bad lungs (it was one of the things they had in common). Gallimard said that he wanted to die before his wife because he couldn't bear to live without her (Camus didn't, however, echo the sentiment). Janine, less sentimentally, said she would rather continue to live, with or without her husband. The two men joked about how, if they both died, their bodies could be embalmed and stuffed and kept in the living room so that Janine could talk to them from time to time. (Janine herself was not so keen on this idea.)

They were driving through Yonne, north of Sens, on Route nationale 5, near a place called Petit Villeblevin. A fine rain was falling; the surface of the road was slick. It was a long straight road but Gallimard swerved, as if he had lost control of the steering, and the car went into a skid. According to one eyewitness the car was going at around 160 kph (100 mph). Gallimard must have been driving at speed because parts of the car would eventually be found scattered over a radius of 150 metres, almost like a plane crash. It is plausible that, as one account has it, the speedo was jammed on 145 kph. The dashboard clock stopped at 1.54 p.m.

It was one of those French roads with plane trees standing along either side, evenly spaced, like sentinels. The car hit one of the trees at an angle, bounced off, then rushed on, completely out of control, and smashed into another tree, this time head-on. The Facel Vega suddenly went from something approaching 160 kilometres an hour right down to zero. You might have expected Camus, beltless, to go flying through the front window. But there was no more front window. The concertina-ing of the car propelled him backwards, right into and out of the back window. His head was outside, his torso inside. He was not decapitated – guillotined, as he might have predicted – but his neck was broken.

There is no record of the contents of his consciousness at the point when it was extinguished. Perhaps it was something like: 'You die. We do the rest'. The closest thing we have to a machine registering the spontaneous thoughts and images and feelings – Lavoisier's blinks – that made up the man Albert Camus is his *Carnets*. This is one of his last thoughts, shortly before the accident, as he watched waves expiring on the shores of the Mediterranean. 'There are waves that reach us from Cape Horn after a journey of ten thousand kilometres.' I am guessing that it was not so much his own past life that flashed before his eyes – all those still confusing, confounding faces – but perhaps the past life of a wave in the moment of breaking apart.

One strange coincidence of a kind he would surely have appreciated: the doctor from the nearby village who attended Camus was called Camus (Marcel).

Two close shaves: Janine and her daughter, sitting in the back of the car, were thrown clear of the wreck, and survived, almost unharmed. Michel Gallimard himself died five days later of his injuries (and was actually prosecuted posthumously for dangerous driving).

Also unscathed: the Camus briefcase, containing the Nietzsche, a school edition of *Othello*, and a blue folder marked 'Elements for The First Man'. Like (as Camus had once written) 'derisory witnesses to this distressing accident'.

One total mystery: the dog vanished without trace.

Sartre and Beauvoir were in Paris when the news filtered through that evening. Beauvoir couldn't sleep and went out roaming the streets of Paris in the rain. The next morning she said to herself: 'He is not here to see this morning.' But he could *be* seen, in a manner of speaking. Newspapers carried headlines and his photograph.

Almost immediately, Sartre dashed off his obituary of this 'Cartesian of the absurd', which appeared in *France-Observateur* on 7 January. He admitted later that he got carried away by the sheer beauty of his prose, as if he couldn't wait to confine Camus to the past tense: he represented a 'movement whose phases and final terminus we tried to foresee'. He stressed Camus' 'silence' (the word occurs no less than five times). Sartre, hammering verbal nails into the coffin, was shocked by Camus' 'scandalous' death, because he was already effectively dead. Hence all the odd, twisted constructions and imperfect subjunctive tenses as if Sartre couldn't quite make his mind up – had he already been dead or, in some equally paradoxical way, was he still alive? Just like Camus' condemned man on – or under – the guillotine. Consider, for example: '*cela suffisait pour que sa présence demeurât vivante* [that was enough in order that his presence might remain alive]', '*dût-on* [even if one were] [. . .]', '*nous eussions su* [we would/should perhaps have known]', and, finally, a triad: '*il était important qu'il sortît du silence, qu'il décidât, qu'il conclût* [it was important that he should break his silence, should make up his mind, should conclude].' The whole of the eulogy is poised on the slippery slopes of the French circumflex, which points uncertainly in two directions, but – like a roof – slopes decidedly down.

The ironic aspect of the preface to Fanon's book, in so far as it is an attack on Camus, is that it was written some time after he was already, technically, dead: dead and yet still needing to be shoved back in his grave. Like a zombie.

Sartre's Camus was a ghostly, haunting presence, even when alive:

> We had a falling-out, he and I: but a falling-out means noth-
> ing – even if we were doomed never to see one another again –
> but another way of living *together* and without ever losing sight
> of what the other is up to in the small world that has been
> given to us. That did not prevent me from thinking of him,
> from sensing his gaze on a page of a book, on the newspaper
> that he was reading, and saying to myself: 'What does he have
> to say? What is he saying about it *at this very moment*?'

In all fairness, Sartre reiterated how entangled they remained, however far apart: 'One lived with or against his thought [. . .] but always through it.' But just as Sartre had once seemed to admire Camus' life to the point of jealousy, so too here he expressed a degree of envy as regards the manner of his death. Camus managed to die young, while he was still a good-looking corpse. Camus' way of dying is exemplary for Sartre, a perfect instantiation of his own theory of absurdity, by virtue of being meaningless. No exit could be more fitting:

> Each life that is suddenly terminated – even that of such a
> young man – is simultaneously a broken disc and a complete
> life. For those who loved him, there is an unbearable absurd-

ity in this death. But we will have to learn to see this muti-lated life's work as a total oeuvre. To the precise extent that Camus' humanism contains a *human* attitude towards the death that would take him by surprise, to the extent that his proud quest for happiness implied and demanded the *inhu-man* necessity of death, we will recognize in this work and in the life that is inseparable from it one man's pure and victo-rious attempt to wrest back every instant of his existence from his future death.

'I know of nothing more idiotic than dying in a car crash,' Camus once said to his friends. But then (as Sartre acknowledged) there was something glamorous about the absurd, something typically film-star; there always would be. In *The Outsider*, Camus wrote: 'Naturally, our hope was to be taken out on the corner of the street, while flying along, by a random bullet.'

Despite all the premonitions and the pervasive death-con-sciousness, we can say with confidence that Camus did not have perfect foreknowledge of his own death. He didn't know it would happen just like that. Death, in other words, is unpre-dictable (even if inescapable): 'unforeseeable and out of the blue' (to quote Sartre). There is a large element of chance involved, in the sense that it could all have worked out differ-ently (if only he had taken the train, for example, and not the Facel Vega; if only that tree had not been just there). It still comes under the heading of contingency, even of freedom, cer-tainly indeterminacy.

And then Camus alone died in just that way. Of course, he is not the only man to have died in a crash. Around the same period, James Dean was the victim of a head-on collision (1955); Jackson Pollock, like Camus, hit a tree (1956). But the differences between these cases are practically infinite. Dean was at the wheel of a Porsche Spyder when a college student, Donald Turnupseed (who escaped with abrasions), crossed into his lane; Pollock, having failed to paint a single picture for the whole of 1956, was almost certainly drunk and depressed when his Oldsmobile convertible went off the road one night on Long Island (and killed a passenger too). That Camus was in the passenger seat of a Facel Vega clearly singles him out: not too many others fit that bill. No one other than Gallimard smashed into that particular tree on that afternoon on the road to Paris.

The aftershock – the repercussions of the crash – continued to ripple out: mediated through police reports, the trial where Gallimard was found posthumously guilty, public homages, tears, obituaries, and biographies. Now conspiracy theorists speculate online about who could have been responsible, invoking a link with the Algerian war. If only a small man with a pipe and one lazy eye – and a spanner in his back pocket – had been seen lurking in the vicinity of the Facel Vega while it was parked outside that restaurant in Sens (which, after all, means 'meaning' as well as 'direction'): it would have been so much simpler. Certainly Sartre had already been assassinating Camus on the page for the best part of a decade. But perhaps we can say that a certain *Monsieur Néant* looked on approvingly, mocking the notion of 'cause and effect'. In any case, a car crash in very slow motion seems to sum up the protracted collision between Sartre and Camus.

The news travelled slowly in those days and didn't reach me until some time later in the sixties, probably after the assassination of President Kennedy, and I haven't written about it until now. Nevertheless, this precise phenomenon had never happened before in the history of the world. Even if we allow for eternal recurrence (for example, with a very powerful telescope, the accident can now be seen again from a planet some fifty-odd light years away), it remains a unique event, a moment unlike any other in this universe. Camus ceased to exist shortly after lunch on a Monday in January 1960. On Route nationale 5. Near Villeblevin. Perhaps this was his way of 'living' the truth, of *being* truth: only by dying could he achieve immortality.

If Camus' death was premature, Sartre's – twenty years later, in April 1980 – was not, even according to his own reckoning. He arrived late for his own funeral. As if he had been expecting him for some time, the Director of the Montparnasse cemetery said: 'I knew he would come to us.'

The realm of the symbolic is immune to death. Sartre wrote in *Being and Nothingness* that (contrary to Heidegger) you cannot 'live towards death', you can only live your life and death is something contrary and negative that lies outside life and cannot be incorporated within it. Death is not something that can be thought either, because it is the opposite of thought. As late as 1978 he was saying something similar. 'Death? I don't

© AFP

Sartre's funeral cortège

think about it. It has no place in my life, it will always be out-side. One day my life will end, but I don't want it to be burdened with death. I want that my death never enter my life, nor define it, that I be always a call to life.'

Sartre was doomed to become prematurely posthumous. Others remarked on his being like the living dead, a zombie. In March 1979, the Palestinian writer Edward Saïd attended a col-loquium in Paris on the Israel-Palestine conflict, where he met Sartre. 'It was a dismal afternoon,' he recalled. 'It rained cats and dogs. We had lunch in the Alsatian brasserie at the Carrefour de l'Odéon. Sartre seemed unable to understand any foreign lan-guage, whether German or English, and even when we spoke French, he was quite absent.' It was now possible to imagine the world without Jean-Paul Sartre. But then it always had been. Sartre was never necessary; he was only ever a contingency, a chance occurrence. A fluke. His whole life was an accident, only his death was inescapable. It is already implicit in *Being and Nothingness*: it is easy to become no-thing because that is exactly what we are from the very beginning; we are never anything other than nothing anyway. The great void that is the guarantee that we are only just beginning (all over again) is also a prom-ise and foretaste of our end.

He had been blind in his right eye since the age of four. In autumn 1973 his left eye, battered by tobacco, alcohol, drugs, went the same way. The philosophy of the gaze gave way to a philosophy of blindness. In his 'Self-Portrait at 70' he gave a brutal assessment of all his handicaps. Again and again, as with Sally Swing, he wrote his own obituary. He allowed himself to be iconized. He knew that he would be anyway and he was trying to put his own swerve on the image he would leave behind. He mapped out a book with his collaborator Pierre Victor (also known as Benny Lévy), to be called *Power and*

Freedom, which would be his way of overcoming death and putting his life into some kind of order. 'This book will be the summa of my political and moral theories. I would like to finish it by the end of my life.' It remained unfinished, a pile of tape recordings and notes and stray thoughts.

When I was a student I had a professor who was trying to write a book about Sartre. But he was finding it hard to finish. 'Every time you think you're done,' he complained, 'the old *salaud* comes out with another book. Completely different to the last one. He is impossible.' Sartre killed him. He came to an end before the book did. There was a feeling – even if it wasn't said flat-out – that it would be easier for all concerned if Sartre were just to drop dead, sooner rather than later. It was the only way to stop him writing and causing further embarrassment.

So it was even with the *Temps modernes* group, his 'guardians' (as he called them). They wanted to control him too, to lay him to rest. 'They're treating me like a dead man who had the gall to appear in public,' Sartre protested. Even Beauvoir didn't like what he was doing. For one thing, it would automatically put in question even the title of her latest work, *All Said and Done* (*Tout compte fait*) – the concluding volume in her autobiography and an overview of their lives together. She could hardly wait to bring out her *Adieux: A Farewell to Sartre*.

'Good morning, monsieur Sartre,' said a young woman fan. 'Thank you for existing!' She was smiling at him. But there was something terminal about that statement too. Another valediction, as if he was about to cease existing. Everybody was killing him, it was to be expected. If Camus died too young, then Sartre died too late. 'Today,' he said in January 1977, 'people speak of me as if I were one of the living dead. I died with my *Flaubert*, and maybe even a little before that [...] I kept on writing but nobody read me any more.' The idea of the living dead, of someone who is dead but doesn't quite know it yet, is present in Sartre's own writing: 'in this darkness that will give way to a new dawn, you are the zombies'.

The imminence of one's own death is always there, like a shadow, in all writing. Sartre already knew it in *Nausea*: the ending is there, in the beginning, overshadowing it. Plato says philosophy is a form of rehearsal for death. And Camus would agree that death is implicit in all thinking, because it involves an abstraction from life, a reduction, a diminution of pure existence. He even joked about it in his letter to *Monsieur le directeur*: 'writing [. . .] comes down to depriving oneself of existence'. The thought is there, sketchily, in the margins of Sartre's earliest philosophy, perhaps too in his fear of invisibility. To think is to die a little. To be and not to be.

The nooks and crevices of negation, the intermittent sense of nothingness that inhabits not just the café or the mountain or the guillotine, but anywhere at any time, that haunting realization of not-quite-being: they are a warm-up for the full-on flat-out state of non-being somewhere further down the road (the Route nationale 5, for example). In this sense, Sartre had already anticipated his own death (and not just that of others) again and again. This is why so many of his characters – in *Huis clos*, in *Les jeux sont faits,* most obviously – have already died. It is not impossible to have a foretaste of death. It is probably unavoidable. Sartre in particular was capable of seeing his own, a symbolic death. And of feeling what it feels like to be dead.

I think therefore I am, says Descartes; I think therefore I am *not*, corrects Sartre.

23

BEYOND THE TEXT

BY WAY OF FURTHER ATONEMENT, the neo-existentialist book-thief ended up doing time here:

The New York Public Library

And, purely by chance, the first book I stumbled upon, sitting on the most visible, accessible shelf, virtually the first one you come to when you walk into the reading room (pictured above), and turn left, was a fat volume, with this title on the spine: *Being and Nothingness* (in the English translation). It was like sending a kleptomaniac into Harrods. Was this heaven or hell? Fortunately, the thief had changed his ways and no longer 'borrowed' books without telling anyone, remorsefully trying to return them years later. It seemed unlikely that by removing this single book from the shelf the whole of the mighty New York Public Library would come tumbling down, but I decided to play it safe. I felt, by not taking it off the shelf, that it was virtually as if I was returning it, to an enormous bookstore, so many years after first making off with it.

Rather like Roquentin, I spent many months in the library, but it struck me every day that, even if so many books were here, the authors themselves remained elusive. Barthes said that the author is dead (and he was dead too as if to prove his case), and technically, where Camus and Sartre were concerned, he surely had a point. They were both on the guest-list of ghosts. Nevertheless, having in mind the twilight zone that both writers did so much to explore, the strange state that we like to call 'existential', poised between being and non-being, I couldn't quite bring myself to believe that Sartre and Camus were entirely extinct.

So naturally I left the library and went to Paris in search of them, returning to the still thriving Café de Flore on the Boulevard Saint-Germain where they met with Simone de Beauvoir. The *garçons* seemed to have read their Sartre (it was probably part of the job specification) and now overacted more than ever – and charged a lot more too. Perhaps there was still a sense of 'plenitude' here; there was certainly the sound of saucers and spoons clinking. But the philosophers had all gone, leaving only the occasional plaque and tributes on the website, and ushering in women in complicated hats and men in smart suits and a flourishing tourist trade. Nobody smoked any more. No one wrote here either, but there were plenty of people tapping out messages on their phones or iPads.

I went next to the La Louisiane hotel on the Rue de Seine, where Beauvoir lived and hosted Sartre and Camus for the first performance of *No Exit* nearly seventy years ago. The hotel still exists and it is possible to rent a room for the night and enter and even exit the very same hell that Sartre and Camus and Beauvoir once so vividly conjured up. It could do with a lick of paint but it's not infernal. There were no Nazis strutting by outside, nor were there any old philosophers inside – zombies, ghosts, or otherwise. Only a man at the reception desk who enthused about all the other great writers who had stayed there over the years (he mentioned Ernest Hemingway and Henry Miller and said not to forget Miles Davis). 'This,' he said, 'is an *hôtel littéraire.*' It was all perfectly fine and bohemian and yet just a little disappointing. Sartre and Camus could no longer be found slugging it out on the streets or in the bars of Paris. Of course not, how could they be?

I went back to New York and the public library and Think Coffee and sought out the ghosts of Sartre and Camus in their books and diaries, as if their words were a magic formula capable of summoning up lost souls. Surely here, if anywhere, they were still to be discovered, immortally uttering their great mantras of love and death and eternal angst. And then, one day in the middle of winter – it was January and much colder than Algiers – I resolved to get up from my desk and set aside all books for twenty-four hours and relinquish entirely my tenuous hold on language, adopting instead the degree-zero minimalism of Camus, taken to its logical conclusion. I would eschew not just books but songs, conversation, newspapers, the radio, television, phones, emails, the endless static of the Internet, any forms of communication that relied on words. I'd had enough of aiming my armchair in any direction. I went out into the world again, on that cold, clear winter's day, like Camus climbing up a mountain outside Algiers, with only a hat, a scarf, and a coat: no books, no paper, no computer, no pen. It was a strange feeling, almost like walking down the middle of the street, naked, vulnerable, unarmoured, without crutches. As if I had landed from another planet.

On any other day, how many conversations would I have had with random strangers on the subway? Today of all days they were lining up to have a chat, talking about the clothes I was wearing ('Cool jacket, man!' – on the platform at Bleecker Street), the weather, the economy, anything. There was no end to them, as if my very silence was a provocation. But I could say nothing in reply. Perhaps they even preferred it this way, as if having a one-way conversation with a dumb animal. I had taken to describing myself as a 'neo-existentialist', but it was not a phrase I came out with too often and less than ever on this particular day.

I wandered into the library on 5th Avenue, by way of testing my nerve. Not only did I not steal anything – I didn't read anything either. Not one word of the billions on offer. I had resisted the ultimate temptation. In the evening, I went as far as the Lincoln Center to go to a jazz concert, but had to back out again when there were complicated negotiations over timing. Maybe it was better that way, there was always a risk somebody might break into song.

But in truth the siren call of words could never be banished, only resisted. We live (as Camus would say) in a *society of signs*. It was impossible to cross the street without seeing the word CROSS. Everywhere street signs, brandishing their information about parking and directions. Everywhere word of bakeries, dentists, radio shacks, buns and burgers, pizzas galore, and Broadway smash-hits – flashing out, endlessly, inescapably, with or without neon. As Derrida said, there was 'nothing beyond the text', even if that now tended to suggest (in a deconstructive twist that he would surely have approved of) that everybody was fetishistically attached to their cell phones.

So it was that I headed west, still on foot, towards the Hudson, and walked along the shore for a mile or two, gazing across at the New Jersey side of the river. And then I saw this:

Without words

(Not carrying a camera at the time, I returned the following day to take the picture.) And I felt, suddenly – there was no smoke from a cigarette, but perhaps a flash of sunlight – as if I had somehow rediscovered Sartre and Camus and the epic struggle between them. True, they had been there before me, prowling the same mean streets, venturing among the ruins of skyscrapers, looking for New York and not finding it, coming upon atmospheres, longitudinally elongated, striped with parallel meanings, or an orgy of violent lights and Camel advertising, unforgettable faces (both very ugly and very beautiful) and looking down on the Hudson from Riverside and seeing the traffic as if it were waves breaking on the shore. I too was anybody anywhere. But that wasn't it.

It wasn't that I was reliving some classic Sartrean or Camusian experience or walking in their footsteps. Maybe they had once looked out on a scene just like this, maybe not. No: it was more that, as I looked out on the half-frozen river, over here all ice and stasis, over there all free-flowing water, it seemed to me that I was looking right into the eyes of Sartre and Camus. Or rather that they were looking out at the Hudson. Arctic immobility on one side (it would be hard to commit suicide – you would have to saw your way through); and then, on the other, warmth and motion and the current and waves. You could try to argue that Sartre was more ice, Camus more flow: all that cold, calculating intelligence, the great unsinkable, the un-relatedness, the symbolic, on the one hand, and then in contrast, the expanding sympathies, the striving after fraternity, the love of dogs and the desert and the sea. Laborious/effortless; prosaic/poetic. Winter and 'invincible summer'. But it was more that there was a split, a divide between two adjacent states, and this was something that both writers came back to, one way or another, again and again.

Sartre and Camus, the boxer and the goalkeeper: they were almost like Rimbaud and Verlaine, except that they hadn't had sex together and neither pulled a gun on the other. But it was close. Their story ended as badly as if they had had a love affair and then broken it off, each of them feeling monumentally betrayed. It was a disaster waiting to happen from the moment they met – and even before. The divorce was as romantic, in its way, as the honeymoon. They were as much a conjunction of opposites as the dream team. The agon between them was long-lasting and profound but turned around and at different times took different forms. But if there was conflict between them they also brought out, at the same time, the conflict within, since consciousness is riven, split, torn, double in its very formation.

'Like': one of the most overused words of our era, especially in New York. Not so much as a verb. 'He was like . . .' 'She was like . . .' 'I mean, like . . .' As I roamed around the city or rattled around the subway, the sentences that still screamed out at me merged into a long string of 'likes'. There was a degree of epistemological indeterminacy implicit in this habit: everything was only approximately true, it was 'like' this or that, but never quite coincided perfectly with the truth. But then perhaps too there was a series of implied comparisons or similes: my love is *like* a red, red rose; the city lies around us *like* a cloak of glittering shells. Everybody was now constantly *like* something or someone, everyday discourse was shot through with implied family resemblances. 'To say' was now 'to be like'. At one level it was a form of stuttering, a series of suspensions of meaning, semantic hiccups; at another it was poetry, of a kind Camus would probably have sympathized with. The unalike were secretly alike. Alikeness, similitude, connectedness: the sensation of an invisible continuum infiltrates his thinking and his writing, like a strong current through water.

By the same token, there must be unalike-ness too. I can hardly begin to doubt unless I have beliefs, said Wittgenstein. So too we cannot think in terms of different things being alike unless there is some rule of difference built into the original perception (and vice-versa). Roman Jakobson reckoned that it was all one, similarity and dissimilarity, subsumed within the same metaphorical (or paradigmatic) axis of thought and language. Sartre and Camus, in contrast, make the case for a fundamental friction between two modes of cognition, two ways of apprehending the world, associative and differentiating. While Camus perpetually sought some underlying relationship, Sartre was always alert to the alterity in the same, the lack of identity even in the seemingly identical. I am not what I am and am what I am not. The human is the realm of non-identity and conflicted-ness. Alikeness/unalike-ness. These subtly, dramatically different ways of thinking and seeing are embodied in the fraught, fractured relationship between Sartre and Camus, in their philosophy and their politics. Or, to put it another way, all philosophy and politics reside in the dissonance between them. In their convergence and divergence they give us something like a definition of existentialism.

S/C: Split Consciousness. The philosophical fight club is emblematic of our 'dual-process' cognition, the two-phase brain, forever affected by the faint delay or deferral that generates the phenomenon of *déjà vu*. Haven't I been here before? In this very bookshop, this café, this hotel? Ah yes, of course, just a few nanoseconds ago, when I was making an initial reconnaissance, processing the information in a different way. Camus captures the vacillation between two phases in his flashbacks to a lost paradise, the network of trees and seas; Sartre, conversely, harks forward to an elusive future transcendence.

That feeling of being the 'first man', of making some primordial discovery of the world, and an elusive, perfect alikeness, is the narrative Camus spent his life trying (and of course failing) to piece back together; while Sartre dedicated himself to exploring the immense possibilities and horizons opened up by the conviction of being a detotalized totality 'doomed to failure'. But reconciled in the universal singular that is each one of us, the boxer and the goalkeeper also provide an unintentional X-ray map of the psyche. the psyche. Henri Bergson seems to sum up their-and-our binary praxis when he writes that:

> Our real existence, as it unfolds in time, is doubled-up by a ritual existence, a mirror-image. Each moment of our lives thus offers us two aspects: it is real and virtual, savage and symbolic, perception and memory. It is split, put in question at the same time as it is lived. Or rather, it consists in this very split.

We are, like it or not, in two minds. Always, everywhere. Right here, right now. I think therefore I am Sartre/Camus. Camus/Sartre, *c'est moi*.

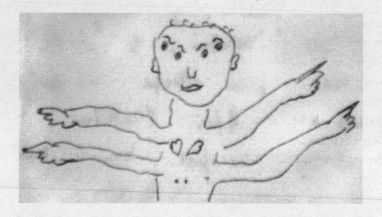

Notes

I. WHAT IT FEELS LIKE TO BE ALIVE

p. 5 **Every existent is born for no reason,** Sartre, *La Nausée* (Folio), 188.

p. 7 **That means nothing to me,** *L'Etranger*, part 1, chapter 4.

p. 8 **A vast hospital in which all the patients want to change beds,** Charles Baudelaire, opening of prose poem 'N'importe où hors du monde'.

p. 9 **We are always in two minds,** For an account of 'dual process cognition', see Jonathan. Evans and Keith Frankish, eds, *In Two Minds: Dual Processes and Beyond* (2009).Daniel Kahneman's recent work *Thinking, Fast and Slow* (2011) likewise develops some of the insights already found in R. D. Laing's classic of existential psychoanalysis, *The Divided Self* (1960).

p. 9 **a binary praxis of antagonistic reciprocity,** Sartre, *Critique of Dialectical Reason*, II, 5 (1985).

2. THINK COFFEE

p. 12 **striped [. . .] with parallel (but not interconnecting) meanings,** Sartre, 'New York, ville coloniale', *Situations* III (1949).

p. 13 **the *agon*,** See Harold Bloom, *The Anxiety of Influence* (1973). Reason is made for arguing, argue Mercier, H. & Sperber, D. 'Why do humans reason? Arguments for an argumentative theory', *Behavioral and Brain Sciences,* 2011.

p. 15 **[the waiter] has brisk and emphatic gestures,** *L'Etre et le Néant* (henceforth *EN*), 95.

p. 17 **nothingness haunts being**, *EN*, 46.

p. 18 **Camus' parody of a philosopher**, *L'Impromptu des philosophes*, *Oeuvres complètes* (Pléiade ed. Jacqueline Lévi-Valesi), 2.

p. 19 **When you see who is against him, you have to be with him**, Camus, *Correspondance Albert Camus Jean Grenier* (1981), 99.

p. 22 **I have to choose between making a bomb and concentrating on philosophy**, Camus, *Correspondance Albert Camus Jean Grenier*, 85.

p. 22 **I do not think that the war is finished**, Camus, *Correspondance Albert Camus Jean Grenier*, 106.

p. 23 **Towards midnight one heard the sound**, Sartre, 'Paris sous l'Occupation', *Situations* III.

p. 23 **Being is discovered as *fragile***, *EN*, 43.

p. 25 **You have to choose. To live or tell stories**, Sartre, *La nausée*, 62.

p. 26 **God is not an artist; and neither is Mauriac**, Sartre, 'M. François Mauriac et la liberté', *Situations* I (1947), 52.

p. 27 **a book exists *against* its author**, *EN*, 25.

3. THE INVITATION

p. 28 **malevolent goblin or gargoyle**, Arthur Koestler/Cynthia Koestler, *Stranger on the Square*, 67.

p. 28 **Camus deliberately cultivated a trenchcoat.** Sam Fussell, in an email, comments: 'Do you remember when Belmondo looks at his reflection in an automobile mirror and says, to himself, "Ah, Bogie." The thing is what they seemed to idolize was Bogie's incarnation in specific Hemingway-esque movies. Which keys into the eternal quest to be "real men" that plagued Camus and Sartre. The irony of Bogie is that he grew up wealthy in NYC as the son of a famous female magazine illustrator. He was sent to the US equivalent of Eton (Andover), where, naturally, he flunked out. I don't believe he ever actually fired a weapon in WW II (not sure which direction his armchair was facing). As Cary Grant once supposedly said, "Everyone wants to be Cary Grant. Even Cary Grant."'

p. 29 **Françoise picked up a piece of toast**, Beauvoir, *L'Invitée* (1943), 407.

p. 30 **Hesitantly, incredulously, she caressed the surface of this hard, smooth young body.** Beauvoir, *L'Invitée,* 403.

p. 30 **It is not always easy to be a man**, Camus, *Noces* (followed by *L'Été*), 61.

p. 35 **When she was not there, this scent of dust, this penumbra,** Beauvoir, 13.

p. 36 **It is impossible to conceive that other people are conscious beings too**, Beauvoir, 15.

p. 42 **'irregular' features**, Beauvoir, 47.

p. 45 **the unbearable and obscene indiscretion of your gaze**, *Huis clos* (suivi de *Les mouches*, Folio), 17.

p. 47 **priests, executioners, martyrs, Martians**, Sartre, *Situations* V, 28.

p. 48 **odourless, colourless, blindingly white landscape**, Beauvoir, *The Prime of Life* (trans. Peter Green, Penguin), 207.

p. 51 *The History of Private Perrin*, Sartre, see Annie Cohen-Solal, *Sartre, A Life* (1988), 48.

4. LYING IN BED IN THE AFTERNOON, LOOKING OUT OF THE WINDOW

p. 54 **He began by thinking**, Camus, *Carnets* 1, 21.

p. 55 **I am the world**, Camus, *Carnets* 1, 22.

p. 59 **set off in search of a time that has not yet come**, Camus, *Carnets* 2, 44.

p. 59 **When I was younger**, Camus, *Carnets* 1, 19.

p. 60 **Between this sky and these faces turned up towards it**, Camus, 'Summer in Algiers', *Noces*, 47.

p. 60 **The book falls open at a much thumbed page**, Camus, *Carnets* 1, 22.

p. 61 **I am not in the least concerned to be happy**, Camus, *Carnets* 1, 23.

p. 62 **When am I truer and more transparent**, Camus, *Carnets* 1, 23.

p. 62 **Beauty is unbearable and drives us to despair**, Camus, *Carnets* 1, 22.

5. BAD HAIR DAY

p. 64 **'Brigitte Bardot and the Lolita Syndrome'** first appeared in *Esquire*, August 1959. This is the unexpected front cover:

p. 67 **the gorgeous head of long blond locks.** Sartre, *Les Mots* (Folio), 89-91.

p. 71 **Fifty years ago**, Sartre, *Les Mots*, 89.

p. 71 **The grey thing has just appeared in the mirror**, Sartre, *La Nausée*, 31-2.

p. 71 **I was born from writing**, Sartre, *Les Mots*, 130.

p. 71 **the dirtiest, worst dressed, and also, I think, the ugliest**, Beauvoir, in *Sartre* (the text of the film by Alexandre Astruc and Michel Contat, 1972), 34.

p. 72 **impressed by how ugly he was, bordering on disabled**, Michel

Houellebecq, *Les particules élémentaires*, 26-7.

p. 72 **Who is this bum with one eye that says *merde* to the other?** cited in Bernard-Henri Lévy, *Sartre* (Polity, 2003), 259.

p. 73 **Desire, for example, 'is itself doomed to failure'**, Sartre, *EN*, 447.

p. 73 **Human reality is what it is not**, Sartre, *EN*, 94.

p. 73 **I am not born a woman**, Beauvoir, *Second Sex* (1949), 267.

p. 74 **Some time after the war.** In 1947, see Olivier Todd, *Albert Camus, Une Vie*, 583.

6. FIGHT CLUB

p. 75 **I fought constantly**, *Writing Against: a Biography of Jean-Paul Sartre*, Ronald Hayman (1987), 36.

p. 75 **technically, a featherweight**, according to his own estimation: Beauvoir, *La Cérémonie des Adieux: entretiens avec Jean-Paul Sartre* (1981), 403.

p. 75 **I unloaded on to the writer the sacred powers of the hero**, Sartre, *Les Mots*, 129.

p. 76 **I could easily have smashed him on the table**, Sartre, *La Nausée*, 234.

p. 76 **He taught me how to box**, Beauvoir, *Adieux*, 410.

p. 77 **someone who could fight anyone and win**, Sartre, Beauvoir, *Adieux*, 410.

p. 77 **a binary praxis of antagonistic reciprocity**, Sartre, *Critique of Dialectical Reason* II, 5.

p. 77 **the incarnation of a pre-existing violence**, Sartre, *Critique of Dialectical Reason* II, 26.

p. 77 **The two boxers gather within themselves**, Sartre, *Critique of Dialectical Reason* II, 26.

p. 77 **the fight is everywhere**, Sartre, *Critique of Dialectical Reason* II, 27.

p. 78 **even if Engels was right**, Sartre, *Critique of Dialectical Reason* II, 50.

p. 78 **proud of his boxing skills**, Marius Perrin, *Avec Sartre au Stalag 12D*.

p. 79 **Le Central Sporting Club**, Camus, *L'Été*, (Gallimard, 1954), 33-45.

p. 79 **what I know most surely about morality and the duties of men**, Camus, originally published in 'RUA', now accessible at http://esm-maix.pagesperso-orange.fr/rua/Camus-n.HTM.

p. 81 **Camus had plenty of time to reflect on the absurdist nature of his position**, Jim White, http://www.telegraph.co.uk/culture/books/6941924/Albert-Camus-thinker-goalkeeper.html.

p. 82 **the once familiar smell of embrocation in the dressing-rooms**, Camus, *La Peste*, 260.

p. 83 **In a few seconds they were naked**, Camus, *The First Man*, 40-1.

p. 83 **I have to write in the same way that I have to swim**, Camus, *Carnets* 1, 25.

p. 84 **And he went into the water**, Camus, *Carnets* 1, 62.

p. 84 **Everything** *flows*. In *Flow: The Psychology of Optimal Experience,* the psychologist Mihaly Csikszentmihalyi has described this state of 'flow' as 'a state of effortless concentration'.

p. 85 **Oran 'turns its back on the bay,** Camus, *La Peste,* 15.

p. 85 **Tarrou and Rieux, carving through the water,** Camus, *La Peste,* 279-80.

p. 86 **I was hearing all that, and at the same time,** Camus, 'Return to Tipasa', *L'Été,* 155–6.

p. 86 **If I were to die, in the midst of the cold mountains, unknown to the world,** Camus, 'Summer,' *Lyrical and Critical Essays* 1970, 140.

p. 86 **What else can I desire other than to exclude nothing?** Camus, *L'Été,* 159.

p. 86 **In the midst of winter,** Camus, *L'Été,* 158.

p. 87 **the featherweight boxing champion,** Beauvoir, *Second Sex,* 350.

p. 88 **What is the meaning of skiing?** Sartre, *EN,* 641-50.

7. PEN ENVY

p. 92 **it is too close to a certain part of me for me not to fall for its charms,** Camus in Todd, *Albert Camus, une vie,* 273.

p. 92 **the way he explores the extremes of conscious thought,** Camus, *Essais,* (Pléiade), 'La Nausée de Jean-Paul Sartre', 1417-9.

p. 95 **M. Camus has the affectation of quoting,** Sartre, *Situations* I, 'Explication de *l'Etranger.*'

p. 97 **Most of his criticisms are fair,** Camus, cited in Todd, 427.

p. 97 **I am thinking about a clean-shaven American, with thick black eyebrows,** Sartre, *La Nausée,* 245.

p. 99 **He loved the big body of that stooping athlete,** Sartre, 'The Defeat', cited in Cohen-Solal, 72.

p. 99 **contemporary philosophy has established that meanings [*significations*] are immediate givens,** Sartre, *Situations* I, 'Explication de *l'Etranger.*'

p. 100 **Doubtless, I really loved Ma, but that meant nothing',** Camus, *The Outsider,* part 2, chapter 1.

p. 100 **I didn't understand too well what he [the judge] meant,** *The Outsider,* part 2, chapter 1.

p. 100 We tend to take the speech of a Chinese for inarticulate gurgling, Wittgenstein, *Culture and Value*, 1.

p. 100 He is 'mindblind' (1995). See Simon Baron-Cohen, *Mindblindness* (1995).

8. HELL IS OTHER PEOPLE

p. 104 **Many fledgling moralists in those days**, Camus, *La Peste*, 149.

p. 104 **the real tragedy is not being alone**, Camus, *Carnets* 3, 60.

p. 104 **place of my dreams**, Beauvoir, *La Force de l'âge*, 569.

p. 107 **Separation is the master theme**, Camus, *Carnets* 2, 80.

p. 108 **I am bent over, peering through the keyhole**, Sartre, *EN*, 277.

p. 112 **There was a passage in Faulkner**, Sartre, *EN*, 457.

p. 122 **Camus, Carnet, Chalet . . .** Sartre, *Les jeux sont faits*, 96.

p. 122 **The door mysteriously opens**, Sartre, *Huis clos*, 86.

p. 124 **Terrible as a woman.** Beauvoir, typically, disagreed: 'Sartre dressed as a woman. Curiously, drag suited him,' *La Force de l'âge*, 255.

p. 124 **[WANDA *laughs*.]** We know that Camus and Sartre and Beauvoir joined forces with Wanda for rehearsals. See Todd, 461.

9. AN OCTOPUS AND SOME TREES

p. 125 **You are an octopus!** Sartre, *Huis clos*, 85.

p. 126 **I would willingly compare it to an octopus**, Sartre, 'Paris sous l'Occupation', *Situations* III, 21.

p. 126 **An octopus? He grabbed his knife**, Sartre, *La mort dans l'âme*, 9.

p. 127 **what lies beneath the surface**, Sartre, *La Nausée*, 114.

p. 128 **Between the man and the tree**, Camus, *Carnets* 1, 91.

p. 128 **nature = equivalence**, Camus, *Carnets* 1, 40.

p. 128 **I *was* the root of the chestnut tree**, Sartre, *La Nausée*, 187.

p. 129 **[. . .] everything seemed alive with a dark, angry life**, Sartre, 'A Defeat', Cohen-Solal, 72.

p. 131 *It* **[. . .] – an octopus with fiery eyes**, Sartre, *Les Mots*, 129-30.

10. THE X OF SEX

p. 133 **What did Wanda think she was doing, running after Camus?** Sartre, *Lettres au Castor* I, 241.

p. 134 **I'd trample on the whole world (including the Beaver)**, Beauvoir, *Letters to Sartre*, 283.

p. 134 **purely symbolic**, Sartre, *Lettres au Castor* I, 219.

p. 135 **they spoke more about women than about philosophy**, Todd, *Camus*, 462.

p. 135 **Why are you going to so much trouble?** Todd, 464.

p. 136 **I'm more intelligent than you**, Todd, 464.

p. 139 **the chambermaid is liable to be rather surprised**, Bianca Lamblin, *Mémoires d'une jeune fille dérangée*, 55.

p. 139 **I quite profoundly and sincerely feel myself to be a bastard**, Sartre, *Lettres au Castor* II, 94. 24 February 1940.

p. 140 **literary labour**, Sartre to Beauvoir, cited in Hazel Rowley, *Tête-à-Tête*, 77.

p. 141 **a cardboard box in the reading room**, Letters from Jean-Paul Sartre to Sally Swing, 1947-55, the Morgan Library & Museum, MA 4991. I am also indebted to Jean Nathan's essay 'My Dear Little Animal'. *Tin House* (2009).

p. 153 **That was a wild, and I admit very deep, affair**, John Gerassi, *Talking with Sartre*, 33.

p. 153 **More a masturbator of women than a copulator**, Beauvoir, *Adieux*, 385.

p. 153 **I mount and I perform**, Sartre, *Lettres* 2, 342.

p. 154 **And a very good thing too**, V. S. Ramachandran, *Phantoms in the Brain*, chapter 5.

p. 154 **The real is never beautiful; only the imaginary can be beautiful**, Sartre, *L'Imaginaire* (1940), 245.

11. SNOW ON FIRE

p. 156 **The hot beast of desire**, Camus, *Carnets* 1, 59.

p. 156 **If I had to write a book of ethics**, Camus, *Carnets* 1, 71.

p. 157 **to love is to want to be loved**, Sartre, *EN,* 425.

p. 157 **Hence the lover's perpetual dissatisfaction**, Sartre, *EN,* 426.

p. 157 **The greatest misfortune is not to be unloved**, Camus, *Carnets* 3, 51.

p. 157 **I must learn to tame my ardour**, Camus, *Ecrits de jeunesse,* 'Notes de lecture'. Readers can judge for themselves whether my translation is valid or not. Here is the original: (*Le Premier Camus, cahiers Albert Camus 2,* 201). 'Il me faudrait apprendre à dompter ma sensibilité, trop prompte à déborder. Pour la cacher sous l'ironie et la froideur, je croyais être le maître. Il me faut déchanter. Elle est trop vive, trop prodigue, importune, inopportune. Elle me rend trop complaisant à l'impressionnisme, à l'immédiat, au facile, au "fatal". Par elle, je me complais dans d'insignifiants alanguissements.' And this is the official translation: 'I ought to learn to master my sensitivity, too ready to spill over. I thought I was past master at the art of concealing it beneath irony and coolness. I must come down a few pegs. It is too vivid, too obtrusive, inopportune. It makes me too prone to impressionism, to the immediate, to the facile, to the "fatal". Through it I take delight in insignificant languor.' *Youthful Writings,* trans. Ellen Conroy Kennedy (1976, Knopf).

p. 158 **I ought to keep a notebook of the weather**, Camus, *Carnets* 1, 28.

p. 158 **the fusion of the Hindu wiseman and the western hero**, Camus, *Carnets,* 1, 39.

p. 158 **integrating himself into this rocky, aromatic world**, Camus, *Carnets* 1, 61.

p. 158 **I also remember those small seaside villages**, Camus, *Ecrits de jeunesse,* 216.

p. 159 **At that time not a single wrinkle**, Camus *Carnets,* 1, 32.

p. 157 **Sartre called this technique**, 'La liberté cartésienne', *Situations* I, 294.

p. 160 **Above me, I admire the light falling from the sky**, Camus, *Carnets* 1, 32.

p. 160 **The ultimate sensual pleasure is attained**, Camus, *Le Mythe de Sisyphe,* 105.

p. 161 **withdraw from time itself**, Sartre, 'La liberté cartésienne', *Situations* I.

p. 161 **a mistress with whom one goes out into the street**, Camus, *Carnets* 1, 91.

p. 161 When the world is bathed in light and the sun beats down, *Carnets* 1, 86.

p. 161 When 'the world is grey all over', Camus, *Carnets* 1, 86.

p. 162 We use the word love for this mix of desire, tenderness, and intelligence, Camus, *Le Mythe de Sisyphe*, 102.

p. 162 May I be granted a long extension! Camus, *Le Mythe de Sisyphe*, 99.

p. 162 It will collapse, Camus, 'Maison Mauresque', *Ecrits de jeunesse*, 207.

p. 162 We have to fall in love, Camus, *Carnets* 1, 96.

p. 163 Wretchedness and greatness of this world, Camus, *Carnets* 1, 116.

p. 164 Being able to keep on going all the way, Camus, *Carnets* 1, 60.

p. 164 I distrust my facility. It is too natural, Camus, 'Notes sur Stendhal'.

p. 164 Art is born from constraints, Camus, 'Discours de Suède', *Essais*.

p. 165 To write, lean always towards understatement, Camus, *Carnets* 1, 118.

p. 165 You have to choose: you can make it last or you can be on fire, Beauvoir, *La Force des choses*, 65.

12. SARTRE AND CAMUS GO TO WAR

p. 166 He crawled up to the parapet, Sartre, *La Mort dans l'âme*, 244.

p. 168 I don't really believe in the war, Sartre, Letter August 1939 to Wanda, cited in Cohen-Solal, 127.

p. 169 fear was the organ, Sartre, *Carnets de la drôle de guerre*, 13.

p. 169 something equivalent to a bar in Montmartre, Sartre, *Carnets,* 63.

p. 169 Since my mobilization I have often thought about Kafka, Sartre, letter to Jean Paulhan, cited in Cohen-Solal, 133.

p. 170 You work sixteen hours a day, Sartre, *Carnets*, 89.

p. 171 There is always one guy who does something stupid, Sartre, *Carnets*, 31.

p. 171 He recalled the experience of standing at a station, Sartre, *Carnets*, 14.

p. 173 Only pigeon fanciers, Sartre, *Cohen-Solal*, 135.

p. 173 Tu m'as cloué, Sartre, *Carnets*, 20.

p. 174 **he put us in charge of sending a daily letter**, Cohen-Solal, 144.

p. 174 **Unfaithful wives and cuckold husbands**, Sartre, *Carnets*, 217.

p. 174 **I've never written as much in my whole life**, Sartre, *Lettres* 2, 17.

p. 175 **I can only see my writing as a symbolic gesture**, Sartre, Cohen-Solal, 145.

p. 175 **When his hair starts falling out**, Sartre, *Carnets*, 101.

p. 176 **Your mother is ironing. Describe her**, Cohen-Solal, 146.

p. 177 **phalanstery of inverts**, Cohen-Solal, 154.

p. 177 **They can beat us all they want**, Cohen-Solal, 152.

p. 178 **I wonder if the Beaver's terror does not include some obscure measure of pleasurable excitement**, Sartre, *Carnets*, 188.

p. 178 **All in all, I was happy there**, Beauvoir, *Adieux*.

p. 178 **affected by a partial blindness of the right eye, entailing difficulties of orientation**, Cohen-Solal, 159.

p. 178 **Please allow the bearer and two accompanying prisoners to pass**, Hayman, *Sartre*, 170.

p. 179 **Where are the dead and the wounded?** Sartre, *La Mort dans l'âme*, 376.

p. 179 **phantom war, a phantom defeat**, Sartre, *La Mort dans l'âme*, 62.

p. 180 **a great wave of death**, Camus, letter to Francine, summer 1939, cited in Todd, 77.

p. 180 **One of the journalists, much younger than the others**, Camus, *L'Etranger*, part 2, chapter 3.

p. 180 **In this very place, some minutes later, only a few scattered vegetables**, Herbert R. Lottman, *Camus* (Gallimard), 207.

p. 181 **Still the same desolate wasteland**, Camus, *Carnets* 1, 150.

p. 181 **War has broken out. But where is the war?** Camus, *Carnets* 1, 165.

p. 182 **Hence the absolute necessity of proving oneself ... Through rigorous chastity**, Camus, *Carnets* 1, 193.

p. 182 **It is so difficult ... not to yield to beings and to beauty**, *Correspondance Camus Grenier*, 86.

p. 183 **A single constant subject for meditation, and refuse anything else**, *Carnets* 1, 193.

p. 183 **I want so much to embrace you, and also to turn away**, Todd, *Camus*, 331.

p. 183 **All French people [. . .] look like *émigrés***, Camus, *Carnets*.

p. 183 **The people who create,** *Carnets* 1, 99.

p. 184 **One fine morning in the month of May,** Camus, *La Peste,* 224.

p. 184 **I don't know how to define it very well,** Camus, *Carnets* 2, 51.

p. 184 **Literature [...] Distrust this word.** Camus, *Carnets* 2, 35.

p. 185 **The temperature varies from one minute to the next,** Camus, *Carnets* 1, 120.

p. 186 **There are times when the only companions I feel good with are animals,** Todd, 124.

p. 186 **To be able to remain in a bare room for a year,** Camus, *Carnets* 1, 206.

p. 186 **Until now ... I have always known what I wanted to do with my life,** Camus, letter to Yvonne, February 1941, quoted in Todd, 123.

p. 186 **The Frenchman has kept the habits and traditions of great thinking,** Camus, *Carnets* 2, 13.

p. 187 **Illness is a monastery with its own rules,** Camus, *Carnets* 2, 57.

p. 188 **the poet of 'fraternity'.** See his war articles for *Combat,* collected in *Combat: éditoriaux et articles d'Albert Camus, 1944-1947,* ed. Jacqueline Lévi-Valensi.

p. 188 **like walking on a 'tightrope, in passionate and solitary tension',** cited in Todd, 335.

p. 190 **You aimed your armchair in the direction of history!** Camus, in Todd, 188.

13. NEW YORK/NEW YORK

p. 193 **atmospheres, gaseous masses longitudinally elongated,** Sartre, 'New York, ville coloniale', *Situations* III.

p. 194 **Her passion literally scares me,** Sartre, *Lettres au Castor* II, 334.

p. 194 **killed by passion and lectures,** Sartre, *Lettres au Castor* II, 335.

p. 195 **I notice that I have not noticed the skyscrapers, they seemed to me perfectly natural,** Camus, *Journaux de Voyage,* 30.

p. 195 **an American soldier, his mouth open, puffing out clouds of real smoke,** Camus, *Journaux de Voyage,* 29.

p. 196 **an army of long-legged young starlets, lazing on the lawn,** Camus, *Journaux de Voyage,* 39.

p. 197 **it is necessary to be either very ugly or very beautiful**, Camus, *Journaux de Voyage*, 41.

p. 197 **Afternoon with students. They don't feel the real problem**, Camus, *Journaux de Voyage*, 39.

p. 198 **Marvellous night on the Atlantic**, Camus, *Journaux de Voyage*, 51-2.

p. 201 **The one thing that I would like to say**, Camus, *Journaux de Voyage, 47.*

14. PHILOSOPHERS STONED

p. 202 **No one in our circle was reluctant to get drunk**, Beauvoir, *La Force des choses*, 47.

p. 202 **I get drunk [...] but only every other night**, Sartre, *Lettres au Castor 2*, 328.

p. 202 **little crematory sacrifice**, *EN*, 658.

p. 204 **I would wake up in the morning and say**, Gerassi, *Talking with Sartre*, 80.

p. 204 **I would have liked my crabs to come back**, Gerassi, *Talking with Sartre*, 81.

p. 205 **Sartre's true drug was neither mescaline nor corydrane, but writing**, Bernard-Henri Lévy, *Sartre*, 214.

p. 206 **it is time to create new worlds**, Camus, cited in Todd, 100.

p. 206 **We would like to break through the all too narrow frames of thought**, Todd, 101.

15. SQUARING UP

p. 209 **I am a battleship. I can't be sunk**, Sartre, in a conversation with Jean Cau, recorded in Todd, 572.

p. 210 **I cannot leave you**, Camus, letters, Todd, 585.

p. 210 **Beauvoir, at her bitchiest**, Beauvoir, *La Force des choses*, 126.

p. 210 **As writers we are traitors to ourselves**, Camus, *Carnets 2*, 186.

p. 211 **You are a better novelist than I am, but not such a good philosopher**, Koestler, cited in Beauvoir, *La Force des choses*, 123.

p. 211 **An anti-communist is a dog!**' cited in Aronson, *Camus and Sartre*, 128.

p. 213 **Individuals are paramount for us**, Camus, cited in Lottman, 414.

p. 214 **Unbearable solitude**, Camus, *Carnets* 2, 189.

p. 214 **never got much beyond page 179.** So he told Grenier, but Todd, 679, notes that he reads it carefully at least up to page 183, and then more intermittently after that point.

p. 217 **Isaiah Berlin's terminology.** See *Two Concepts of Liberty.*

p. 217 **He is condemned to fragmented and semi-automatic tasks**, Sartre, *The Communists and Peace* (New York), 51.

p. 219 **After ten years of ruminating, I had come to the breaking point**, Sartre, cited in Beauvoir, *La Force des choses*, 280.

p. 220 **If only . . . we could write the truth!** Camus, cited in Beauvoir, *La Force des choses*, 65.

16. THE REBEL

p. 221 **I must be *really* famous**, Sartre, *Lettres au Castor* II, 329.

p. 222 **What has done me the most harm is abstract ideas**, Camus, *Carnets* 1, 37.

p. 224 **'the immoderate energy of desire'**, 'the inexhaustible law of desire', Camus, *L'Homme révolté*, 60, 63.

p. 224 **the unlimited liberty of desire entails the negation of the other and the suppression of pity**, Camus, *L'Homme révolté*, 66.

p. 225 **Dalí, for instance, who claims**, in *Investigating Sex: Surrealist Research 1928-32* (1992).

p. 226 **these dozens of volumes stuffed full of atrocities and philosophy**, Camus, *L'Homme révolté*, 68.

p. 227 **I abhor nature**, Camus, *L'Homme révolté*, 69.

p. 227 **At the same instant that sexual crime suppresses the object of pleasure**, Camus, *L'Homme révolté*, 66.

p. 228 **infinitely demanding**, Simon Critchley, *Infinitely Demanding.*

p. 230 **Revolt, for human beings, is the refusal to be a thing**, Camus, *L'Homme révolté*, 22.

p. 230 **Man is the only creature who refuses to be what she is**, Camus, *L'Homme révolté*, 21.

17. THE LAST SUPPER

p. 232 **According to Beauvoir, Camus 'just took it for granted**, Beauvoir, *La Force des choses,* 279.

p. 233 **Revolt is not clearly defined when it is said, as it is by our existentialists,** Camus, *L'Homme révolté,* 219.

18. EASTER 1952

p. 236 Jeanson's review of *The Rebel* and the exchange between Camus, Jeanson and Sartre has been collected in English, *Sartre and Camus: A Historic Confrontation,* ed. and trans. David A. Sprintzen and Adrian van den Hoven (New York, 2004).

p. 236 **I tried to find someone who would be willing to review it,** Sartre, in Beauvoir, *Adieux,* 344.

p. 237 ***Modern Times.* They allow sin and refuse grace,** Camus, *Carnets* 3, 62.

p. 237 **The tragedy is not being alone, but rather *not* being alone,** Camus, *Carnets* 3, 60.

p. 238 **Everyone is on my case, they all want to destroy me,** Camus, *Carnets* 3, 50.

p. 238 **This explosion of long-suppressed hatred,** Camus, letter to Francine, September 1952, Todd 790.

p. 238 **Who will bear witness for us? Our works,** Camus, *Carnets* 3, 62.

19. GLOVES OFF

p. 241 **My dear Camus.** Sartre's 'letter' is in *Situations X.*

p. 244 **In other times, now regarded as backward,** Camus, *Carnets* 3, 102.

p. 244 **Art is a revenge,** Camus, *Critical Essays,* 159.

20. WAR OF WORDS

p. 247 As Tony Judt observed, *Past Imperfect: French Intellectuals, 1944-1956* (1994), 119.

p. 247 No one today can be unaware, Sartre, *Situations* V, 161.

p. 247 I have defended all my life, Camus, *Actuelles* III, 127.

p. 247 These reforms, Sartre, *Situations* V, 26.

p. 247 Some kind of progress, Camus, *Actuelles* III, 74.

p. 248 Colonization is neither, Sartre, *Situations* V, 43.

p. 248 From what you say, Camus, *Actuelles* III, 139.

p. 248 It is not true, Sartre, *Situations* V, 45.

p. 248 Speaking for my own family, Camus, *Actuelles* III, 22.

p. 248 The colonist has even created, Sartre, *Situations* V, 43.

p. 248 The time of imperialism is over, Camus, *Actuelles* III, 23.

p. 249 Any intention, Sartre, *Situations* V, 26.

p. 249 Presuppositions and a bundle of ideas, Camus, *Actuelles* III, 49.

p. 249 The system is pitiless, Sartre, *Situations* V, 38.

p. 249 We need a confederation of peoples, Camus, *Actuelles* III, 28.

p. 249 A lot of fine words, Sartre, *Situations* V, 187.

p. 249 It is absurd to describe a whole country as racist, Camus, *Actuelles* III, 151.

p. 249 Our beautiful souls are racist, Sartre, *Situations* V, 182.

p. 249 Everything we do for truth, Camus, *Actuelles* III, 49.

p. 249 Colonialism is in the process of destroying itself, Sartre, *Situations* V, 51.

p. 249 The world today is immersed in hatred, Camus, *Actuelles* III, 122.

p. 250 We have to confront this unexpected spectacle, Sartre, *Situations* V, 186.

p. 250 When violence responds to violence in an escalating delirium, Camus, *Actuelles* III, 18.

p. 250 There is no 'Third Way', Sartre, *Situations* V, 185.

p. 250 Some of our pundits seem to have the obscure idea, Camus, *Actuelles* III, 18.

p. 250 It is not their violence in the first place, Sartre, *Situations* V, 178.

p. 250 We must condemn with the same force, Camus, *Actuelles* III, 17.

p. 251 They don't give a fuck, Sartre, *Situations* V, 182.

p. 251 **Whatever the origins of the Algerian tragedy**, Camus, *Actuelles* III, 173.

p. 251 **The signs of violence will not be wiped away**, Sartre, *Situations*, V, 183.

p. 251 **Someone will always reply: the time for reconciliation is past**, Camus, *Actuelles* III, 129.

p. 251 **Too many of our pseudo-intellectuals**, Sartre, *Situations* V, 192.

p. 251 **Gandhi demonstrates that one can struggle**, Camus, *Actuelles* III, 17.

p. 251 **Understand this if you can**, Sartre, *Situations* V, 187.

p. 252 **Then we are returning to the jungle**, Camus, *Actuelles* III, 17

p. 252 **On the solution to the Algerian problem**, Sartre, *Situations* V, 64.

p. 252 **Reprisals against civilians**, Camus, *Actuelles* III, 14.

p. 252 **Can we cure ourselves?** Sartre, *Situations* V, 192.

p. 252 **Then we are locked into an agon**, Camus, *Actuelles* III, 126.

p. 252 **You, so liberal, so humane**, Sartre, *Situations* V, 174.

p. 252 **And yet you and I, we resemble one another so much**, Camus, *Actuelles* III, 126.

21. THE CALL

p. 253 **He muttered that Malraux**, Todd, 689.

p. 254 **He didn't steal it**, Sartre, quoted in Todd, 950.

p. 254 **Strange feeling of despondency and melancholy**, Camus, *Carnets* 3, 214.

p. 254 **Without your teaching and your example**, Camus, Todd, 957.

p. 255 **'Reflections on the Guillotine'**, Camus, *Essais*.

p. 257 **You are zombies!** Sartre, *Situations* V, 'Preface to *The Wretched of the Earth*', 174.

p. 258 **Remember that shit thou art**, Camus, Todd, 954.

p. 259 **When he got in a taxi**, see Todd, 976.

p. 259 **SARTRE DOES THE DOUBLE**, Cohen-Solal, 455.

p. 259 **This great writer is also a true man**, Mauriac, cited in Cohen-Solal, 445.

p. 261 **Today, the Nobel prize appears**, Sartre, Cohen-Solal, 447.

p. 262 **to call a cat a cat**, Sartre, *Qu'est-ce que la littérature?* Or, less literally, 'a spade a spade'.

p. 263 **With the sum the laureate receives**, Sartre, Cohen-Solal, 448.

22. WHAT IT FEELS LIKE TO BE DEAD

p. 266 **This car is a coffin on wheels**, cited in Herbert R. Lottman's biography of Camus, who provides the most detailed – forensic – analysis of the crash.

p. 267 **Michel, you have no experience of poverty**, Camus, cited Todd, 467.

p. 268 **My life is at this instant at its meridian**, Camus, *Carnets* 3, 266.

p. 268 **The intense light, the infinite space transport me**, Camus, *Carnets* 3, 258.

p. 268 **I am at the steering wheel for 11 hours**, Camus, *Carnets* 3, 259.

p. 269 **I feel as if I only have to stretch out my hand and I can touch Algeria**, Camus, Todd, 1016.

p. 270 **Grey sky. In the garden marvellous roses**, Camus, *Carnets* 3, 266, 28 April 1958.

p. 270 **For years I have tried to live according to a collective code**, Camus, *Carnets* 3, 266.

p. 270 **a mix of Fernandel, Humphrey Bogart, and a samurai**, Camus, cited by Todd, 843.

p. 271 **a kung fu of philosophy**, Peimin Ni, *New York Times* (http://opinionator.blogs.nytimes.com/2010/12/08/kung-fu-for-philosophers/).

p. 271 **Tomorrow, yes, in this fortunate valley, we will find the nerve to die happy**, Camus, *The Posterity of the Sun*.

p. 271 **Bad night. It is raining on the golf course and the hills**, Camus, *Carnets* 3, 263.

p. 272 **I make war against myself**, Camus, *Carnets* 3, 267.

p. 272 **I love the little lizards**, Camus, *Carnets* 3, 268.

p. 272 **It is myself that, for the last five years, I have put on trial**, Camus, *Carnets* 3, 267.

p. 273 **140,000 people dying per day**, Camus, *Carnets* 3, 273.

p. 274 **The lie is a form of sleep or dream**, Camus, *Carnets* 3, 233.

p. 274 **Destroy everything in my life that is not this poverty**, Camus, *Carnets* 3, 264.

p. 275 **I am a writer. But it is not I but my pen that thinks**, Camus, *Carnets* 3, 275.

p. 275 **man of the North**, Camus, *Carnets* 3, 265.

p. 276 **But one should not marry one's sister**, Camus, Todd, 1018.

p. 276 **It is in the sea that life is born**, Camus, *Carnets* 3, 274.

p. 277 **this is the kind of love that expands to encompass all beings at once**, Camus, *Carnets* 3, 255.

p. 277 **For the mature man, only happy love affairs**, Camus, *Carnets* 3, 273.

p. 277 **I am so in love with love**, Camus, *Carnets* 3, 272.

p. 278 **Carnal love has always been tied for me**, Camus, *Carnets* 3, 274.

p. 278 **There is no more Don Juan since love is free**, Camus, *Carnets* 3, 277.

p. 279 **By giving, when you can. And by not hating, if you can**, Todd, 1030.

p. 281 **Let Jean-Paul Sartre philosophize about revolution**, cited in Cohen-Solal, 399.

p. 282 **They are as stupid and brutish as we are**, Camus, *The First Man*, 141.

p. 284 **There are waves that reach us from Cape Horn after a journey of ten thousand kilometres**, Camus, *Carnets* 3, 275.

p. 285 **He is not here to see this morning**, Beauvoir, *La Force des choses*, 509.

p. 285 **Cartesian of the absurd**. Sartre's obituary is collected in *Situations* IV.

p. 287 **I know of nothing more idiotic than dying in a car crash**, Camus, Lottman, 683.

p. 287 **Naturally, our hope was to be taken out on the corner of the street**, Camus, *The Outsider*, part 2, chapter 5, first paragraph.

p. 289 **I knew he would come to us**, Cohen-Solal, 523.

p. 291 **This book will be the summa of my political and moral theories**, Cohen-Solal, 513.

p. 291 **people speak of me as I were one of the living dead**, Cohen-Solal, 494.

p. 292 **in this darkness that will give way to a new dawn**, Sartre, 'Preface to *The Wretched of the Earth*'.

23. BEYOND THE TEXT

p. 297 **nothing beyond the text**, Derrida's original takes different forms; for example, 'il n'y a pas de hors-texte' (*De la grammatologie*).

p. 299 **I can hardly begin to doubt unless I have beliefs**, Wittgenstein, *On Certainty.*

p. 300 **Roman Jakobson reckoned that,** Taken from his essay on 'Two Aspects of Language and Two Types of Aphasia'.

p. 301 **Our real existence**, Bergson, 'Le souvenir du présent et la fausse reconnaissance', *L'Energie spirituelle* (1979), p. 136.

Short Lists

CAMUS

Noces (*Nuptials*), 1938
L'Etranger (*The Outsider/ The Stranger*), 1942
Le Mythe de Sisyphe (*The Myth of Sisyphus*), 1942
La Peste (*The Plague*), 1947
L'Homme révolté (*The Rebel*), 1951
L'Eté (*Summer*), 1954
La Chute (*The Fall*), 1956
Carnets (*Notebooks*), 1962, 1964, 1989

SARTRE

La Nausée (*Nausea*), 1938
L'Etre et le Néant (*Being and Nothingness*), 1943
Huis clos (*No Exit*), 1944
L'Age de raison (*Age of Reason*), the first volume of *Les Chemins de la liberté* (*Roads to Freedom*), 1945
Qu'est-ce que la littérature? (*What Is Literature?*), 1948
Les Mots (*Words*), 1964
Carnets de la drôle de guerre (*War Diaries: Notebooks from the Phoney War*), 1983, 1995

OTHERS

Roland Aronson, *Camus and Sartre: The Story of a Friendship and the Quarrel That Ended It* (2004)

Roland Barthes, *Writing Degree Zero* (1953)

Simone de Beauvoir, *L'Invitée* (*She Came to Stay*) (1943)
The Second Sex (1949)
Brigitte Bardot and the Lolita Syndrome (1959)

Harold Bloom, *The Anxiety of Influence* (1973)

Annie Cohen-Solal, *Sartre, 1905–1980* (1985)

Simon Critchley, *Infinitely Demanding* (2007)

John Gerassi, *Talking with Sartre* (2009)

Roman Jakobson, 'Two Aspects of Language and Two Types of Aphasia' in *Fundamentals of Language* (1956)

Daniel Kahneman, *Thinking, Fast and Slow* (2011)

Bernard-Henri Lévy, *Sartre, The Philosopher of the Twentieth Century* (2003)

Herbert R. Lottman, *Albert Camus, A Biography* (1981)

V. S. Ramachandran (with Sandra Blakeslee), *Phantoms in the Brain* (1998)

Hazel Rowley, *Tête à tête: The Lives and Loves of Jean-Paul Sartre and Simone de Beauvoir* (2006)

Olivier Todd, *Albert Camus, une vie* (1996)

Acknowledgements

This book could not have been written without the generosity and intellectual stimulus of the University of Cambridge, the Dorothy and Lewis B. Cullman Center for Scholars and Writers, New York, and the Rutgers Center for Historical Analysis. I am also grateful to the Morgan Library and Museum, New York, for their assistance. Parts of this book first appeared in *Raritan* and *The New York Times*.

Index